Moses
the Reluctant Leader

Discipleship and Leadership Lessons

and Bible Study Commentary for Personal Devotional Use, Small Groups or
Sunday School Classes, and Sermon Preparation for Pastors and Teachers

JesusWalk® Bible Study Series

by Dr. Ralph F. Wilson
Director, Joyful Heart Renewal Ministries

Additional books and reprint licenses are available at:
http://www.jesuswalk.com/books/moses.htm

Free Participant Guide handout sheets are available at:
http://www.jesuswalk.com/moses/moses-lesson-handouts.pdf

JesusWalk® Publications
Loomis, California

Paperback
ISBN-13: 978-0-9832310-1-1
ISBN-10: 098323101X

Library of Congress Control Number: 2011905020

Library of Congress subject headings:
Moses (Biblical Leader)
Bible. O.T. – Biography.

Suggested Classifications
Dewey Decimal System: 222.1
Library of Congress: BS 580.M6

Published by JesusWalk® Publications, P.O. Box 565, Loomis, CA 95650-0565, USA.

JesusWalk is a registered trademark and Joyful Heart is a trademark of Joyful Heart Renewal Ministries.

Unless otherwise noted, all the Bible verses quoted are from the New International Version (International Bible Society, 1973, 1978), used by permission.

1103026

Preface

Moses is awe-inspiring. From a distance he is a grand and epic figure. But close up, he can be studied as a somewhat reluctant leader trying desperately to learn to lead under God's direction. My interest is on what we can learn from Moses as a man of faith and as a leader of God's people.

You may be a church member and disciple. But, more likely than not, you're also a leader in your church, perhaps as a deacon or elder or pastor. As you take the time to look at Moses the man, you'll learn a lot that can benefit you in your ministry. Even as a seasoned pastor myself, I am struggling to learn afresh the lessons that this 80-year-old, newly-minted leader was learning from God during his on-the-job training.

To get through the Moses material in the Pentateuch, we'll move right along, studying four to six chapters from the Bible each lesson – or even more. We'll focus, however, on particular passages that illuminate Moses' situation, his

James J. Tissot, "Moses" (1896-1900), watercolor, Jewish Museum, New York.

faith, his leadership challenges, and the decisions he made as a leader of God's people.

I want to thank the dear people at First Baptist Church of Nevada City, California, who gave me an opportunity to appreciate at a deeper level and practice along with them the principles of leadership pioneered by Moses.

I invite you to join me on this quest to learn from Moses, the man of God.

Dr. Ralph F. Wilson
April 1, 2011
Loomis, California

Table of Contents

Preface   3

Table of Contents   4

Reprint Guidelines   11

References and Abbreviations   12

Introduction to Moses and the Exodus   15
    Dating of the Exodus   15
    Who Wrote the Books of Moses?   18

1. The Birth and Call of Moses (Exodus 1-4)   21
    A. Introduction (Exodus 1:1-22)   21
       The Pharaoh Who Knew Not Joseph (Exodus 1:6-10)   21
       Oppressing the Israelites (Exodus 1:11-14)   22
       Killing the Male Babies (Exodus 1:15-23)   23
    B. Infancy (Exodus 2:1-10)   23
       The Birth of Moses (Exodus 2:1-4)   23
       Moses Is Adopted by Pharaoh's Daughter (Exodus 2:5-10)   24
    C. Moses the Activist (Exodus 2:11-22)   24
       Moses Commits Murder (Exodus 2:11-15a)   24
       Leadership Is Influence   25
       Moses Flees to Midian and Delivers Jethro's Daughters (Exodus 2:15-17)   27
       Middle Eastern Hospitality (Exodus 2:18-22)   27
    D. The Call of Moses (Exodus 2:23-4:17)   28
       God Hears His People's Cry (Exodus 2:23-25)   28
       The Burning Bush (Exodus 3:1-5)   29
       God's Promise (Exodus 3:6-9)   31
       Moses' Call (Exodus 3:10-12)   31
       God Reveals Himself as Yahweh (Exodus 3:13-15)   32
       Directions and Signs (Exodus 3:16-22; 4:1-9)   33
       Send Someone Else (Exodus 4:10-17)   33
    E. Moses Obeys God (Exodus 4:18-31)   34
       The Circumcision of Moses' Son (Exodus 4:24-26)   34
       Moses Returns to Egypt (Exodus 4:27-31)   35

2. Finding Courage to Stand (Exodus 5-11)   38
    A. Moses' Early Failure (Exodus 5:1-3)   38

The Word of the Lord (5:1)   38
Courage in the Face of Raw Power (5:1)   39
Pharaoh's Response (Exodus 5:2)   39
A Three-Day Pilgrimage in the Desert (Exodus 5:3)   40
B. Discouragement and the Lord's Instruction (Exodus 5:4-7:7)   41
Blame the Leader (Exodus 5:4-21)   41
Blaming God (Exodus 5:22-23)   42
The Lord Encourages Moses (Exodus 6:1-8)   43
The Lord Commands Moses (Exodus 6:9-13)   43
I Will Harden Pharaoh's Heart (Exodus 7:1-6)   45
C. God's Increasing Judgment on Egypt (Exodus 7:8-11:10)   45
The Plagues upon Egypt (Exodus 7:8-11:9)   45
Moses' Staff   48
The Staff and Ancient Concepts of Magic   49
Distinction between Egypt and the Israelites   49
D. Leadership Lessons   50
1. The Leader Must Confront When Necessary   50
2. The Leader Must Deal with Criticism and Pressure   51
3. The Leader Must Know When to Compromise – and When Not To   52
4. The Leader Must Know that the Battle Is the Lord's   53

3. Passover and Crossing the Red Sea (Exodus 12-15)   **56**
A. Passover (Exodus 12:1-28)   56
A Lamb for Every Household (Exodus 12:1-6)   56
The Blood of the Passover (Exodus 12:7)   56
What Kind of Sacrifice Is the Paschal Lamb?   57
Christ Our Paschal Lamb   57
Commemorating the Passover (Exodus 12:14-20)   58
Final Preparations for Passover Night (Exodus 12:21)   59
B. Leaving Egypt (Exodus 12:29-36)   60
The Tenth Plague, the Slaying of the Firstborn (Exodus 12:29-33)   60
Plundering the Egyptians (Exodus 12:35-36)   61
C. On the Move (Exodus 12:37-51)   61
The Israelites Begin Their Journey (Exodus 12:37-40)   61
The Lord Brought the Israelites Out of Egypt (Exodus 12:50-51)   62
The Pillar of Cloud and the Pillar of Fire (Exodus 13:21-22)   64
The Desert Route (Exodus 13:17-18a)   64
Location of the Red Sea (yām sûp)   65

D. Pharaoh Pursues (Exodus 14:1-14) 65
  Encamping West of the Sea (Exodus 14:1-4) 65
  Pharaoh Rises to the Bait (Exodus 14:5-9) 66
  Blaming the Leader – Again! (Exodus 14:10-12) 67
  Moses Encourages the People (Exodus 14:13-14) 67
E. Crossing the Red Sea (Exodus 14:15-31) 69
  The People March through the Red Sea (Exodus 14:15-16, 21-22) .. 69
  Gaining Glory over the Egyptians (Exodus 14:4, 17-18) 71
  The Destruction of Pharaoh's Army (Exodus 14:23-30) 73
F. Celebration (Exodus 15:1-21) 74
  The Song of Moses (Exodus 15:1-19) 74
  The Song of Miriam (Exodus 15:20-21) 76

4. Grumbling, Conflict, and Delegation (Exodus 15-18) **78**
A. Grumbling (Exodus 15:22-17:7) 78
  Finding Drinkable Water at Marah (Exodus 15:22-25a) 78
  Grumbling, Complaining, Murmuring, and Quarreling against Leaders ... 79
  None of These Diseases (Exodus 15:26) 82
  Grumbling about Food (Exodus 16:2-3) 83
  Grumbling against the Lord, not Moses (Exodus 16:7b-8) 83
  The Glory of the Lord Revealed (Exodus 16:6-12) 84
  God's Provision of Quail and Manna (Exodus 16) 86
  The People Grumble about Water (Exodus 17:1-7) 87
  Including the Elders and Officers (Exodus 17:5-7) 89
  Double References to Water and Quail Miracles 89
B. Battle (Exodus 17:8-16) 90
  Fighting the Amalekites (Exodus 17:8-16) 90
  Yahweh Is My Banner (Exodus 17:15-16a) 91
C. Jethro (Exodus 18) 92
  Jethro Learns about Yahweh (Exodus 18:1-12) 92
  Jethro Teaches Moses to Delegate Responsibility (Exodus 18:13-27) ... 93
  Learning to Delegate 94
  Delegating to the 70 Elders (Numbers 11:10-30) 95

5. The Covenant at Mount Sinai (Exodus 19-24) **98**
A. Invitation to the Covenant (Exodus 19:1-9) 98
  Invitation to a Unique Covenant Relationship (Exodus 19:3-6) .. 98
  Requirement: Keeping the Covenant (Exodus 19:5a) 99
  God's Treasured Possession, Personal Property, Chosen People (Exodus 19:5) ... 101

A Kingdom of Priests (Exodus 19:6a)   102
A Holy Nation (Exodus 19:6b)   103
Identity Statement (Exodus 19:5-6)   104
Initial Agreement to Enter into Covenant (Exodus 19:7-8a)   105
Moses the Go-Between (Exodus 19:8b-9a)   105
B. Preparing for the Covenant (Exodus 19:10-25)   105
Consecrate the People (Exodus 19:10-11)   105
The People Witness the Lord at the Mountain (Exodus 19:16-21)   107
C. Requirements of the Covenant (Exodus 20-23)   108
The Ten Commandments and Book of the Covenant (Exodus 20-23)   108
The Book of the Covenant (Exodus 20-23)   108
D. Confirming the Covenant (Exodus 24)   109
The Formal Ratification of the Covenant (Exodus 24:4-8)   109
The Blood of the Covenant (Exodus 24:8)   109
The Old Covenant and the New Covenant   110
Eating and Drinking on the Mountain (Exodus 24:9-11)   111
Moses Ascends the Mountain for Forty Days (Exodus 24:12, 18)   111

6. The Golden Calf and Moses' Intercession (Exodus 32-34)   **113**
A. Idolatry (Exodus 32)   113
The Israelites Worship the Golden Calf (Exodus 32:1-6)   113
A Stiff-Necked People (Exodus 32:7, 9)   115
God's Righteous Anger (Exodus 32:10)   115
Moses Intercedes for the People (Exodus 32:11-13)   116
Moses Breaks the Tablets (Exodus 32:15-16, 19)   117
Moses Destroys the Golden Calf (Exodus 32:20)   118
Moses Reprimands Aaron (Exodus 32:21-24)   119
Levites Slaughter the Idolaters (Exodus 32:26-29)   120
B. Interceding (Exodus 32:30-33:23)   122
Moses Intercedes for the People – Again (Exodus 32:30-35)   122
Repentance and Mourning (Exodus 33:1-6)   123
Moses Intercedes One More Time (Exodus 33:12-17)   123
Lessons for Leader-Intercessors   124
Teach Me Your Ways (Exodus 33:13)   125
God with Us (Exodus 33:15-16)   126
Moses' "Tent of Meeting" Outside the Camp (Exodus 33:7-11)   126
Moses Sees God's Glory (Exodus 33:18-23)   128
C. A Second Chance (Exodus 34)   129

The Second Giving of the 10 Commandments (Exodus 34:1-4)   129
Proclamation of the Name of Yahweh (Exodus 34:5-7)   130

7. The Tabernacle, Priesthood, and Sacrifices (Exodus 20-31, 35-40; Leviticus 1-17; Numbers 6-10)   **131**
A. The Kingdom of God   *131*
Yahweh's Presence in the Midst of His People (Numbers 2:1-3:39)   132
B. The Laws of the Covenant   *133*
1. Civil Law   134
2. Religious or Ceremonial Law   134
3. Moral Law   135
Is the Mosaic Law Binding on Christians?   135
C. The Tabernacle   *136*
Craftsmen and Materials   136
Three Names for the Tabernacle   137
The Tabernacle Itself (Exodus 26-27)   137
Tabernacle Furniture (Exodus 25, 27, 30)   140
Completing the Tabernacle (Exodus 39-40)   142
The Cloud and the Glory (Exodus 40:34-38)   142
Dedicating the Tabernacle   143
Flow of Worship in the Tabernacle   143
D. The Priests, Levites, and Sacrifices   *144*
Priests   145
Levites   145
Tithing   146
Priestly Garments (Exodus 28 and 39, Leviticus 8:7-9)   146
The Aaronic Blessing (Numbers 6:22-27)   148
The Sacrifices   149
Repentance Is Necessary   150
Special Sacrifices   150
Steps in a Burnt Offering (Leviticus 1:3-9)   151
Priests Participate in the Sacrifice (Leviticus 10)   153
The Cloud above the Tabernacle (Numbers 9:15-23)   155

8. Rebellion against Moses' Leadership (Numbers 11-17)   **157**
A. Demand for Other Food (Numbers 11)   *157*
Complaints and Fire at Taberah (Numbers 11)   157
Moses' Complaint to the Lord (Numbers 11:11-15)   158
The Quail and Plague at Kibroth Hattaavah (Numbers 11:31-34)   159

B. *Handling Criticism (Numbers 12)* *159*
Miriam's and Aaron's Criticism and Punishment (Numbers 12:1-15) 159
Power Struggles and Pride 160
Moses, the Humble (Numbers 12:3) 161
Aaron and Miriam Rebuked for Speaking Against Moses (Numbers 12:4-9) 162
Miriam's Punishment (Numbers 12:10-15) 162
C. *Faltering at the Edge of Canaan (Numbers 13-14)* *163*
Spying Out the Land (Numbers 13:1-25) 163
Fear and Unbelief Spread (Numbers 14:1-9) 165
The Glory and Wrath of Yahweh (Numbers 14:10-12) 166
Moses Intercedes Again (Numbers 14:13-20) 167
Caleb's Faith (Numbers 14:24) 168
The Command to Leave Kadesh-Barnea (Numbers 14:25) 168
The Israelites Presume to Enter the Land Anyway (Numbers 14:39-45) 168
Discipleship and Leadership Lessons 169
D. *Authority Challenged (Numbers 16)* *171*
Korah's Rebellion (Numbers 16) 171
Moses Intercedes Once More (Numbers 16:42-50) 173
Aaron's Rod that Budded (Numbers 17) 174

9. Conquering the Transjordan and Moses' Death (Numbers 20-27; Deut 32, 34) **176**
A. *Moses and Aaron Displease the Lord (Numbers 20)* *176*
Moses Strikes the Rock at Kadesh and Is Disciplined (Numbers 20:1-13) 176
B. *Conflict with the People of the Land (Numbers 20-25)* *179*
Conflicts with Edom and Arad (Numbers 20:14-21:3) 179
Vipers Attack the Israelites (Numbers 21:4-9) 179
Conquering Kingdoms East of the Jordan (Numbers 21:10-35) 182
Balak Hires Balaam to Curse Israel (Numbers 22-24) 182
Israelite Men Sin with Moabite Women (Numbers 25) 183
The Census (Numbers 26) 184
C. *Succession (Numbers 27; Deuteronomy 32, 34)* *185*
Commissioning of Joshua (Numbers 27:12-18) 185
The Song of Moses, Blessings, and Death (Deuteronomy 32) 185
The Death of Moses 187

Epilogue: Moses' Leadership Legacy **189**
Moses: Leadership by Listening and Obeying 189
The Prophet Who Was to Come (Deuteronomy 18:15, 18-19) 190

Jesus: Leadership by Listening and Obeying   190
Can This Leadership Pattern Be Replicated?   191
Jesus Modeled Spirit-led Leadership   192

Appendix 1. Participant Handouts for Classes & Groups   **193**

Introduction to the Moses and the Exodus   194
1. The Birth and Call of Moses (Exodus 1-4)   196
2. Finding Courage to Stand (Exodus 5-11)   198
3. Passover and Crossing the Red Sea (Exodus 12-15)   201
4. Grumbling, Conflict, and Delegation (Exodus 15-18)   204
5. The Covenant at Mount Sinai (Exodus 19-24)   208
6. The Golden Calf and Moses' Intercession (Exodus 32-34)   211
7. The Tabernacle, Priesthood, and Sacrifices (Ex 20-31, 35-40; Lev 1-17; Num 6-10)   214
8. Rebellion against Moses' Leadership (Numbers 11-17)   221
9. Conquering the Transjordan and Moses' Death (Numbers 20-27; Deuteronomy 32, 34)   224

Appendix 2. The Route of the Exodus   **226**

1. Northern Sinai Route   226
2. Central Sinai Route   226
3. Southern Sinai Route (Traditional)   227
Ramses, Pithom, and Succoth (Exodus 12:37)   228
Location of the Red Sea or *yām sûp*   228
The Sinai Coast   229
Marah (Exodus 15:23)   230
Elim (Exodus 15:27)   230
Mount Sinai   230
Kadesh-Barnea   231
Mount Hor   232
Ezion-geber (Numbers 33:35; Deuteronomy 2:8)   232
Dizahab (Deuteronomy 1:1)   232
Jotbathah (Numbers 33:33)   232

Appendix 3. References to Moses in the New Testament   **233**

Moses as Lawgiver   233
Contrast between Old and New Covenants   234
Miscellaneous References   234
Moses as the Prophet Prototype of Jesus Christ   234

Reprint Guidelines

Copying the Handouts. In some cases, small groups or Sunday school classes would like to use these notes to study this material. That's great. Appendix 1 provides copies of handouts designed for classes and small groups. There is no charge whatsoever to print out as many copies of the handouts as you need for participants.

All charts and notes are copyrighted and must bear the line: "Copyright © 2011, Ralph F. Wilson. All rights reserved. Reprinted by permission."

You may not resell these notes to other groups or individuals outside your congregation. You may, however, charge people in your group enough to cover your copying costs.

Copying the book (or the majority of it) in your congregation or group, you are requested to purchase a reprint license for each book. A Reprint License, $2.50 for each copy is available for purchase at

www.jesuswalk.com/books/moses.htm

Or you may send a check to:

Dr. Ralph F. Wilson
JesusWalk Publications
PO Box 565
Loomis, CA 95650, USA

The Scripture says,

"The laborer is worthy of his hire" (Luke 10:7) and "Anyone who receives instruction in the word must share all good things with his instructor" (Galatians 6:6).

However, if you are from a third world country or an area where it is difficult to transmit money, please make a small contribution instead to help the poor in your community.

References and Abbreviations

ABD — David Noel Freedman (editor-in-chief), *The Anchor Bible Dictionary* (Doubleday, 1992)

Ashley, *Numbers* — Timothy R. Ashley, *The Book of Numbers* (New International Commentary on the Old Testament; Eerdmans, 1993)

BDAG — Walter Bauer and Frederick W. Danker, *A Greek-English Lexicon of the New Testament and Other Early Christian Literature* (Third Edition; based on a previous English edition by W.F. Arndt, F.W. Gingrich, and F.W. Danker; University of Chicago Press, 1957, 1979). This is the standard NT Greek-English Lexicon.

BDB — Francis Brown, S.R. Driver, and Charles A. Briggs (eds.), *A Hebrew and English Lexicon of the Old Testament* (Oxford: Clarendon Press, 1907). Used in an electronic edition.

Beitzel, *Atlas* — Barry J. Beitzel, *The Moody Atlas of Bible Lands* (Moody Press, 1985)

Cole, *Exodus* — R. Alan Cole, *Exodus* (Tyndale Old Testament Commentaries; Inter-Varsity Press, 1973)

Childs, *Exodus* — Brevard S. Childs, *The Book of Exodus* (The Old Testament Library; Westminster Press, 1974)

Craigie, *Deuteronomy* — P. C. Craigie, *The Book of Deuteronomy* (New International Commentary on the Old Testament; Eerdmans, 1976)

Davis, *Moses* — John J. Davis, *Moses and the Gods of Egypt: Studies in Exodus* (Baker Book House, 1971)

DOTP — T. Desmond Alexander and David W. Baker (editors), *Dictionary of the Old Testament: Pentateuch* (InterVarsity Press, 2003)

Durham, — John I. Durham, *Exodus* (Word Biblical Commentary; Nelson, 1987)

Exodus

God's Wilderness	Beno Rothenberg, in collaboration with Yohanan Aharoni and Avia Hashimshoni, *God's Wilderness: Discoveries in Sinai* (Thomas Nelson, 1961-62)
Harrison, *Leviticus*	R. K. Harrison, *Leviticus* (Tyndale Old Testament Commentary; Inter-Varsity Press, 1980)
Harrison, *Numbers*	R. K. Harrison, *Numbers: An Exegetical Commentary* (Baker Book House, 1992)
Holladay	William L. Holladay (editor), *A Concise Hebrew and Aramaic Lexicon of the Old Testament, based upon the Lexical work of Ludwig Koehler and Walter Baumgartner* (Eerdmans/Brill, 1971, 1988)
Hyatt, *Exodus*	J. Philip Hyatt, *Exodus* (New Century Bible Commentary; Eerdmans, 1971)
ISBE	Geoffrey W. Bromiley (general editor), *The International Standard Bible Encyclopedia* (Eerdmans, 1979-1988; fully revised from the 1915 edition)
Keil and Delitzsch	Carl Friedrich Keil and Franz Delitzsch, *Commentary on the Old Testament* (10 volumes; Eerdmans, 1976, reprinted from earlier editions, originally appearing in 1861. The Pentateuch portion was written by Keil and translated from the German by James Martin)
Kitchen	K.A. Kitchen, *On the Reliability of the Old Testament* (Eerdmans, 2003)
KJV	King James Version (Authorized Version, 1611)
NASB	New American Standard Bible (The Lockman Foundation, 1960-1988)
NIV	New International Version (International Bible Society, 1973, 1978)
NJB	New Jerusalem Bible (Darton, Longman & Todd Ltd, 1985)
NRSV	New Revised Standard Version (Division of Christian Education of the

National Council of Churches of Christ, USA, 1989)

TDNT   Gerhard Kittel and Gerhard Friedrich (editors), Geoffrey W. Bromiley
               (translator and editor), *Theological Dictionary of the New Testament*
               (Eerdmans, 1964-1976; translated from *Theologisches Wörterbuch zum Neuen
               Testament*, ten volume edition)

Thompson,   J. A. Thompson, *Deuteronomy* (Tyndale Old Testament Commentaries;
Deuteronomy Inter-Varsity Press, 1974)

Thompson,   J. A. Thompson, *The Ancient Near Eastern Treaties and the Old Testament*
Treaties   (London: Tyndale Press, 1964)

Wenham,   Gordon J. Wenham, *The Book of Leviticus* (New International Commentary
Leviticus   on the Old Testament; Eerdmans, 1979)

Wenham,   Gordon J. Wenham, *Numbers* (Tyndale Old Testament Commentaries;
Numbers   Inter-Varsity Press, 1981)

Introduction to Moses and the Exodus

The Exodus was certainly an historical event, as was Moses, the Reluctant Leader. But they're so far back in history that it's difficult to know some of the details that interest historians. Archaeological clues are scanty and there are no contemporaneous mentions of Moses and his feat. But here, let's discuss some issues such as dating of the Exodus and the sources for the Pentateuch.

Dating of the Exodus

When did the Exodus take place? If we can determine that, we'll know something about the historical setting of the people of Israel at this time. There are two popular theories of the date of the Exodus:

- Early date, about 1470 BC, end of the Middle Bronze Age
- Late date, about 1250 BC, Late Bronze Age IIB

James J. Tissot, "Moses on the Mountain during the Battle" (1896-1900), watercolor, Jewish Museum, New York.

A number of factors go into dating. This is not a matter of liberals vs. conservatives, but a matter of weighing the evidence carefully. Evidence comes from several sources: references in the Bible that can be tied to specific dates, archaeological excavations of ancient cities, and inscriptions found on ancient monuments and buildings. Weighing this evidence is quite difficult, since some of it seems ambiguous. But here's the major evidence that has come to light so far.

Store Cities of Rameses and Pithom

There are two Egyptian store-cities mentioned in the Exodus account – Pithom and Rameses (Exodus 1:11). The Exodus began when "the Israelites journeyed from Rameses to Succoth" (Exodus 12:37).

Scholars identify Rameses ("house of Rameses") as Qantir or Tell el-Dab'a, the ancient Avaris/Pi-Ramesse, dating to the beginning of the Eighteenth Dynasty of Egypt. The first city on that site was founded by Seti I (1294-1279 BC). Major development, however, took place under his son, Rameses II, a great builder, whose 67-year reign extended from 1279-1213 BC.[1] Rameses II established Pi-Ramesse as his capital city. It consisted of a mud-brick citadel associated with storage facilities to support military efforts in Canaan. It declined from 1130 BC onward. Its

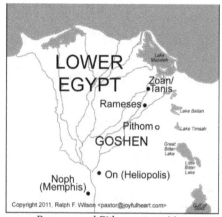

Rameses and Pithom, store cities

temple stonework was reused to build new temples at Tanis (Zoan) and elsewhere. The disused mud-brick structures crumbled back into the Nile mud from which they had been drawn.[2]

Some argue that, since the city (under another name) existed prior to Rameses II, it could have been referred to as Rameses as an anachronism, but I don't find that very likely. To me, the mention of the city of Rameses is evidence for the Late Date of the Exodus.

Merneptah Stela

One piece of hard evidence dated between 1220 and 1207 BC[3] is the Merneptah Stela, sometimes called the Israel Stela, a black granite stela or commemorative pillar found in the ruins of a pharaoh's mortuary temple at Thebes. Merneptah was a pharaoh of the Nineteenth Dynasty (c. 1213-1203 BC), successor of Rameses II, who inscribed on this stela a series of victory hymns that appear to mention *Ysr'r* (Egyptian for *Ysr'l*) among his conquests in Syria-Palestine This seems to indicate that the Israelites were in Palestine at this time, so it marks the latest possible date for the conclusion of the Exodus period.[4]

[1] K. A. Kitchen, *Ancient Orient and Old Testament* (InterVarsity Press, 1966), pp. 57-58, fn. 6, sees his accession taking place in either 1304 or 1290, based on a combination of lunar and historical data. William S. LaSor ("Ramses," ISBE 3:41-42) pegs the date at 1304 BC. Other sources state his accession as 1279 BC.

[2] K. A. Kitchen, "Egypt, Egyptians," DOTP, p. 210.

[3] The stela was placed in the fifth year of Merneptah's reign. Using Kuhrt's "middle chronology" this would be c. 1220. Using Kitchen's "low chronology," adopted here, the date would be about 1208.

[4] Gary Pratico, "Merneptah," ISBE 3:324-325.

Amarna Letters

In 1887, more than 300 clay tablets were discovered in Upper Egypt at Amarna. They are written in Akkadian cuneiform, and consist of correspondence that spans 15 to 30 years during the reign of Pharaoh Amenhotep III (1390-1352 BC). They consist of letters between Egypt and various vassal city-states or administrative centers, including several in Palestine. There is no mention of Israel or the Israelites. However, the `apiru referred to are probably "warlords, brigands, and disenfranchised peoples on the outskirts of society." The word cannot be etymologically related to the word "Hebrew" and the word cannot be equated with the Israelites.[5] For those who contend for an Early Date for the Exodus, the Amarna Letters present several problems since they contain no clear reference to the Israelites who (according the Early Date theory) should be in Canaan by this time.[6]

Conquest of Canaanite Cites

The results of archaeological digs in ancient Canaanite cities don't provide consistent support for either a late or early date. The data is controversial and often incomplete. In Jericho, the only discovery of city walls that would seem to match the Conquest account in Joshua is found in Stratum IV, usually dated about 1550 BC. After that, there seems to have been no significant occupation until well into the Iron Age. This might argue for an earlier date for the Exodus and Conquest.

Reference in 1 Kings

An Early Date of about 1446 BC (fifteenth century, Late Bronze I) can be derived by adding up numbers in the Bible. The key text says:

> "In the four hundred and eightieth year after the Israelites had come out of Egypt, in the fourth year of Solomon's reign over Israel, in the month of Ziv, the second month, he began to build the temple of the LORD." (1 Kings 6:1)

Since the dedication of Solomon's temple occurred in 966 BC, this gives a date of 1446 BC for the Exodus. But to complicate matters, the Masoretic Hebrew text reads 480 years, while the Greek Septuagint text reads 440 years, which would make the date of the Exodus about 1406 BC.

But how does this fit with the historical data that we can glean from other documents and from the evidence of archaeological digs? An event of the magnitude of the Exodus

---

[5] Ibid., p. 263.
[6] Ibid., pp. 263-264.

should synch with at least some events in the surrounding cultures. Unfortunately, the resulting data at this point just isn't that clear-cut.

Is there another way of understanding 1 Kings 6:1? To pioneering Bible archaeologist William F. Albright, the number looks less like an exact figure, but rather a round figure of 12 generations of 40 years each, the usual conventional length. But if men were 20 to 30 at the birth of their eldest son as often seemed the case, the period of 12 generations would actually bring the date of the Exodus to the 13th century BC.[7]

Old Testament scholar K. A. Kitchen observes,

> "In principle, this problem is not quite so contradictory as it may appear, if we remember that the Old Testament is also part of the Ancient Near East, and therefore that Ancient Oriental principles must be applied. Thus, in ordinary king lists and historical narratives, ancient scribes and writers did not usually include synchronistic tables[8] and cross-references as we do today."[9]

Summing Up

So which date has the most support? This is difficult. My own tentative conclusion is the Late Date. Evangelical Old Testament scholar R.K. Harrison agrees.

> "The beginning of the Conquest can be dated about 1235 BC, or slightly later, on the assumption that the Exodus occurred in the thirteenth rather than the fifteenth century BC."[10]

This would make

- Seti I (1294-1279 BC) the pharaoh of the oppression, and
- Rameses II (1279-1213 BC) the pharaoh of the Exodus

But, as Durham puts it,

> "The chronology of the events described in Exodus is of little importance to the theological message of the book in its present form."[11]

Who Wrote the Books of Moses?

The second question I'd like to explore briefly is: Who wrote the Books of Moses? Of course, the traditional answer is Moses himself. But note that nowhere in the Pentateuch

---

[7] Cole, *Exodus*, p. 42.

[8] For example, it is likely that the reigns of the judges overlapped. We also see princes co-reigning with their fathers for a period, before the reigning king died.

[9] Kitchen, *Ancient Orient*, p. 72.

[10] Harrison, *Introduction to the Old Testament*, p. 177. Cecil B. DeMille's epic movie "The Ten Commandments" (1956) and the animated film "Prince of Egypt" (1998) assume a late date for the Exodus.

[11] Durham, *Exodus*, p. xxvi.

does the author speak in the first person, but always in the third person voice of a narrator.

Moses didn't have any difficulty writing. After all, he was well educated. Moreover, the Scripture specifically says that he wrote down God's revelation (Exodus 17:14; 24:4, 12; 34:27; etc.). Surely, Moses was the original author of a considerable part of the Pentateuch!

But when you read the Pentateuch carefully, you begin to see "seams" between some of the various stories narrated, as if they were put together by a final editor or redactor from various documents in existence when the final version was complete.

The most celebrated and complex theory of authorship was advanced by German Old Testament scholar Julius Wellhausen (1844-1918), which is referred to as "the Documentary Hypothesis." He posited four strands of sources, which are abbreviated JEDP:

J	Yahwistic
E	Eloistic
D	Deuteronomic
P	Priestly

The Yahwistic strand could be identified, so goes the theory, by the editor's use of Yahweh (Jehovah) or LORD for God; the Eloistic strand by the use of El for God. Wellhausen was widely influential and the theory grew more and more complex – and speculative. These days, however, Wellhausen's JEDP theory is in disarray. R.N. Whybray commented in 1995 on the state of Pentateuchal studies:

> "There is at the present moment no consensus whatever about when, why, how, and through whom the Pentateuch reached its present form, and opinions about the dates of composition of its various parts differ by more than five hundred years."[12]

Certainly, Jesus, the Jews, and the early church all believed that the Pentateuch (which the Jews referred to as "the law") was inspired by God and attributed it as a whole to Moses. It's likely that the materials Moses or other early editors worked with represent oral and written traditions dated much earlier than Moses himself. Whether Moses was the first to write down the stories of Abraham and his descendents or served as an editor himself, we just don't know.[13] Our focus will not be on speculative theories

---

[12] R.N. Whybray, *Introduction to the Pentateuch* (Eerdmans, 1995), pp. 12-13, cited in T. Desmond Alexander, "Authorship of the Pentateuch," DOTP 61-72.

[13] Alexander, DOTP 61-72; Hamilton, *Genesis* 1:11-38.

of sources, but on the text that comes down to us in the Bible and the meaning of that revelation.

We'll look at the route of the Exodus in Appendix 2 and New Testament references to Moses in Appendix 3. Other questions will be covered in the appropriate lesson.

1. The Birth and Call of Moses (Exodus 1-4)

The Book of Exodus begins with a recital of the names of the patriarchs, the sons of Jacob, who had gone to Egypt centuries before when Joseph had been at the pinnacle of power as second to Pharaoh over all Egypt. But now things had changed.

A. Introduction (Exodus 1:1-22)

The Pharaoh Who Knew Not Joseph (Exodus 1:6-10)

James J. Tissot, "Pharaoh Notes the Importance of the Jewish People" (1896-1900), watercolor, Jewish Museum, New York. The pyramids in the background aren't accurate, however, since the largest were at Giza, far south of Pi-Rameses.

The family that had emigrated with 70 members (1:5) had now become a multitude.

> "The Israelites were fruitful and multiplied greatly and became exceedingly numerous, so that the land was filled with them." (Exodus 1:7)

I see two themes in chapter one:
  1. Increase and
  2. Oppression

The text uses the phrase "multiplied greatly" (NIV), "were prolific" (NRSV), "increased abundantly" (KJV). The Hebrew word is interesting – *shāras*, "teem, swarm,"[1] the same word used to describe the swarm of frogs that overtook Egypt in the second plague (Exodus 8:3). The Israelites were everywhere in Goshen!

This increase caused fear among the Egyptian leaders. Since the Israelites hadn't been assimilated and didn't consider themselves as Egyptians, Pharaoh feared that such a large group could pose an internal security threat in time of war. Verse 12 uses the word "dread."[2] If Egypt were attacked by an enemy at their front, the Israelites might use the

---

[1] *Shāras*, BDB 1056.

[2] "Dread" (NIV, NRSV), "be grieved" (KJV) is *qûs*, "feel a loathing, abhorrence, sickening dread" (BDB 880), "feel a disgust for," here "feel a horror of." (Holladay, pp. 316-317).

opportunity to (1) fight against the Egyptian army from behind and then (2) escape from the country (Exodus 1:10).

The Pharaoh, who reigned centuries after Joseph's time, concluded that a new policy towards the Israelites was required. He would "deal shrewdly"(NRSV) or "deal wisely" (NIV, KJV) with them strictly in the Egyptians' self-interest.[3]

Instead of allowing them relative freedom as subsistence farmers, their freedoms would be curtailed. Pharaoh began a policy of systematic oppression and forced labor.

Oppressing the Israelites (Exodus 1:11-14)

The oppression or affliction[4] escalated as the threat the Israelites posed became more apparent, as verse 14 tells us.

1. **Construction projects** with forced labor under slave masters.[5] Their labor built the empire's storage or supply depot cities[6] at Pithom and Rameses.
2. **Brick[7] making**, described in Exodus 5:7. These bricks, which built the buildings, were made of the clay along the Nile mixed with straw and stubble to add strength, and then joined to other bricks with mortar.[8]
3. **Field labor**.

None of this was voluntary or paid labor. It was the ancient institution of tribute or corvee that involved service for a superior power – a feudal lord, a king, or a foreign ruler.[9] It left precious little time to till their own fields and eke out a living for their families. Life was exceedingly bitter (1:14).

---

3 *Hākam*, "be wise, act wise(ly)." "The essential idea of *hākam* represents a manner of thinking and attitude concerning life's experiences; including matters of general interest and basic morality. These concerns relate to prudence in secular affairs, skills in the arts, moral sensitivity, and experience in the ways of the Lord" (Louis Goldberg, TWOT #647).

4 "Oppressed" (NIV, NRSV), "afflicted" (KJV) in 1:11 is *ānâ*, with the primary meaning of "to force," or "to try to force submission," and "to punish or inflict pain upon." Here, "afflict, oppress, humble" (Leonard J. Coppes, TWOT #1652).

5 "Slave masters" (NIV), "taskmasters" (KJV) is *mas*, body of forced laborers, task-workers, labor-band or gang," here, of chief of *mas*, "gang-overseers" (BDB 586, 2a).

6 "Store cities" (NIV), "treasure cities" (KJV), "supply cities" (NRSV) translates "city" (*îr*) plus *miskenôt*, "storage house, magazine," designating a place of service, particularly storage cities (1 Kings 9:19; 2 Chronicles 16:4; 17:12) (R.D. Patterson, *miskenôt*, TWOT #1494a).

7 "Brick" is *lebēnâ*, "brick, tile," from the whiteness of clay or the light color of sun-baked bricks. (BDB 526).

8 "Mortar" is *hōmer*, "Cement, mortar, clay." This noun was also a term for the reddish clay of that area, particularly Palestine (Gerhard Van Granigen, TWOT #683d).

9 G. Lloyd Carr, *mas*, TWOT #1218.

This was not a mild oppression. This was a full-out subjugation of a people into slavery. In verse 14b, it says, "In all their hard labor the Egyptians used them ruthlessly."[10] Harshness and severity were the rule of the day.

Killing the Male Babies (Exodus 1:15-23)

Harsh oppression may have kept the Israelites under better control to prevent a rebellion, but their numbers kept increasing. To stop this, Pharaoh ordered the midwives to kill the male babies. When this didn't work, he decreed that all boy babies be exposed as infants and left to die.

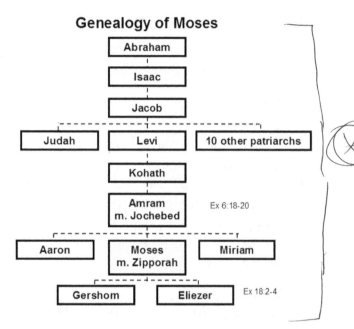

Genealogy of Moses

Abraham — Isaac — Jacob — Judah / Levi / 10 other patriarchs — Kohath — Amram m. Jochebed (Ex 6:18-20) — Aaron / Moses m. Zipporah / Miriam — Gershom / Eliezer (Ex 18:2-4)

B. Infancy (Exodus 2:1-10)

The Birth of Moses (Exodus 2:1-4)

In verse 1 we learn that Moses is a descendant of Levi, one of the 12 sons of Jacob. Exodus 6:20 gives Moses' and Aaron's parents as Amram and Jochebed, who is his father's younger sister. The weight of Pharaoh's edict is heavy upon this couple. Jochebed sees Moses as all mothers see their sons – "a fine child"![11]

She can't expose him, but neither can she keep him. So she weaves a basket[12] for him from the reeds,[13] then waterproofs it with tar[14] and pitch so that it won't leak. She obeys

---

[10] "Ruthlessly" (NIV, cf. NRSV), "with rigor" (KJV) in verses 13 and 14 is *perek*, "harshness, severity" (BDB 827).

[11] "Fine" (NIV, NRSV), "goodly" (KJV) is *tôb*, which refers to "good" or "goodness" in its broadest senses." It can mean, "good, pleasant, beautiful, delightful, glad, joyful, precious, correct, righteous," or it could mean "happy" (Andrew Bowling, TWOT #793a).

[12] "Basket" (NIV, NRSV), "ark" (KJV) is *tēbâ*, "ark," properly, "chest, box." It is the same word used for Noah's ark.

[13] "Papyrus" (NIV, NRSV), "bulrushes" (KJV) is *gōme'*, "rush, reed, papyrus" (BDB 167).

[14] "Tar" (NIV), "bitumen" (NRSV), "slime" (KJV) is *ḥēmār*, "bitumen, asphalt" (BDB 330).

the letter of the law, but sends her daughter Miriam to watch over the floating basket, deliberately placed among the reeds[15] along the Nile where one of Pharaoh's daughters was known to bathe.[16]

Moses Is Adopted by Pharaoh's Daughter (Exodus 2:5-10)

So God arranged for Moses to be raised in his earliest years in his mother's and father's home. This way he got a clear idea who he was – that he was a Hebrew, a descendent of Abraham, Isaac, and Jacob.

If the Pharaoh at the time is Rameses II (and we can't be sure) then this daughter is one of 60 daughters. She may have lived in one of his numerous hunting lodges scattered over the delta area.[17] Harrison sees her as the adolescent offspring of one of the pharaohs by a concubine or some lesser paramour, and not one of the chief princesses of full royal blood.[18] If so, Moses didn't necessarily grow up in the royal palace as a royal prince, but he certainly benefited from his status as an adopted royal. In Acts we read:

> "When he was placed outside, Pharaoh's daughter took him and brought him up as her own son. Moses was educated[19] in all the wisdom of the Egyptians and was powerful in speech and action." (Acts 7:21-22)

C. Moses the Activist (Exodus 2:11-22)

Moses Commits Murder (Exodus 2:11-15a)

Moses is now about 40 (Acts 7:23) and seems to have adopted the arrogance of a member of the ruling class. The next incident tells us a lot about his character.

---

[15] "Reeds" (NIV, NRSV), "flags" (KJV) is *sûp*, "reeds, rushes" (BDB 693).

[16] Scholars have drawn attention to the fact that a similar story was told centuries later about the Assyrian ruler Sargon. Whether it draws upon the Moses story, we don't know. The Legend of Sargon, a much-later neo-Assyrian text from the seventh century BC. Sargon was an Akkadian emperor (reigned c. 2270 to 2215 BC) who conquered the Sumerian city-states.

[17] Cole, *Exodus*, p. 58; Harrison (*Intro*, p. 575) cites R.A. Caminos, *Literary Fragments in the Hieratic Script* (1956), pp. 19ff.

[18] Harrison, *Intro*, p. 575.

[19] Harrison observes, "Children of the *harîm* [harem], especially male princes, were frequently educated under the supervision of the *harîm* overseer, and at a rather later date the princes were educated by the priestly caste in reading and writing, the transcription of classical texts, civil administration, and in certain physical accomplishments" (Harrison, *Intro*, p. 575, citing F.L. Griffiths and P.E. Newberry, *El Bersheh* (1894), II, p. 40).

> "One day, after Moses had grown up, he went out to where his own people were and watched them at their hard labor. He saw an Egyptian beating a Hebrew, one of his own people. Glancing this way and that and seeing no one, he killed the Egyptian and hid him in the sand." (Exodus 2:11-12)

Moses, of course, wasn't seen by most as a Hebrew, but a prince of Pharaoh's family. He has a predictable reaction when he sees his countrymen being abused. "Beating" (NIV, NRSV), "smiting" (KJV) in verse 11 is the same Hebrew word as "killed" (NIV, NRSV), "slew" (KJV) in verse 12 – *nākâ*, "smite, strike, hit, beat, slay, kill." It can vary from a single stroke, to a beating, to mean even "strike dead."[20]

Moses' response is interesting. He doesn't seek legal justice in Pharaoh's court. Rather, "glancing this way and that," provides his own rough but illegal justice. This suggests several things about Moses:

1. He identifies himself as a Hebrew.
2. He has a strong sense of basic justice.
3. He is willing to take charge of a situation, a man of action. On this occasion he is decisive, perhaps to the point of being rash. But he is not a timid man.
4. He is physically strong.
5. He seems to have no sense yet of acting for God.

But he is not seen as a leader or even having authority by his own people. Here's the take-charge leader asserting himself again, but his authority isn't recognized. I would guess that he was well-known among the Hebrews as "one of our people made good," but his intervention in this quarrel doesn't seem to be appreciated. He may be a prince in Egypt, but that doesn't win him real respect among his own people. They question Moses' right to be either a ruler[21] or judge[22] over them.

Leadership Is Influence

Pause here for a moment. Moses is a member of the ruling class, but not a ruler. Why? He has neither office nor influence among those he seeks to lead. We often mistake holding a leadership position or office as "leadership." You can impose your will if you hold an office, perhaps, but is that leading?

---

[20] Marvin R. Wilson, *nākâ*, TWOT #1364.

[21] "Ruler" is *śar*, from the verb *śārar*, "rule, reign, act as a prince, govern." The noun can refer to leaders and chieftains, military commanders, as well as various ranks of government officials, nobles, and courtiers (Gary G. Cohen, *śārar*, TWOT #2295a).

[22] "Judge" is the verb *shāpaṭ*, "to judge, govern." It's the most common word for governing in the Old Testament, and the term for the series "judges" who ruled as leaders in Israel between Joshua and Saul (Robert D. Culver, *shāpaṭ*, TWOT #2443).

John C. Maxwell, in his classic *21 Irrefutable Laws of Leadership*, asserts that leadership is influence, pure and simple.[23] Many a pastor has come to a church expecting to be the congregation's leader, only to find that the real leaders, the people who calls the shots, are a couple of the old-time members who everyone in the congregation turns to – even if they no longer have any official leadership role.

Moses is influential later because he has encountered God and is able to speak with an authority and miracles that are recognized by his peers.

Is leadership a part of a person's personal charisma or can it be learned? There are people who are "natural leaders," of course, who carry themselves as leaders and whose leadership is accepted by those around them, even if they're new to a situation. But notice that Moses was not one of these. He emerged as a leader as he was transformed by God. You can learn to be a leader – and if you're already a "natural leader," you can become a better leader.

At this point, however, Moses is clearly not a "natural leader." He has no response to his countrymen's challenge, "Who are you?" Moreover, he is suddenly frightened – frightened enough to run[24] for his life. Dear friends, there is a time for everything under heaven. Jesus and his apostles knew when it was time for a strategic retreat also.[25]

You may have fled from situations in your life. But don't think that this is the end of you as a leader. God has a way of retooling and equipping his leaders for future tasks. God hasn't given up on you!

Q1. (Exodus 2:11-15a) What do we learn about Moses' motivations, character, and leadership ability from the incident of him killing the cruel Egyptian taskmaster? What positive things do you see in his character? What negative things do you discern?
http://www.joyfulheart.com/forums/index.php?showtopic=1034

---

[23] John C. Maxwell, *The 21 Irrefutable Laws of Leadership* (Thomas Nelson, 1998, revised 2007).

[24] "Fled" is *bārah*, "to go or pass through, and to flee or hurry." It occurs mostly in narratives, referring to flight from an enemy (Earl S. Kalland, TWOT #248).

[25] Luke 4:30; John 8:59; 10:39; Acts 8:1; 12:17; 14:6; etc.

Moses Flees to Midian and Delivers Jethro's Daughters (Exodus 2:15-17)

Where is Midian? Probably east of the Gulf of Aqaba or in the eastern Sinai peninsula.[26]

Moses stops by a well – doubtless near a settlement, and a great place for this wanderer to meet people. As he is there, shepherds – young, beautiful shepherd girls – are watering their father's flock. The shepherds would lower down into the well a pot or jar, let it fill, then pull it up and pour the water into troughs where the sheep could drink. Now Moses watches while some

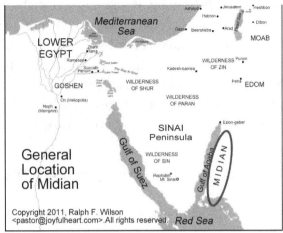

Location of Midian

male shepherds push their way in and threaten[27] the girls who got there first.

> "Some shepherds came along and drove them away, but Moses got up and came to their rescue and watered their flock." (Exodus 2:17)

Moses has just gotten in trouble trying to see justice done in Egypt. Now he takes it upon himself to fight off these bullies. This may mean that Moses is physically strong, but more likely it means that he is just assertive. It's likely that these male shepherds are young – older children or teenagers – and not very confident in the face of a grown man, an Egyptian, threatening them with his staff.

Moses not only "came to their rescue,"[28] but finished watering the girls' flock himself – a menial task you would not expect a grown man to perform in this culture.

Middle Eastern Hospitality (Exodus 2:18-22)

Now we meet a man who will be linked to Moses' future success – Jethro, here called Reuel. The girls' father asks them why they didn't invite the man into their home. In our culture, it would be very wrong for girls to invite a strange man home. But in the Middle

---

[26] George E. Mendenhall, "Midian," ABD 4:815-818; T.V. Brisco, "Midian," TDNT 3:349-351.

[27] "Drive away" is gārash, which can mean variously, "cast up, drive out/away, divorce, expel, put away, thrust out, trouble" (TWOT #388).

[28] "Came to the rescue" (NIV), "came to the defense" (NRSV), "helped" (KJV) is the verb yāsha', in the Hiphil stem, "save, deliver, give victory, help." The noun form of this word is yeshû'â, "salvation," from which the names Joshua and Jesus are derived. Moses is the girls' savior. This prefigures Yahweh's salvation that Moses brings to the whole people of Israel at the Red Sea (Exodus 14:13).

East, strangers are treated well – especially strangers who assist in time of danger. To fail to offer hospitality is a grievous social breach. The father rebukes his daughters.

So they run back to the well to fetch the stranger and bring him home. The father then extends the invitation and finally offers his daughter to Moses in marriage.[29]

The father is identified as a "priest of Midian" (Exodus 2:16), a designation marking him as a person of status with a strongly religious role in the hierarchy of Midianite society.[30] Moses' father-in-law is identified by several names in the Bible,[31] but for the most part in Exodus, he is known by the name Jethro.

D. The Call of Moses (Exodus 2:23-4:17)

God Hears His People's Cry (Exodus 2:23-25)

Moses' life can be roughly divided into three periods, each about 40 years.[32] Here's one way to describe his life:

1.	Prince of Egypt	Proud in man's knowledge and status	40 yrs
2.	Shepherd in Midian	Humbled and molded by God	40 yrs
3.	Leader	Obedient servant	40 yrs

By the time the third phase of Moses' life begins, he is about 80 years of age. He has been a humble shepherd for half his life, far away from the hustle and bustle of Egyptian

---

[29] It's likely that Moses came with no bride price, like Jacob when he wanted to marry Rachel, Laban's daughter (Genesis 29:14-30). So Moses, like his ancestor Jacob, is later employed by Jethro as a far-ranging shepherd, taking this father-in-law's flock far afield to find pasture (Exodus 3:1).

[30] Hughes, "Jethro," DOTP, p. 467.

[31] Reuel (re'û'ēl, "friend of God"; Exodus 2:18); Jethro (yitrô, "his excellence"; Exodus 3:1; 4:18; 18:1-12); Hobab (ḥōbāb, "cherished," Judges 4:11). In Numbers 10:29, Hobab is said to be the son of Raguel the Midianite. W.F. Albright saw Reuel as a clan name and Jethro as his proper name, with Numbers 10:29-32 explained by a misvocalization of the Hebrew text, which should have been ḥōtēn, "son-in-law" referring to Moses (W.F. Albright, "Jethro, Hobab, and Ruel," CBQ 25 (1963) 1-11, cited by P.E. Hughes, "Jethro," DOTP, pp. 467-469).

[32] Exodus 7:7; Acts 7:23-24, 29-30, 36; Numbers 32:13; Deuteronomy 34:7. Forty years may be a literal number (Deuteronomy 2:14), but often it is used as a round number used for a relatively long period of time, specifically, the traditional number of years in a generation (Judges 3:11; 5:31; 8:28; 1 Samuel 4:18; etc.). In the Exodus, 40 years is the period of time that it took for one generation to die out and be replaced by a new one. A sense of completeness or maturity is attached to the number. A man was considered to reach full adulthood at 40 (Joshua 14:7; 2 Samuel 2:10). See Bruce C. Birch, "Number," TDNT 3:558.

society and culture. For the most part, his life has been quiet, solitary, out in the desert pastures, except when he is home in his family's tent.

So far, the narrator has offered an introduction to Moses' character. But now the real story of the Exodus begins.

> "23 During that long period, the king of Egypt died. The Israelites groaned in their slavery and cried out, and their cry for help because of their slavery went up to God. 24 God heard their groaning and he remembered his covenant with Abraham, with Isaac and with Jacob. 25 So God looked on the Israelites and was concerned about them." (Exodus 2:23-25)

Notice three things from these verses:

1. **God's compassion**.[33] The Exodus isn't about Moses at all. It is about God's compassion and plan. God is the main player in the story. Moses is only his servant – a great servant, but still only a servant.
2. **God's faithfulness**. God has made promises to Abraham and his descendants called covenants. He is faithful to keep his promises!
3. **Sustained prayer**. The deliverance took place through anguished prayer[34] to God. God hears our prayers and answers them. All significant revivals have taken place as a result of consistent, urgent prayer before God for help. Don't give up, even if it seems like God isn't answering immediately!

The Burning Bush (Exodus 3:1-5)

Now God begins his plan in answer to the prayers of the Israelites. He appears to Moses. Wide-ranging shepherds had probably seen shrub fires lit by lightning strikes. But this bush wasn't consumed.[35] Moses came closer to see if he could find an explanation for this phenomenon.

---

[33] "Was concerned" (NIV), "took notice" (NRSV), "had respect unto" (KJV), is the very common verb *yāda'*, "to know." Here it is used in the sense of "most intimate acquaintance with" (Paul R. Gilchrist, TWOT #848).

[34] "Groaned" (NIV, NRSV), "sighed" (KJV) is *'ānah*, "sigh, groan, gasp" from mental or physical distress" (Charles L. Feinberg, TWOT #127). "Cried" is *zā'aq*, "to cry for help in time of distress… In the Qal stem [as here], the word is used almost exclusively in reference to a cry from a disturbed heart, in need of some kind of help. The cry is not in summons of another, but an expression of the need felt. Most frequently, the cry is directed to God" (Judges 6:6-7; Leon J. Wood, TWOT #570).

[35] "Burn up" (NIV, NRSV), "consume" (KJV) is *'ākal*, "to eat, consume, devour, burn up" (Jack B. Scott, TWOT #85).

The narrator tells us that this was "the angel of the LORD," who appears elsewhere in the Pentateuch. Often the "angel of the LORD" is referred to earlier in the passage, while later in same the passage the person speaking is identified as the LORD (Yahweh) himself.[36] The angel "appears"[37] here in the flame itself, not as a person. Elsewhere, God appears as a "consuming fire,"[38] and his "glory" as a brightness that cannot be looked at with the naked eye. The tongues of fire (flames) that appeared over the believers on the Day of Pentecost typify the presence of God in his Holy Spirit.

Eugene Pluchart (French painter, 1809-1880), "God Appears to Moses in Burning Bush" (1848), St. Isaac of Dalmatia Cathedral, St. Petersburg.

God attracts Moses' attention with the flames. Now he calls to him, with his voice coming from the burning bush. God calls[39] Moses by name, and Moses answers. Then God informs him of the holiness[40] of the place and instructs him to act appropriately by taking off his sandals.[41]

---

[36] Genesis 16:7-13 (revealed to Hagar); 22:15-16 (to Abraham on Mt. Moriah); Numbers 22:22-35 (to Balaam); Judges 6:11-22 (to Gideon); Judges 13:3-21 (to Sampson's parents); as well as to Elijah, Elisha, etc.

[37] "Appeared" is the common verb rā'â, "see, look at." Here in the Niphal stem, it carries the passive idea, "to be seen or to reveal oneself" (Robert D. Culver, TWOT #2095).

[38] Exodus 24:17; Deuteronomy 4:24, 36; Hebrews 12:18, 29.

[39] "Called" is qārā', "call, call out." "The root qr' denotes primarily the enunciation of a specific vocable or message. In the case of the latter usage it is customarily addressed to a specific recipient and is intended to elicit a specific response (hence, it may be translated 'proclaim, invite')" (Leonard J. Coppes, TWOT #2063).

[40] "Holy" is qōdesh, "apartness, holiness, sacredness, hallowed, holy." "The noun qōdesh connotes the concept of "holiness," i.e. the essential nature of that which belongs to the sphere of the sacred and which is thus distinct from the common or profane" (Thomas E. McComiskey, TWOT #1990a).

[41] Na'al is the generic Hebrew word for footwear, either a shoe or a sandal (David M. Howard, Jr., "Shoe, Sandal," ISBE 4:491-492). Holy places in the Old Testament are seen in the tabernacle precincts where priests are obliged to take off their regular clothing and wear priestly garments that have been consecrated to God (Exodus 28-29). Apparently, the priests went about their duties barefoot. When Joshua meets "the commander of the LORD's army" outside of Jericho, he, too, is told, "Take off your sandals, for the place where you are standing is holy" (Joshua 5:15). Jacob was awed by his vision of angels ascending to and from heaven, senses the holiness of the place, and said, "How awesome is this place! This is none other than the house of God ... the gate of heaven" (Genesis 28:16-17).

God's Promise (Exodus 3:6-9)

"[7] The LORD said, 'I have indeed seen the misery of my people in Egypt. I have heard them crying out because of their slave drivers, and I am concerned about their suffering. [8] So I have come down to rescue them from the hand of the Egyptians and to bring them up out of that land into a good and spacious land, a land flowing with milk and honey....'" (Exodus 3:7-8)

God's message to Moses from the burning bush is four-fold:
1. **Seeing.** I have seen my people's misery and oppression.
2. **Hearing.** I have heard their cries and prayers.
3. **Rescuing.** I will rescue them.[42]
4. **Giving.** I will bring them into a land that I will give them.

God's

This is a wonderful promise, the fulfillment of the covenant that God had spoken to Abraham and the patriarchs hundreds of years previously.[43]

in us too!

Moses' Call (Exodus 3:10-12)

"So now, go. I am **sending you** to Pharaoh to bring my people the Israelites out of Egypt." (Exodus 3:10)

After stating the promise, God explains that he is appointing[44] Moses to fulfill this promise. When God appoints you and gives you a mission, you don't question – you go!

But Moses questions God: "Who am I, that I should go...?" This statement and others in Moses' running dispute with God in Exodus 3-4 indicate a profound humility. Later, the Scripture explains,

"Now Moses was a very humble[45] man, more humble than anyone else on the face of the earth." (Numbers 12:3)

Written by Moses! ☺

---

[42] "Rescue" (NIV), "deliver" (NRSV, KJV) is *nāṣal*, "deliver, rescue, save." An Arabic cognate verb indicates that the basic meaning is one of "drawing out or pulling out" (Milton C. Fisher, TWOT #1404).

[43] Genesis 13:14-18; 15:14; 50:24; etc.

[44] "Sending/send" in verse 10 is *shālah*, which is often used where God is sending people on an official mission as his envoys or representatives (for example, Isaiah 6:8; Jeremiah 1:7; etc.). (Hermann J. Austel, TWOT #2394). The corresponding Greek word in the New Testament is *apostellō*, from which we get our word "apostle," which means, "one who is sent."

[45] "Humble" (NIV, NRSV), "meek" (KJV) is ʿânâv, from ʿānâ, "afflict, oppress, humble," with the primary meaning "to force" or "to try to force submission." The adjective "stresses the moral and spiritual condition of the godly as the goal of affliction implying that this state is joined with a suffering life rather than with one of worldly happiness and abundance" (Leonard J. Coppes, TWOT #1652a).

Moses had experienced a kind of brokenness. As a prince of Egypt he operated with a sense of entitlement and arrogance because of both his place in the ruling class of society and his superior education. But 40 years before he had fled from Egypt as a common criminal. Now he was a lowly shepherd at age 80, watching flocks that were not even his own. "Who am I?" asks Moses.

But his question also betrays a lack of faith. He assumes that he must carry out this task by himself. Nothing could be further from the truth. God says to him, "I will be with you" (Exodus 3:12a). This profound promise from God has encouraged God's people throughout the ages.[46] If we can believe that God is with us, on the basis of that faith, we can do anything God asks of us. Nothing will be impossible to us!

Q2. (Exodus 3:10-12) Does Moses' response to God's call reflect a low self image, true humility, or lack of faith? How does God reassure him? How does God reassure us when we are called to impossible situations?
http://www.joyfulheart.com/forums/index.php?showtopic=1035

Yes!

"I will be with you"

→ Reporter NOT Orator

God Reveals Himself as Yahweh (Exodus 3:13-15)

"[13] Moses said to God, 'Suppose I go to the Israelites and say to them, "The God of your fathers has sent me to you," and they ask me, "What is his name?" Then what shall I tell them?' [14] God said to Moses, 'I AM WHO I AM. This is what you are to say to the Israelites: "I AM has sent me to you."'" (Exodus 3:13-14)

Moses asks for God's name and is given a new revelation of God as the Great I Am. One who is always present and eternally existent seems to be the etymological basis of God's revealed name Yahweh, from the Hebrew verb meaning "to be." We see echoes of it in the New Testament, as well.

"Jesus Christ is the same yesterday and today and forever." (Hebrews 13:8)

---

[46] Exodus 4:12, 15; Genesis 31:3; Deuteronomy 31:23; Joshua 1:5; Isaiah 41:10; 43:2; Matthew 28:20; Romans 8:31; Hebrews 13:5.

> "'I am the Alpha and the Omega,' 'says the Lord God, 'who is, and who was, and who is to come, the Almighty.'" (Revelation 1:8)

I discuss the name Yahweh in detail in another study in this series.[47]

Directions and Signs (Exodus 3:16-22; 4:1-9)

Now God gives Moses specific instructions: "Go, assemble the elders of Israel and say to them...." (Exodus 3:16). He gives Moses the message to give to them and to Pharaoh, as well as promises of deliverance and a new land. But Moses still protests:

> "What if they do not believe me or listen to me and say, 'The LORD did not appear to you'?" (Exodus 4:1)

The Lord shows him how his staff can turn into a snake. When put into his cloak, his hand becomes leprous, and is then restored. Turning water into blood is a third sign.

Send Someone Else (Exodus 4:10-17)

Now Moses complains about lack of eloquence.[48] God's answer: I will help you. Consider God's amazing promise:

> "I will be with your mouth, and teach you what you are to say." (Exodus 4:12)

God promises to take care of Moses' inadequacies in public speaking. Even more important, he promises to coach[49] him on what to say – help with both delivery and content! And still, Moses tries to wriggle out of the call.

Ever since God had called him, Moses had come up with a series of excuses and "what ifs," plus another fear revealed in verse 19:

1. Who am I? (3:11-12)
2. What if they ask your Name? (3:13-15)
3. What if they don't believe me? (4:1-9)
4. But I'm not eloquent (4:10-12)
5. People will kill me (4:19)

Each of these God has answered. But now, after God has peeled back each of his excuses, Moses comes to the underlying reason: he just doesn't want to do it! God responds with anger![50]

---

[47] Ralph F. Wilson, *Names and Titles of God* (JesusWalk Publications, 2010).

[48] *Dābār*, "speech, word." The phrase is literally, "I have never been a man of words" (NASB, margin).

[49] *Yârâ'*, "teach" (Hiphil). A related word *tôrâ* or Torah is "teaching."

[50] "Burned" (NIV), "was kindled" (NRSV, KJV) is *hārâ*. "This word is related to a rare Aramaic root meaning 'to cause fire to burn,' and to an Arabic root meaning 'burning sensation,' in the throat, etc." In Hebrew,

"¹³ But Moses said, 'O Lord, please send someone else to do it.' ¹⁴ Then the LORD's anger burned against Moses…." (Exodus 4:13-14a)

Q3. (Exodus 4:13-14a) Why is God angry with Moses? What is Moses' basic sin? Unbelief, fear, or disobedience? Do you think the Lord has ever been angry with you? How did Moses appease God's anger?

http://www.joyfulheart.com/forums/index.php?showtopic=1036

In spite of his anger, God provides a second way to convince Moses to take the assignment – his brother Aaron. As I ponder Moses' chutzpah in resisting God, I am amazed at God's grace in spite of his anger. God is not rigid. He is willing to work with us and find ways to fill in for our weaknesses, so that he can use our strengths.

E. Moses Obeys God (Exodus 4:18-31)

Convinced and rebuked, Moses makes plans to returns to Egypt. On the long trip back, the Lord explains what will happen. Pharaoh will not give in right away, God says, but don't be afraid, this is part of a plan. God tells him ahead of time so Moses won't be as discouraged when the deliverance drags on and on.

The Circumcision of Moses' Son (Exodus 4:24-26)

An incident occurs on Moses' trip back to Egypt that is difficult to understand.

"²⁴ At a lodging place on the way, the LORD met [Moses] and was about to kill him. ²⁵ But Zipporah took a flint knife, cut off her son's foreskin and touched [Moses'] feet with it. 'Surely you are a bridegroom of blood to me,' she said. ²⁶ So the LORD let him alone. (At that time she said "bridegroom of blood," referring to circumcision.)" (Exodus 4:24-26)

ḥārâ is always used in conjunction with anger and with related words is found 139 times in the Old Testament (Leon J. Wood, TWOT #736).

There are dozens of theories about the meaning of the passage. What makes the most sense to me is that Moses had neglected circumcision (of Gershom and perhaps of himself), in accordance with the ancient rite revealed to Abraham as a sign of the Covenant (Genesis 17:9-14), and this neglect arouses God's anger. At any rate, God stops him while they are at an overnight desert camp. Zipporah intervenes, takes a flint knife, circumcises Gershom, and then apparently touches Moses' genitals with it. "Feet" (*regel*) here is likely a euphemism for male genitalia, as in Isaiah 7:20 (with reference to pubic hair) and in Judges 3:24 and 1 Samuel 24:3 (with reference to relieving oneself).[51] After this rite has been performed, God backs off from his threat to Moses.

Of course, this doesn't answer all our questions. Why does Zipporah touch Moses' genitals with Gershom's foreskin? It's possible that Moses himself hasn't been circumcised as a baby, or fully circumcised as an adult. Egyptian circumcision, performed on adults, was only a partial circumcision. Perhaps Gershom's circumcision is being vicariously transferred to Moses by touching his penis.[52] And what do Zipporah's words mean: "Bridegroom of blood"? Scholars have speculated that in Midian culture, circumcision was performed at puberty as a premarital rite, and that Zipporah's words echo this.[53] But it is merely speculation. We don't really know.

The point seems to be that only those who have been circumcised will escape God's judgment – especially God's judgment upon the Egyptians in Egypt (Exodus 12:44-49; Joshua 5:5). When Zipporah's rite has been completed, God allows Moses and his family to continue to Egypt.

Fortunately this obscure event isn't important to the primary story of Moses' character and ministry.

Moses Returns to Egypt (Exodus 4:27-31)

As Moses is returning to Egypt, God calls Aaron too. They meet at Mt. Horeb, "the mountain of God," where Moses lets Aaron know what his part will be as divine spokesman. When they arrive in Egypt, they go together to the leaders of God's people, the elders. Aaron knows these men, but it is likely that Moses does not. Moses is terrified, but does what he is told.

---

[51] William White, *regel*, TWOT #2113a. See Durham, *Exodus*, p. 58.

[52] Durham, *Exodus*, p. 58, citing J.M. Sasson, "Circumcision in the Ancient Near East," *Journal of Biblical Literature* [1966] 473-474. So also Paul R. Williamson, "Circumcision," DOTP, p. 124.

[53] Durham, *Exodus*, p. 58. Durham speculates that Zipporah circumcises not Moses, "who would have been temporarily incapacitated by the surgery" (Genesis 34:18-31), but Gershom, and then vicariously transfers the effect of the rite to Moses.

Notice that before the elders, Moses doesn't point to himself, but to the Lord. His message is that God has heard the Israelites' prayers and has compassion on them. The result is faith and thankfulness on the part of the elders, evidenced by worship. The elders' worship is described by two words, *qādad*, "bow down,"[54] and the Eshtafel stem of *ḥāwâ*, "prostrate oneself, worship,"[55] demonstrating their deep submission to Yahweh who had loved them and heard their prayers.

James J. Tissot, "Moses and Aaron Speak to the People" (1896-1900), watercolor, Jewish Museum, New York.

God has done what Moses had doubted could happen – that people would really believe him and take him seriously. I can almost hear God's thoughts echoed by his Son centuries later:

"You of little faith, why are you so afraid?" (Matthew 8:26)
"You of little faith, why did you doubt?" (Matthew 14:31)

Moses has taken the first steps and learned some important lessons. But what God will ask him to do in days to come builds on this earlier reluctant obedience. Moses doesn't begin as a man of great faith, but gradually God builds faith within him, and as he operates in that faith, he becomes a leader whom God can use.

[54] "This root refers to the bowing of one's head accompanying and emphasizing obeisance" (Leonard J. Coppes, *qādad*, TWOT #1985).

[55] This word is cognate with the Ugaritic *ḥwy* "to bow down" and originally meant to prostrate oneself on the ground (Nehemiah 8:6; Edwin Yamauchi, *ḥāwâ*, TWOT #619).

Q4. Why are we so afraid to obey God when he puts on our heart to do something decisive? How are we to deal with fear when we feel it? What is the relationship of fear to courage? Why is courage required in leaders and disciples?

http://www.joyfulheart.com/forums/index.php?showtopic=1037

Prayer

Father, we have felt doubt and fear, just like Moses. Forgive us for our unbelief. Forgive us for being so slow to obey. Build your faith in us, so that you can use us to do mighty things that are part of your plan for us. With confidence in your faithful work in us, we pray in Jesus' name. Amen.

2. Finding Courage to Stand (Exodus 5-11)

When Moses was ready to pass on his leadership to Joshua, he commanded him to be strong and courageous. But where did Moses learn courage? He learned it here in Egypt under the insults and taunts of both Pharaoh and his own people. Moses learned courage to stand.

He has gone to the elders of Israel to explain his mission as God had instructed him (Exodus 3:16). Now he goes to Pharaoh himself.

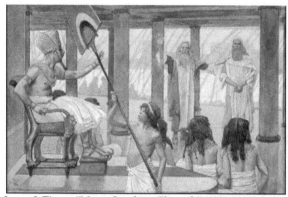

James J. Tissot, "Moses Speaks to Pharaoh" (1896-1900), watercolor, Jewish Museum, New York.

"Afterward Moses and Aaron went to Pharaoh and said, 'This is what the LORD, the God of Israel, says: "Let my people go, so that they may hold a festival to me in the desert."'" (Exodus 5:1)

A. Moses' Early Failure (Exodus 5:1-3)

The Word of the Lord (5:1)

Moses begins with the words echoed by nearly every prophet who followed him throughout the Old Testament.

"Thus saith the LORD" (KJV)
"This is what the LORD says" (NIV)

These words resound century after century with the power of a mighty hammer (Amos 1:3, 6, etc.)

One of the lessons of Moses' leadership is that he doesn't come with his own words, but bearing God's words, which will ultimately prevail!

"... My word that goes out from my mouth:
... will not return to me empty,
but will accomplish what I desire
and achieve the purpose for which I sent it." (Isaiah 55:11)

Leaders today are tempted to come with their own words, their own message, their own spin. They quote Scripture, but that doesn't mean they are speaking the *message* of the Lord. Dear friends, we must listen to God for his direction to make things clear to us, then come obediently speaking the words, the message that *he* gives us to say.

A second lesson is patient persistence. The fulfillment of God's word didn't come immediately for Moses. He came to his adversary again and again with, "This is what the LORD says."[1] Only at the end does God act. But when he acts, he acts with a power that none can withstand.

Courage in the Face of Raw Power (5:1)

A third lesson is courage. The dictionary defines "courage" as "mental or moral strength to venture, persevere, and withstand danger, fear, or difficulty."[2]

Moses exercises great courage before Pharaoh. An 80-year-old man, who once had been adopted by one of the many daughters of a pharaoh, an alien Hebrew at that, has the temerity to tell Pharaoh what he must do. Remember, Egypt was not a democracy but a totalitarian state where, at Pharaoh's word, a man who did not please him could be struck down and killed.

Courage is required of leaders. When Moses commissions his successor Joshua, he says:

> "The LORD himself goes before you
> and will be with you;
> he will never leave you nor forsake you.
> Do not be afraid; do not be discouraged." (Deuteronomy 31:8)

I don't know about you, dear friend, but many times I have been both afraid *and* discouraged. God help me! As did Moses, we must find our courage in the Lord's promise that he will go with us and that he will teach us what to say. Then we must act!

Pharaoh's Response (Exodus 5:2)

Pharaoh's response to Moses' message is abrupt and proud:

> "Who is the LORD, that I should obey him and let Israel go? I do not know the LORD and I will not let Israel go." (Exodus 5:2)

You speak of the LORD, Yahweh, says Pharaoh, but I don't know him and have no obligation to obey him. These defiant words against the Lord will come back to bite

---

[1] Exodus 4:22; 7:17; 8:1; 9:1; etc.
[2] *Merriam-Webster's Collegiate Dictionary*, 11th Edition.

Pharaoh as Moses' staff and later the Ten Plagues serve as the powerful proof of Yahweh's presence with his people. God's words roll like waves to answer Pharaoh's arrogance as Moses announces the plagues upon Egypt:

Plague of Blood: "By this you will know that I am the LORD." (7:17)

Plague of Flies: "... so that you will know that I, the LORD, am in this land." (8:22)

Plague of Hail: "... so you may know that the earth is the LORD's." (9:14, 29)

Plague on the Firstborn: "Then you will know that the LORD makes a distinction...." (11:7)

A Three-Day Pilgrimage in the Desert (Exodus 5:3)

Pharaoh says "No," but Moses persists, saying to Pharaoh what the Lord tells him to say (Exodus 3:18):

> "Then they said, 'The God of the Hebrews has met with us. Now let us take a three-day journey[3] into the desert to offer sacrifices[4] to the LORD our God, or he may strike us with plagues or with the sword.'" (5:3)

In verse 1, the phrase, "hold a festival" (NIV), "celebrate a festival" (NRSV), "hold a feast" (KJV) is *ḥāgag*,[5] from which derives Arabic *hajj*, the word used for Muslims' pilgrimage to Mecca.

Harrison notes:

> "Work-journals belonging to the New Kingdom period have furnished, among other reasons for absenteeism, the offering of sacrifices by workmen to their gods, and in view of the widespread nature of animal cult-worship in the eastern Delta region it is not in the least unrealistic to suppose that the Hebrews could request, and expect to receive, a three-day absence from work in order to celebrate their own religious feast in the Wilderness without at the same time provoking Egyptian religious antagonism."[6]

But for the Hebrew slaves to ask to leave their jobs for a three-day feast was unacceptable to Pharaoh. God had hardened his hard heart.

---

[3] *Derek*, from the verb *dārak* "to tread, trample." Here the noun refers to a journey (Herbert Wolf, TWOT #453a).

[4] "Sacrifice/offer sacrifices" in Exodus 5:3, 8, 17 is *zābaḥ*, "sacrifice, slaughter." *Zebaḥ* is the generic noun linked with offerings of various kinds (Herbert Wolf, TWOT #525).

[5] "The basic idea of this root is 'keep a feast' or 'celebrate a holiday' but the word usually refers to the three main pilgrimage-feasts of Israel" (Carl Phillip Weber, *ḥāgag*, TWOT #602).

[6] Harrison, *Intro*, p. 577. He cites A. Erman, *Life in Ancient Egypt* (1894), pp. 124f., and P. Monet, *L'Égypte et la Bible*, pp. 99ff.

B. Discouragement and the Lord's Instruction (Exodus 5:4-7:7)

Blame the Leader (Exodus 5:4-21)

Pharaoh blames Moses and Aaron for threatening a work stoppage. He retaliates "that same day" (5:6) by requiring the Israelites to work even harder.

The sun-dried mud bricks the Israelites were making were commonly used to build houses, palaces, and temples. Bricks were made of soil and water mixed with chopped straw that gave the bricks additional strength. The mud mixture was poured into a frame-like mold. The rectangular mud brick was then tapped from the frame and left to dry in the sun.[7]

Pharaoh commands:

> "You are no longer to supply the people with straw for making bricks; let them go and gather their own straw. But require them to make the same number of bricks as before; don't reduce the quota." (5:8)

Mud brick and wooden frame for making bricks. Oriental Institute Museum, University of Chicago. Photos: Ralph F. Wilson.

In the process, Pharaoh turns the Israelite foremen[8], who are employed by the Egyptian slave-masters, against Moses. If the Israelites don't meet the daily quota of bricks, the foremen are beaten. Now they come accusing Moses:

---

[7] Inscription on brick and wood frame in Oriental Institute Museum, University of Chicago.

[8] "Foremen" is shāṭar, "official, officer," from a root meaning "to write." "The word is used of a subordinate official. In distinction to many other known officials, these were probably originally trained in the scribal

"When they left Pharaoh, they found Moses and Aaron waiting to meet them, and they said, 'May the LORD look upon you and judge you! You have made us a stench[9] to Pharaoh and his officials and have put a sword in their hand to kill us.'" (5:20-21)

This is so typical of what leaders face. When something goes wrong, blame the leader, especially when the leader took an action that precipitated the calamity. Of course, Pharaoh is at fault, not Moses, but Moses takes the heat.

Perhaps you've seen this at work. When a pastor has to rebuke a person in the church, the retaliation is to blame the leader for something – whether it is legitimate or not doesn't matter. Now, the leader is so busy trying defend himself that he loses sight of the mission and the opponent wins. The blame game is a diversion tactic.

Blaming God (Exodus 5:22-23)

And Moses falls for this tactic, at least initially. Moses follows the same pattern as the people and *blames God himself.*

"Moses returned to the LORD and said, 'O Lord, **why have you brought trouble**[10] upon this people? Is this why you sent me? Ever since I went to Pharaoh to speak in your name, he has brought trouble upon this people, and **you have not rescued**[11] your people at all.'" (5:22-23)

According to Moses, "You [Yahweh] have brought trouble upon this people." This sounds so like us! If I hadn't done what you told me, Lord, none of this would have happened. It's your fault, God!

What we forget is that the job of a leader is not to be liked or even to be understood. The job of a leader is to act for God to accomplish God's will on earth. It is often a thankless job fraught with brutal criticism.

If we quit when the going gets rough, if we don't persist in faith, we won't see what God will do to resolve the issue. We begin in obedience to God, and we must not falter along the way. As Moses quieted the people on the edge of the Red Sea:

"Do not be afraid. Stand firm and **you will see the deliverance** the LORD will bring you today…. The LORD will fight for you; you need only to be still." (Exodus 14:13-14)

---

arts, as the root would indicate" (R.D. Patterson, TWOT #2374a). Here it refers to the Jewish foremen who had been appointed by the Egyptians (Exodus 5:14, 19).

[9] *Bā'ash*, "stink, abhor…. This word either describes objects that have a foul odor, bad relationships between people creating abhorrence, and the general principle that evil deeds are so rotten that they have a bad smell in God's nostrils" (Louis Goldberg, TWOT #195).

[10] "Brought trouble" (NIV), "mistreated" (NRSV), "evil entreated" (KJV) is *rā'a'*, "be bad, evil," here, "bring/cause evil" (G. Herbert Livingston, TWOT #2191).

[11] *Nāṣal*, "deliver, rescue, save."

"We want each of you to show this same diligence to the very end, in order to make your hope sure. We do not want you to become lazy, but to imitate those who **through faith and patience inherit what has been promised**." (Hebrews 6:11-12)

The Lord Encourages Moses (Exodus 6:1-8)

But Moses is not yet ready to quiet the people; God must quiet him. What follows is a passage where God reminds Moses of what he had already said: that Pharaoh's heart would be hardened and that "because of my mighty hand he will let them go" (Exodus 6:1). God reminds Moses of his covenant with the patriarchs.

"I have remembered my covenant," he says. "**I will redeem you** with an outstretched arm and with mighty acts of judgment" (6:6b)[12]

The word "redeem" here is *gā'al*, "redeem, avenge, revenge, ransom, do the part of a kinsman." It refers to the responsibilities of a next of kin to rescue family members from difficulty, redeem them from slavery, avenge them when they have been mistreated, etc.[13] Thus Abraham raises a private army to rescue his nephew Lot who had been kidnapped (Genesis 14) and Boaz acts as kinsman-redeemer for Ruth and Naomi, the widows of his kinsman (Ruth 2:20). Yahweh is the kinsman-redeemer to Israel, fulfilling his covenant obligations made to Abraham, Isaac, and Jacob centuries before.

The Lord Commands Moses (Exodus 6:9-13)

"Moses reported this to the Israelites, but they did not listen to him because of their discouragement and cruel bondage." (Exodus 6:9)

Even Moses' own people won't listen to him! Moses is moping. But God doesn't quit talking to Moses. He commands him to act! Observe the dialog:

"Then the LORD said to Moses, '**Go, tell Pharaoh** king of Egypt to let the Israelites go out of his country.'

But Moses said to the LORD, 'If the Israelites will not listen to me, why would Pharaoh listen to me, since I speak with faltering lips[14]?'

---

[12] Exodus 6:3, "by my name the LORD I did not make myself known to them," is a fascinating verse, but outside the scope of this study. For more on this verse, see Ralph F. Wilson, *Names and Titles of God* (JesusWalk, 2010), lesson 3, p. 57.

[13] R. Laird Harris, *gā'al*, TWOT #300.

[14] "I speak with faltering lips" (NIV), "poor speaker that I am" (NRSV), is literally, "who am of uncircumcised lips" (KJV). "Uncircumcised" is *ārēl*, "'having foreskin, uncircumcised,' became a word of contempt, used particularly with reference to the Philistines who did not practice circumcision. This term was associated with moral and spiritual uncleanness (Isaiah 52:1) as well as with organs that did not function

Now the LORD spoke to Moses and Aaron about the Israelites and Pharaoh king of
Egypt, and **he commanded them** to bring the Israelites out of Egypt." (6:10-13)

Notice: God won't take "no" for an answer. The Lord says, "Go tell Pharaoh." Moses
says, "He won't listen to me." Now the Lord *commands* Moses and Aaron. "Commanded" (NIV), "gave them a charge" (KJV, cf. NRSV) is *ṣāwâ*, "command, charge,"
used of instruction of a father to a son, a farmer to his laborers, and of a king to his
servants. The word reflects a society where a leader is in a position to command the
people and to expect their obedience.[15]

Sometimes, dear friends, we get stubborn and God needs to tell us, in no uncertain
terms, what we must do. There is no argument that we can win against God. If you are a
leader for God, then he expects you to follow his instructions, no matter how hard. It's
not a good sign when he needs to tell you the equivalent of, "Because I'm the mother,
that's why!"

God has taken Moses and Aaron to the "woodshed" for a whipping. But finally, to
their credit, they obey.

"Moses and Aaron **did just as the LORD commanded them**. Moses was eighty years
old and Aaron eighty-three when they spoke to Pharaoh." (7:6-7)

How does God deal with his reluctant leader Moses? By command, but also by
reasoning with him, encouraging him, and helping him to see the vision ahead of time of
what God will do. When Moses can see it with his eye of faith, then he can act on God's
behalf and be a leader.

Q1. (Exodus 7:6-7) Why did Moses blame God for his troubles? Why do you think Moses
and Aaron are so stubborn? Was it fear? Was it unbelief? Or both, perhaps? Why does
God have to command Moses and Aaron?
http://www.joyfulheart.com/forums/index.php?showtopic=1038

---

properly (Exodus 6:12, "uncircumcised lips" do not speak well; Jeremiah 6:10, "uncircumcised ears"
cannot listen)" (Ronald B. Allen, TWOT #1695b).

[15] John E. Hartley, *ṣāwâ*, TWOT #1887.

2. Finding Courage to Stand (Exodus 5-11)   45

I Will Harden Pharaoh's Heart (Exodus 7:1-6)

Following a genealogical insertion in 6:14-25, the narrative continues:

> "But **I will harden Pharaoh's heart**, and though I multiply my miraculous signs and wonders in Egypt, he will not listen to you. Then I will lay my hand on Egypt and with mighty acts of judgment I will bring out my divisions, my people the Israelites." (Exodus 7:3-4)

Theologians have spent lots of time discussing Pharaoh's hard heart. Was it hard initially? If God hardened it, is Pharaoh really responsible for his actions? The word "hardened" (*ḥāzaq*[16]) appears 12 times in Exodus 4-14. Notice three different statements:

- Yahweh hardens Pharaoh's heart (active) – Exodus 4:21; 7:3, 13; 9:12; 10:1, 20, 27; 11:10, 14:4, 8, (17)
- Pharaoh's heart is hardened (passive) – Exodus 7:13, 14, 22; 8:19; 9:7, 35
- Pharaoh hardens his own heart (reflexive) – Exodus 8:15, 32; 9:34

In fact, Pharaoh is an unrepentant sinner from the start. Harris observes,

> "All of God's hardening of an obstinate sinner was judicial and done that God's deliverance should be the more memorable."[17]

Certainly, Pharaoh is guilty of sin and rebellion against God. This instance is similar to how God treats hardened sinners elsewhere. In Romans 1, for example, Paul notes that it is because of their gross sins, "God gave them over" to even greater sin (Romans 1:24, 26).

C. God's Increasing Judgment on Egypt (Exodus 7:8-11:10)

The Plagues upon Egypt (Exodus 7:8-11:9)

Now come the Ten Plagues against Egypt. The word "plague" is *maggēpâ*, "blow, pestilence," from *nāgap*, "to strike."[18] God himself is striking Egypt with his own hand. Of course, since our study is primarily on Moses the leader, we can't analyze each plague in detail.

---

[16] The basic meaning of *ḥāzaq* in the Qal stem is "be(come) strong." The Piel stem is the causative, "make strong, strengthen, harden" (Carl Philip Weber, *ḥāzaq*, TWOT #636). Two synonyms are also used in this passage, *qāshâ* once (Exodus 7:3), "be hard, severe" and *kābēd*, "be heavy, grievous" five times (Exodus 7:14; 8:15, 32; 9:7, 34; 10:1).

[17] R. Laird Harris, *ḥāzaq*, TWOT #636, editorial comment.

[18] Leonard J. Coppes, *maggēpâ*, TWOT #1294b.

There have been various attempts to explain these plagues as naturally occurring phenomena, either seasonal or cyclical events occurring in nature. Unfortunately, any explanation we might offer is mere speculation, not scientific fact. Of course, God may have *used* nature to bring these judgments. But they are presented as miracles, so, unless we believe that miracles are impossible, or that these are merely natural phenomena that *seemed* like miracles to primitive, unsophisticated minds, we'll refrain. However, observe three things:

1. The Egyptians saw the God of the Israelites as the cause of the judgments.
2. The plagues did not fall on the Israelites, only on the Egyptians.
3. The timing was exquisite.

The plagues may have occurred over a period as long as six months.[19] These are the plagues:

1. **Blood** (7:14-24).[20] The blood of the plague makes the Nile's water undrinkable and kills the fish (7:21) – a major industry along the Nile.
2. **Frogs** (8:1-15). Frogs in Egypt were associated with the god Hopi and the goddess Heqt, who assisted at childbirth, and were thus a fertility symbol.[21] For all the frogs to die and rot must have been seen as a defeat of the Egyptian gods.
3. **Gnats** (8:16-19). "Gnats" (NIV, NRSV), "lice" (KJV) is Hebrew *kēn*. We don't really know what kind of insect is intended by the word. "Fleas" or "sandflies" have been suggested, but more likely it refers to "mosquitoes."[22]
4. **Flies** (8:20-32). "Swarm [of flies]" in verse 20 is literally *'ārōb*, "swarm" ("mixture," from incessant involved motion).[23] We're not told what kind of flies they were, but perhaps flies attracted by the decaying frogs. The Septuagint translates the word as *kynomuia*, "dog-fly," perhaps our modern gadfly or Monarch fly, with a painful bite.[24] This plague it is described as a "severe[25] swarm." Whatever it was, it must

[19] Cole, *Exodus*, p. 91.

[20] There is a reference in ancient Egyptian literature describing catastrophes that took place about 2300-2250 BC, that reads: "Why really, the River is blood. If one drinks of it, one rejects (it) as human and thirsts for water." What relationship this has to the first plague, we're not sure. Found in James B. Pritchard (ed.), *Ancient Near Eastern Texts* (Third Edition, with Supplement; Princeton University Press, 1969), p. 441, ii 10, cited by Durham, *Exodus*, p. 98. The date of the text we have is from the approximate period of the Exodus.

[21] Cole, *Exodus*, p. 91.

[22] Cole, *Exodus*, p. 92-93.

[23] *'Ārōb*, BDB 786.

[24] Cole, *Exodus*, p. 94.

[25] *Kābēd*, "great," from *kābēd*, "be heavy, grievous, hard," the same root from which *kābôd*, "glory" derives.

have been pretty awful, since Pharaoh is induced to send the Israelites away, though he relents.

5. **Livestock** (9:1-7). Since many varieties of "livestock" (NIV), "cattle" (KJV)[26] were considered sacred animals by the Egyptians, this plague "on your horses and donkeys and camels and on your cattle and sheep and goats" (9:3), was a direct blow against Egypt's gods. The statement that "all the cattle of Egypt died" (9:6) is sometimes contrasted with the fact that the Egyptians still had livestock prior to the plague of hail (9:19).

James J. Tissot, "The Plague of Locusts" (1896-1900), watercolor, Jewish Museum, New York. The pyramids in the background aren't accurate, however, since the largest were at Giza, far south of Pi-Rameses.

Childs comments, "The discrepancy is not a serious one, since the narrative style should not be overtaxed."[27]

6. **Boils** (9:8-12). "Ashes of the furnace" that Moses and Aaron threw into the air would be black and fine like soot. "Festering boils" (NIV, NRSV) consists of two words, translated by Childs as "boils breaking out into pustules."[28] It sounds pretty ugly.

7. **Hail** (9:13-35). Hailstones have been measured as large as 8 inches in diameter[29] and can be terribly destructive. I once had a rental car pockmarked by hail in an intense storm near St. Cloud, Minnesota. The storm that devastated Egypt was much more severe, destroying crops in the fields and trees, as well as livestock left in the open.

8. **Locusts** (10:1-20). Locusts are still a dreaded pest in areas bordering the desert. In Amos 7:1-3 and Joel 1:1-7 they are seen a terrible figure of God's judgment. Our text

---

[26] *Miqneh*, "cattle in general, including cows, sheep, horses, asses, camels (any or all of them), as purchasable domestic animals" (BDB 889), from *qānâ*, "get, acquire, possess." "Cattle" is the thing possessed.

[27] Childs, Exodus, p. 157.

[28] Childs, *Exodus*, p. 128. *Shehîn*, "boil, enflamed spot," is threatened as a punishment for disobeying the covenant (Deuteronomy 28: 27, 35) and used to describe Job's affliction (Job 2:7) (Elmer A. Martens, TWOT #2364a). An Arabic cognate means "to be hot," perhaps linking the boils with the soot taken from the furnace (Childs, *Exodus*, p. 129). The second word is ʾabaʿbuʿōt, "blisters, boils" (BDB 97).

[29] The largest recorded hailstone in the United States was 8 inches in diameter and weighed 1.93 pounds, in Vivian, South Dakota on July 23, 2010 ("World Record Hailstone Weighed in Vivian," Keloland TV (Souix Falls, SD), 27 June 2010).

reads, "They covered all the ground until it was black. They devoured all that was left after the hail" (10:15a).

9. **Darkness** (10:21-29). This darkness is so intense that it can be "felt."[30] There is speculation that this must have been a sandstorm, but if this were the case, I think the narrator would have said so. Instead of the whirling sand, it is the darkness that is so awful.

10. **Firstborn** (11:1-10; 12:29-32). The final plague is the death of the firstborn son as well as the firstborn of livestock throughout Egypt. We will examine this plague further in Lesson 3.

Moses' Staff

At God's direction, Moses and Aaron use their staffs to work miracles, both before the Israelites and before Pharaoh. Sometimes it is Moses' staff that is employed; other times it is Aaron's. They seem interchangeable, since Aaron is acting as Moses' spokesman.

"Staff" (NIV, NRSV), "rod" (KJV) is *maṭṭeh*, "staff, rod, shaft" from the verb *nāṭâ*, "extend, stretch out." The staff is closely associated with the hand[31] in Exodus, and was used as a support when travelling, a common walking stick that was probably carried by every man. The staff could be used as a weapon, probably much like the medieval quarter-staff (Psalm 2:9; 23; 4; 89:32; Isaiah 10:24; 11:4), and was used for such everyday tasks as to thresh herbs (Isaiah 28:27) and count sheep (Ezekiel 20:37). A staff carried some value (Genesis 38:18), probably since suitable trees were somewhat scarce. It could also represent the authority of a leader (Numbers 17:1-11) as a kind of scepter (Psalm 110:2; Jeremiah 48:17).[32]

At the conclusion of Yahweh's first revelation to Moses at the burning bush, God says:

> "But take this staff in your hand so you can perform miraculous signs with it.... So Moses took his wife and sons, put them on a donkey and started back to Egypt. And he took the staff of God in his hand." (Exodus 4:17, 20)

---

[30] *Māshash*, "to feel, grope" (BDB 606).

[31] In Ugaritic literature, the phrase "staff of the hand" (Exodus 4:2, 17, 20; 7:15, 17; 8:5, 17; 14:16; 17:5, 8-9) is well attested (Marvin R. Wilson, *maṭṭeh*, TWOT #1352b).

[32] Marvin R. Wilson, *maṭṭeh*, TWOT #1352b; Larry G. Herr, "Staff," ISBE 4:608-609; "Rod," ISBE 3:206-207. *Maṭṭeh* seems to be used synonymously in the Bible with *shēbeṭ* as "staff, rod," in the Messianic passage in Genesis 49:10 regarding Judah and as the staff in Psalm 23 with *mish'enet*, staff, support."

This "staff of God" (Exodus 4:20; 17:9) figures in miracles both in Egypt and during their sojourn in the wilderness.

The Staff and Ancient Concepts of Magic

I've wondered, though, if the "staff of God" is used in Moses' ministry as a kind of magical object – an ancient magic wand. Some Christians are troubled by concepts of the miraculous efficacy of objects, such as the bones of saints (relics), anointing oil for healing (Mark 6:13; James 5:14), and "prayer cloths" (Acts 19:12). How do we understand Moses' rod?

Magic was widespread in the ancient near east as an attempt to understand, control, or manipulate the divine realm.[33] But rather than seeking to manipulate God to their own ends, Moses and Aaron use their rods at God's explicit direction, as their obedient response to a specific situation, perhaps as a visible symbol of God's authority.

Why does Jesus sometimes lay on hands for healing, and at other times speak a word or use spittle? We don't know. We do know, however, that sometimes God directs us to use specific physical objects in the pursuit of his purposes. This understanding seems to characterize the biblical description of Moses' rod better than assigning it to the category of magic.

Distinction between Egypt and the Israelites

The Lord says to Pharaoh through Moses,

"I will make a distinction between my people and your people." (Exodus 8:23)

The plagues which fall on the Egyptians don't directly affect the Israelites, who live in a particular part of Egypt, the land of Goshen. This distinction appears explicitly in the:

- Plague of Flies (Exodus 8:22-23)
- Plague on Livestock (Exodus 9:4-6)
- Plague of Hail (Exodus 9:26)
- Plague of Darkness (Exodus 10:23)
- Plague on the Firstborn (Exodus 11:7)

---

[33] O'Mathúna helps define the ancient understanding of magic: "Magic attempts to use supernatural powers to influence people, events, or other supernatural beings. Biblically approved practices emphasize divine initiative and divine prerogative. Magic and divination are human efforts to understand, control, or manipulate the divine realm by methods believed to practically guarantee the desired results" (Dónal P. O'Mathúna, "Divination, Magic," DOTP, pp. 193-197. See also the essay by David E. Aune, "Magic," ISBE 3:213-219).

But this selectivity of the effects of the plagues may have occurred in the other plagues, too, since the narrator emphasizes the effect on the Egyptians and doesn't mention any effects on the Israelites whatsoever. God doesn't punish his people with the punishments of their oppressors.[34]

D. Leadership Lessons

As I reflect on Moses' leadership during these plagues, several leadership lessons occur to me.

1. The Leader Must Confront When Necessary

Moses is asked – no, commanded – to confront the most powerful person on the face of the earth: Pharaoh, king of Egypt.

I don't know about you, but I don't like confrontations. I've learned, however, that leaders must confront when necessary, or their organization will lose its sense of direction and unity. *Not* confronting, when one needs to, hardly ever makes the situation better. And putting it off only makes the situation worse.

Good parents confront their children when they're behaving badly in order to correct them. Undisciplined children are the result of parents who refuse to confront, rebuke, and correct.

Do you have a situation that you need to confront to be a good leader under God? Ask God to give you wisdom and courage. Then do what you need to do. That's the job of a leader.

If you've read the Gospels, you'll see that Jesus did a lot of confronting – of the people he healed, of the people who opposed him, and of his errant disciples. Jesus was not a laissez-faire leader, but one who lovingly, but firmly confronted. So did the Apostle Paul. These are examples for us.

---

[34] In a similar way, in Ezekiel 9:4-6 the faithful saints were marked on their foreheads to avoid the judgment of slaughter. In Revelation the 144,000 servants of God are sealed on their foreheads before the land or sea or trees are harmed by God's angels, presumably to protect them from the plagues (Revelation 7:3; 9:4). Later they are "redeemed from the earth" (Revelation 14:3), perhaps to protect them from the later plagues.

Q2. Why is it so difficult for some church leaders to confront people? What fears in this regard does a leader face? How can confrontation and rebuke be a good thing? What happens when we refuse to confront when we should?
http://www.joyfulheart.com/forums/index.php?showtopic=1039

2. The Leader Must Deal with Criticism and Pressure

I've tried to imagine the kind of pressure Moses was under. After Moses' first encounter with Pharaoh, the Israelites were punished by being required to find their own straw without any reduction in their quota of bricks. Now Moses' own people accuse him of upsetting the status quo for something new and negative.

Then Moses stands before Pharaoh who heaps abuse on him and his God. It's surprising that Pharaoh doesn't just kill Moses at the outset, but to do so would probably have caused riots among the Hebrews and threatened the stability of Pharaoh's oppressive regime.

How well did Moses sleep during this period? How many emissaries did he receive from the Israelites pleading with him to cease and desist and go back where he came from? How many representatives of Pharaoh did he entertain who were trying to find a compromise solution so that Egypt would not be destroyed? How many threats against his life did he have to deal with?

The period of the Ten Plagues took place over months and months. In hindsight, we know that there were ten plagues, but neither Moses nor the Egyptians knew how long the plagues would last.

So how did Moses sustain himself? Through faith in the word that the Lord had given him that Yahweh would deliver Israel from Egypt. Through all the ups and downs of this period, Moses remains steady, trusting in the word of the Lord. So must we.

3. The Leader Must Know When to Compromise – and When Not To

As I read these chapters, I see Pharaoh trying to negotiate a settlement for less than Moses has demanded. That Pharaoh, king of Egypt, feels he must negotiate at all, demonstrates the threat he feels. See his tactics:

- During the Plague of Flies, Pharaoh offers to allow sacrifice to God "within the land" or "in the wilderness, provided you do not go very far away," but Moses does not compromise. (8:25-27, 32).[35]

- Prior to the Plague of Locusts, Pharaoh seems to be willing to let the men sacrifice, but not the women and children. Moses does not compromise (10:10).

- During the Plague of Darkness, Pharaoh seems willing to allow all the people to go and worship, but they must leave their flocks and herds behind. Moses does not compromise (10:24-26).

A lesser leader than Moses would have been tempted to accept a compromise. After all, leaders, both in churches and in statehouses, use compromise as a way to keep from stalemate and to accomplish the business that must be accomplished. You don't always get everything you want. "Half a loaf is better than none," goes the saying. Politics is the art of compromise.

Of course, we church leaders *must* learn to compromise if we want to move the church forward. If you don't have leaders who meet Scriptural qualifications, for example, you work with the leaders you do have, hoping for a better day. You "make do" the best you can. Many a leader has cleaned the church restrooms and mopped the church kitchen when someone else should have done it. Leaders must do what needs to be done to achieve the greater purpose.

But there are times when we leaders must *not* compromise. That is when God has clearly told us what we must do – no matter what. Moses has been charged with obedience to God, and only through his obedience will God bring about the truly impossible – the deliverance of the Israelites from Egypt through the Red Sea as well as the destruction of the Egyptian army. To Moses' credit, he continues to be faithful to the word, the vision that God has given him. And since he *is* faithful, he receives the promised reward (Hebrews 10:35).

---

[35] Moses insists on a full three-day journey lest the Israelite sacrifice spark a race riot (8:26), since the Egyptians considered certain bulls sacred to Apis, cows sacred to Isis, rams sacred to Amon, etc. Sacrifice of sacred animals would be considered blasphemy by the Egyptians. In the fifth century AD, animal sacrifice actually prompted a pogrom against the Jews in the Yeb or Elephantine colony on the upper Nile (Cole, *Exodus*, p. 95).

> "By faith he left Egypt, not fearing the king's anger; he persevered because he saw him who is invisible." (Hebrews 11:27, NRSV)

Leader, don't abandon the vision God has given you!

Q3. Why didn't Moses accept Pharaoh's compromises? In what instances should church leaders accept compromise? In what instances is it wrong for church leaders to compromise?

http://www.joyfulheart.com/forums/index.php?showtopic=1040

---

4. The Leader Must Know that the Battle Is the Lord's

Finally, the leader must know the real protagonists in the battle. This is not really a battle between Moses and Pharaoh at all. The Apostle Paul reminds us:

> "For our struggle is not against flesh and blood, but against the rulers, against the powers, against the world forces of this darkness, against the spiritual *forces* of wickedness in the heavenly *places*." (Ephesians 6:12, NASB)

But it is very easy for us leaders to think that this is a battle of wills between us and a human opponent. When we leaders confront evil people, we sometimes end up demonizing our opponents in what may appear to be a personal battle of wills. But Jesus tells us to love our enemies!

So it is important to recognize that this is a contest not between Moses and Pharaoh – Rather, it is a contest between the God of the Hebrews and the gods of Egypt – including Pharaoh himself. If Rameses II was the pharaoh during the Exodus, it is interesting to observe that he had been deified, declared a god, when he was 30 years old, only halfway through his long 66-year reign. He was one of the false gods of Egypt.

Moses does not speak to Pharaoh as he might as a former prince of Egypt. Moses speaks for Yahweh, the God of the Hebrews. And as God's spokesman, his words are powerful. A mere human would quail to say such things to the most powerful monarch on earth, but as fearful Moses may have felt on the inside, he speaks God's words with clarity. For example:

"This is what the LORD, the God of the Hebrews, says: Let my people go ... or this time I will send the full force of my plagues **against you and against your officials** and your people, so you may know that there is no one like me in all the earth.... **You still set yourself against my people** and will not let them go." (9:13b-14, 17)

"This is what the LORD, the God of the Hebrews, says: '**How long will you refuse to humble yourself before me**? Let my people go, so that they may worship me.'" (10:3)

Finally, after the Ninth Plague, Pharaoh in his anger makes a personal threat against Moses.

"'Get out of my sight! Make sure you do not appear before me again! The day you see my face you will die.'

'Just as you say,' Moses replied, 'I will never appear before you again.'" (10:28-29)

But the threat against Moses is a threat against Moses' God, since Moses speaks for God. Now God brings the tenth and final devastating plague against Egypt, and it is Pharaoh's own son who dies.

It seems that leaders from generation to generation must relearn this lesson: the battle is the Lord's!

1. **Moses:** "The LORD will fight for you." (Exodus 14:14)

2. **David to Goliath and the Philistines:** "All those gathered here will know that it is not by sword or spear that the LORD saves; for the battle is the LORD'S, and he will give all of you into our hands." (1 Samuel 17:47)

3. **Jahaziel:** "Listen, King Jehoshaphat and all who live in Judah and Jerusalem! This is what the LORD says to you: 'Do not be afraid or discouraged because of this vast army. For the battle is not yours, but God's." (2 Chronicles 20:14)

4. **Zechariah**: "This is the word of the LORD to Zerubbabel: 'Not by might nor by power, but by my Spirit,' says the LORD Almighty." (Zechariah 4:6)

My dear friend, it may seem trite to say, "Let the Lord fight your battles," but you must! If you make the battles your own, you'll destroy yourself and your family. These must be battles of faith and of prayer, not mere human strategy and clever words. If you want to be a leader like Moses, then you must learn to listen like Moses, trust like Moses, and lead like Moses. You need to learn to pick only the battles that God wants you to engage on his behalf, and then fight with *his* strength. We are not our own. We have been bought with a price (1 Corinthians 6:20). We are *his* men and women. And he *will* defend us if we represent him clearly and forthrightly as we lead.

Q4. Why do we tend to fight our battles "in the flesh" rather than using spiritual weapons? Why do we so often mistake the human enemy for the spiritual enemy? When will God fight our battles – and when won't he?

http://www.joyfulheart.com/forums/index.php?showtopic=1041

We began this lesson with Moses and Aaron explaining to the people of Israel how Yahweh had revealed himself and promised deliverance. The people rejoice. But when Moses and Aaron go to Pharaoh, things get much worse. Yet Yahweh has shown himself strong against Pharaoh and has promised deliverance and Moses has learned courage. Moses now looks forward to the deliverance of the Lord.

Prayer

Lord, keep me steady when things are difficult. Give me courage. Help me to listen for your voice, be strong in your word, and not waver with compromises that are not mine to make, as your servant. Forgive me where I have failed to lead well on your behalf. Continue to teach me your ways. Let your Spirit in me prevail. In Jesus' name, I pray. Amen.

3. Passover and Crossing the Red Sea (Exodus 12-15)

The months of confrontation and plagues have come to a close as an eerie calm seems to exist between Pharaoh and Moses. After nine plagues, Pharaoh has told Moses never to appear before him again. Moses knows that the tenth plague will be the last and will result in Israel's freedom.

A. Passover (Exodus 12:1-28)

A Lamb for Every Household (Exodus 12:1-6)

Now Moses seeks the Lord to get instructions for the final phase of the deliverance from Egypt.

The Lord's instructions are very specific. A male lamb without defect is indicated for every grouping that Passover night. Notice that these lambs are to be selected from the flock several days ahead of time – ten days after the first day of the month, which began on a new moon.[1] The evening of the fourteenth day of the month, then, will be the full moon, characteristic of Passover ever since.

James J. Tissot, "The Signs on the Door" (1896-1900), watercolor, Jewish Museum, New York.

The Blood of the Passover (Exodus 12:7)

The animals are to be slaughtered and then prepared for the Passover meal. But the blood is to be handled in a very special way on this night.

> [7] Then they are to take some of the blood and put it on the sides and tops of the door-frames of the houses where they eat the lambs…. [13] The blood will be a sign for you on the houses where you are; and when I see the blood, I will **pass over** you." (Exodus 12:7, 13)

---

[1] Donn F. Morgan, "Calendar," ISBE 1:575. The Hebrew word for "month," *hōdesh*, also means "new moon."

The word "Passover" is found in Exodus 12:11, 21, 26, 43, 48; 34:25. What does it mean? The word is *pesah*, is traditionally derived from *pāsah*, "to pass over," and interpreted as "the merciful passing over of a destructive power."[2]

What Kind of Sacrifice Is the Paschal Lamb?

Just what kind of sacrifice is the initial Paschal lamb offered prior to the Exodus? Five offerings were performed in the tabernacle and, later, in the temple.[3] Of these, the sacrifice of the Passover lamb bears some resemblance to the peace or fellowship offering, in which a piece of meat is offered before the Lord and to the priests. The remainder of the sacrifice is eaten by the offerer and his family as a kind of celebration meal – similar to the celebration meal of the Passover. The initial Passover offering seems to be a consecration or setting apart of the people within each household who partook of the sacrifice.[4]

Israel's sin doesn't seem to be in the forefront; rather, the lamb seems to be a kind of substitute or interposition for the firstborn males and animals in the household. However, there may be some idea of expiation or purification present, since hyssop is used to smear the blood (Exodus 12:22).[5] Some Rabbinical writings refer to the redemptive effect of the blood of the Passover lamb.[6]

Christ Our Paschal Lamb

The early church certainly saw Jesus as fulfilling the Passover lamb.

Paul: "Christ, our **Passover lamb**, has been sacrificed." (1 Corinthians 5:7)

John the Baptist: "Look, the **Lamb of God**, who takes away the sin of the world." (John 1:29)

---

[2] Victor P. Hamilton, *pāsah*, TWOT #1786.

[3] Richard E. Averbeck, "Sacrifices and Offerings," DOTP 706-773. There are similarities between the original Passover act of placing blood on the doorpost and lintel and the ordination of priests, where blood is placed on the priest's ear, right thumb, and right big toe as an act of consecration (Leviticus 8:23-24).

[4] Richard Averbeck, telephone conversation, 3/5/03. The term "passover sacrifice" occurs in Exodus 12:27, with similar references in Exodus 23:18 and 34:25. The Hebrew noun *zebach*, "sacrifice" is a generic noun often linked with offerings or burnt offerings. The verb *zābach* is mainly used of killing animals for sacrifice (Herbert Wolf, *zābach*, TWOT #525a).

[5] Keil and Delitzsch, *Commentary on the Old Testament: Pentateuch*, 2:13-14: "Sprinkling with hyssop is never prescribed in the law, except in connection with purification in the sense of expiation (Leviticus 14:4, 6, 49, 51; Numbers 19:18-19; cf. Psalm 51:7)."

[6] Jeremias, *Eucharistic Words*, p. 146, n. 4, cites Pirqe R. *'Eli'ezer* 29 (14d); *Pesahim* 10:6 attributed to Rabbi Akiba, early second century, quoted in I. Howard Marshall, *Last Supper and Lord's Supper* (Eerdmans, 1980), p. 168, fn. 2.)

Peter: "You were redeemed ... with the **precious blood of Christ, a lamb** without blemish or defect." (1 Peter 1:18-19)

We Christians are participants in Christ's blood through the Lord's Supper, says St. Paul (1 Corinthians 10:16). And because our names are written in the Lamb's book of life (Revelation 13:8), we are not condemned for our sins (Revelation 20:12, 15). God's wrath "passes over" us! Hallelujah!

Q1. (1 Corinthians 5:7; John 1:29; 1 Peter 1:18-19) In what sense is Christ our Passover Lamb? In what sense are we marked with his blood? In what sense does God's judgment pass over us because of Christ's blood?

http://www.joyfulheart.com/forums/index.php?showtopic=1042

Commemorating the Passover (Exodus 12:14-20)

Passover is of particular interest to Christians because it is the basis of the original Last Supper Jesus had with his disciples on the night in which he was betrayed.[7] While our focus is on Moses himself, not all the institutions of Israel, let's look briefly at the elements of Passover contained in our passage.[8]

1. **Passover Lamb.** As noted above, the Passover or Paschal lamb is sacrificed. In ancient times, before the institution of the Levitical priesthood, each head of the household performed the sacrifice himself. By Jesus' day the slaughter of the Passover lambs took place in the temple by priests. The lamb is a sacrifice, a substitute for the firstborn who is redeemed. In the language of Exodus, the Lord says, "Israel is my firstborn son" (Exodus 4:22), so in a sense, the Passover lamb

---

[7] For more on this, including dating of the Last Supper, see my book *Lord's Supper: Communion and Eucharist Meditations for Disciples* (JesusWalk Publications, 2006).

[8] Later Jews include other elements in the celebration, as well, such as four cups of wine, which became the basis of Jesus' saying, "This is my blood of the covenant, which is poured out for many for the forgiveness of sins" (Matthew 26:28). Other later elements of the Seder plate include *charoset*, sweet, brown, pebbly paste of fruits and nuts, representing the mortar used by the Jewish slaves to build the storehouses of Egypt; and a roasted egg, symbolizing the festival sacrifice that was offered in the Temple in Jerusalem and was then eaten as part of the meal on Seder night.

is a substitute given for all of God's people, Israel. Christ is our Passover lamb (1 Corinthians 5:7), whose blood was shed to redeem us.

2. **Unleavened Bread.** Since this was the Israelites' final meal prior to fleeing from Egypt – and took place at night before the day's bread was made – "the people took their dough before the yeast was added, and carried it on their shoulders in kneading troughs wrapped in clothing"(Exodus 12:34). So in commemoration, for a week called the Feast of Unleavened Bread, the Jews remove yeast from their homes and eat unleavened bread (Exodus 12:14-20).

3. **Bitter Herbs.**[9] Later Judaism associated the bitter herbs with the hardness of the Israelites' oppression. "They made their lives bitter with hard labor ... the Egyptians used them ruthlessly" (Exodus 1:14).

Passover was to be celebrated year after year as a commemoration or remembrance of the Lord's deliverance. Moses instructed the people:

> "And when your children ask you, 'What does this ceremony mean to you?' then tell them, 'It is the Passover sacrifice[10] to the LORD, who passed over the houses of the Israelites in Egypt and spared our homes when he struck down the Egyptians.'" (Exodus 12:27)

To this day, every Passover, the youngest child in the household has the responsibility to ask, "Why is this night different from all other nights?" Then the story of God's deliverance is told once again to the next generation. In the same way, the Lord's Supper is to be a feast of remembrance, so that we never forget the Lord's great salvation through the cross.

Final Preparations for Passover Night (Exodus 12:21)

The Lord had given Moses specific instructions for the Passover that he had conveyed to the people. But now the time was at hand. Moses summons the elders for the final instructions.

> "21 ... Go at once and select the animals for your families and slaughter the Passover lamb. 22 Take a bunch of hyssop, dip it into the blood in the basin and put some of the blood on the top and on both sides of the doorframe. Not one of you shall go out the door of his house until morning. 23 When the LORD goes through the land to strike down the Egyptians, he will see the blood on the top and sides of the doorframe and

---

[9] The word is *mārōr*, "bitterness, bitter herb," from *mārar*, "be bitter, strengthen" (Victor P. Hamilton, *mārar*, TWOT #1248e).

[10] *Zebah*, "sacrifice," the generic noun often linked with offerings or burnt offerings (Herbert Wolf, TWOT #525a)

will pass over that doorway, and he will not permit the destroyer to enter your houses and strike you down." (Exodus 12:21-23)

Fortunately, "The Israelites did just what the LORD commanded Moses and Aaron" (12:28), as if their lives depended on it – as they did!

B. Leaving Egypt (Exodus 12:29-36)

The Tenth Plague, the Slaying of the Firstborn (Exodus 12:29-33)

Now came the final plague:

"[29] At midnight the LORD struck down all the firstborn in Egypt, from the firstborn of Pharaoh, who sat on the throne, to the firstborn of the prisoner, who was in the dungeon, and the firstborn of all the livestock as well. [30] Pharaoh and all his officials and all the Egyptians got up during the night, and there was loud wailing in Egypt, for there was not a house without someone dead." (Exodus 12:29-30)

The slaughter was carried out by "the destroyer,"[11] elsewhere referred to as the "angel of the Lord"[12] or the destroying angel.[13] This figure was later popularized in Judaism and Christianity as the "angel of death."

No Egyptian household was untouched that night, not even Pharaoh's. Pharaoh summons Moses

Arthur Hacker (English Pre-Raphaelite painter, 1858-1919), "And There Was a Great Cry in Egypt" (1897), oil on canvas, 90.2 x 153.7 cm, private collection.

and commands the Israelites to leave immediately with all their flocks and herds. You can sense the pain in his poignant request, "and also bless me" (12:32b).

---

[11] Exodus 12:23; Hebrews 11:28. "Destroyer" is *mashhît*, "destruction, destroyer," the Hiphil participle of *shāhat*, "destroy, corrupt…. The most familiar usage will be in connection with the angel of destruction at the Passover (Exodus 12:23), 'the destroyer.' He is the messenger entrusted with the execution of God's vengeance" (Victor P. Hamilton, TWOT #2370).

[12] 2 Kings 19:35; 2 Samuel 24:16; 1 Chronicles 21:15; 2 Chronicles 32:21.

[13] 1 Corinthians 10:10.

Plundering the Egyptians (Exodus 12:35-36)

Among the Israelites, no son had been lost. They were fed, packed, and ready to leave. So when the word came, there was just one more thing to do.

> "35 The Israelites did as Moses instructed and asked the Egyptians for articles of silver and gold and for clothing. 36 The LORD had made the Egyptians favorably disposed toward the people, and they gave them what they asked for; so they plundered14 the Egyptians." (Exodus 12:35-36)

It might seem crass to ask families in the middle of the night, families that are in deep mourning for their sons, to give them jewelry, gold, and garments. But to the Egyptians, that was a small price to pay to get rid of this people, who were seen as the reason that Egypt was being ruined, and so they gave their valuables and the Israelites left.

But this had been God's plan from the beginning when he had told Abraham (Genesis 15:13-14) and later Moses (Exodus 3:21-22) that this would come to pass. Perhaps the justice was that the Egyptians, who had bled the Israelites dry with slavery and hard labor, now paid them back at the last. And God had a use for the gold and silver, for it would later be given to decorate the tabernacle in the wilderness!

C. On the Move (Exodus 12:37-51)

The Israelites Begin Their Journey (Exodus 12:37-40)

Now the long-anticipated Exodus begins. Read carefully this paragraph:

> "37 The Israelites journeyed from Rameses to Succoth. There were about six hundred thousand men on foot, besides women and children. 38 Many other people went up with them, as well as large droves of livestock, both flocks and herds…. 40 Now the length of time the Israelite people lived in Egypt was 430 years. 41 At the end of the 430 years, to the very day, all the LORD's divisions left Egypt. 42 Because the LORD kept vigil that night to bring them out of Egypt, on this night all the Israelites are to keep vigil to honor the LORD for the generations to come." (Exodus 12:37-42)

We learn several things from this paragraph.

---

14 "Plunder" (NIV, NRSV), "spoiled" (KJV) is *nāṣal*. "An Arabic cognate confirms the judgment that its basic physical sense is one of drawing out or pulling out. While the Niphal is invariably used with the force of 'be delivered, saved' or 'to escape' (i.e. 'deliver oneself'; literally, 'tear oneself away'), the Piel may express 'strip off' (a garment; cf. 2 Chronicles 20:25; Exodus 3:22)…." So the Egyptians are literally "stripped"(Milton C. Fisher, TWOT #1404).

1. **Route**. The Israelites were primarily living in the area around the store-city of Rameses and travelled to Succoth. We examine what we think was their route in greater detail in Appendix 2.

2. **Number of Israelites**. The text indicates 600,000 men, plus women and children. That probably means upwards of 2 million people were involved in the Exodus. While some have questioned the plausibility of this number, we'll use it for our study.

3. **Time in Egypt**. This completed 430 years from the time Jacob entered Egypt, corresponding to the 400 years God had told Abraham (Genesis 15:13). Probably for about 30 years when Joseph was ruler, the Israelites were treated well.

4. **God's army**. In the phrase "all the LORD's divisions left Egypt" we see a word that relates to armies (cf. Exodus 7:4;12:51).[15] The narrator tells us, "The Israelites went up out of Egypt armed for battle" (13:18b). Their weapons may have been primitive compared to the Egyptians – probably mainly staffs – but they went out with a warrior spirit, not as slaves "with their tail between their legs."

5. **Heterogeneous group**.[16] Not only Israelites left Egypt, but with them large numbers of other oppressed peoples. Later these "rabble" cause some trouble (Numbers 11:4; Leviticus 24:10-11).[17]

6. **Night Watch**. Notice how this paragraph concludes; "the LORD kept vigil that night to bring them out of Egypt" (12:42).[18] The Lord took great care to pass over or to guard his people from the destroyer and bring them through what must have been a terrifying night!

The Lord Brought the Israelites Out of Egypt (Exodus 12:50-51)

Exodus chapter 12 ends with these two verses:

---

[15] "Divisions" (NIV), "companies" (NRSV), "hosts" (KJV) is *ṣābā'*, which has to do with fighting. It has also a wider use in the sense of rendering service (John E. Hartley, TWOT #1865b). One of the chief titles of God is "Yahweh/LORD of hosts," (*ṣebā'ôt*) as Martin Luther's "A Mighty Fortress Is Our God" puts it, "Lord Sabbaoth his name / from age to age the same / and he will win the victory."

[16] "Many other people went up with them" (NIV), "mixed crowd" (NRSV), "mixed multitude" (KJV) uses *'ēreb*, "mixture, mixed company, a heterogeneous body attached to a people" (BDB 786).

[17] "Rabble" (NIV, NRSV), "mixt multitude" (KJV) is *'asapsup*, "collection, rabble," the motley collection of people who followed Israel from Egypt, from *'āsap*, "gather." (Charles L. Feinberg, TWOT #140f).

[18] "Keep vigil" (NIV), "vigil" (NRSV), "observed" (KJV) is *shimmūr*, "night watch," from *shāmar*, "keep, guard, observe, give heed," with the basic idea of "to exercise great care over" (TWOT #2414).

"50 All the Israelites did just what the LORD had commanded Moses and Aaron. 51 And on that very day the LORD brought the Israelites out of Egypt by their divisions." (Exodus 12:50-51)

The people's deliverance is founded on two elements mentioned in verse 50:

1. Moses and Aaron obeyed what God had commanded them.
2. The people obeyed what Moses and Aaron commanded them.

The KJV renders the Hebrew quite literally:

"Thus did all the children of Israel; as the LORD commanded Moses and Aaron, so did[19] they." (Exodus 12:50, KJV)

Very often in the Pentateuch, the people are expected to act on, follow through on, obey what God has said. It is the key to receiving God's blessing.

Leaders must listen to God for direction and then act on that direction. But a real kind of "followership" is required of the people, too. When they recognize and follow Moses, God blesses them. But when they bicker and balk and refuse to recognize God's leadership behind Moses, disaster follows. We leaders can blame ourselves for people not following us – and sometimes it *is* our fault from impatience and lack of skill in leading – but ultimately, following God-appointed leaders is the people's responsibility. We cannot do that for them.

Q2. (Exodus 12:50) Why was obedience so important to the people's deliverance? Why is obedience so important to our deliverance from "sin, the flesh, and the devil"? Is there any discipleship without obedience? Does a person who says he believes in Jesus but doesn't obey him have real faith?

http://www.joyfulheart.com/forums/index.php?showtopic=1043

---

[19] "Did" is *āśâ*, "do, fashion, accomplish," here used with a strong sense of acting with a sense of "ethical obligation." "Aside from the numerous occurrences of the meaning 'do' or 'make' in a general sense, *ʿāsâ* is often used with the sense of ethical obligation. The covenant people were frequently commanded to 'do' all that God had commanded (Exodus 23:22; Leviticus 19:37; Deut. 6:18, etc.). The numerous contexts in which this concept occurs attest to the importance of an ethical response to God which goes beyond mere mental abstraction and which is translatable into obedience which is evidenced in demonstrable act" (Tomas E. McComiskey, *āśâ*, TWOT #1708).

The Pillar of Cloud and the Pillar of Fire (Exodus 13:21-22)

Up until now the people of Israel saw the mighty plagues in response to Moses' meetings with Pharaoh and they obeyed his commands for preparation, for Passover, for asking for jewelry from their neighbors, and for the actual embarkation. But for the next part of the journey, Moses is not their only guide. There is a pillar of cloud by day, and a pillar of fire by night.

> "21 By day the LORD went ahead of them in a pillar of cloud to guide them on their way and by night in a pillar of fire to give them light, so that they could travel by day or night. 22 Neither the pillar of cloud by day nor the pillar of fire by night left its place in front of the people." (Exodus 13:21-22)

"Pillar" is 'ammûd, "pillar, column, post," a common word for the pillars supporting buildings, from the verb 'āmad, "to stand."[20] We see it mentioned a number of places in the Pentateuch and referred to elsewhere in the Bible.[21] We'll discuss it more later.

You and I would often like the clarity of this pillar, to both authenticate our ministry before others and to set the direction clearly for the people. But as the story of the Exodus unfolds, we observe that the continual presence of this pillar of cloud and fire in the camp of Israel doesn't mean that Moses' leadership was easy. The people grumbling against Moses was actually a grumbling against the Lord, whom Moses represented (Exodus 16:8; See 1 Samuel 8:7-8).

The Desert Route (Exodus 13:17-18a)

But God didn't lead them on the easiest path! By far the fastest and direct route between Egypt and Canaan is north to the Mediterranean Sea, and then along a well-developed road on the Philistine coast, technically, the north Sinai Mediterranean coast road. If the Israelites were to travel 10 miles a day, they could have reached Canaan in just a few days.

However, the well-traveled Road to the Philistines had two drawbacks:

1. **The presence of military garrisons**. Since this road was the most natural place that Egypt's enemies would use to invade the country, it was heavily fortified.[22] To travel along the "easiest" route would guarantee that the Israelites would "face war."

---

[20] Ronald B. Allen, 'āmad, TWOT #1637c.

[21] Exodus 14:19-24; 40:34-38; Numbers 9:15-23; 10:34; 14:14; Deuteronomy 1:33; Nehemiah 9:12, 19; Psalm 78:14; 99:7; 105:39; Isaiah 4:5-6; 1 Corinthians 10:1-2.

[22] Archaeological and manuscript evidence indicate that the road between Pelusium and Gaza was dotted with perhaps ten additional forts (Kitchen, *Reliability*, pp. 266-267).

2. **Nation-building time needed**. After 400 years in Egypt, and the final years in forced slavery, Israel was not a unified nation, but a loosely confederated group of twelve tribes led by elders. Before Israel would be ready to enter the Promised Land and conquer its inhabitants, it would have to meet God, submit to his leadership, and learn to work together under the leadership of an overall leader: Moses and, later, Joshua. You can't shortcut the time it takes to mature.

Location of the Red Sea (*yām sûp*)

We just don't know the exact location of the body of water identified in the text as the "Red Sea," since the Hebrew phrase *yām sûp* is a term used in the Old Testament to identify a number of different bodies of water. *Yām* is used in the Old Testament over 300 times to refer to "sea" and about 70 times for "west" or "westward."[23] The word *sûp* means "reed, waterplant," a general term for marsh plants.[24]

No doubt the "Red Sea" (literally "Reed Sea," *yām sûp*) refers to some body of water east of the Nile delta, probably either at Lake Timsah or at the Great Bitter Lake, both of which lie along the present route of the Suez Canal. You can explore this further in Appendix 2 - The Route of the Exodus.

Proposed route of the "Reed Sea" crossing from Rameses to the Red Sea.

D. Pharaoh Pursues (Exodus 14:1-14)

Encamping West of the Sea (Exodus 14:1-4)

"[1] Then the LORD said to Moses, [2] 'Tell the Israelites to **turn back**.... They are to encamp by the sea.... [3] Pharaoh will think, 'The Israelites are wandering around the land in confusion, hemmed in by the desert.' [4] And I will harden Pharaoh's heart, and he will pursue them." (Exodus 14:1-4a)

---

[23] Paul R. Gilchrist, *yām*, TWOT #871a.

[24] R.D. Patterson, *sûp*, TWOT #1479. Used, for example, in Exodus 2:3, 5; Isaiah 19:6; Jonah 2:5.

It's fascinating to see Yahweh's strategy: to have the Israelites "turn back" (NIV, NRSV), "turn" (KJV)[25] in order to appear that they are confused and directionless, a tempting target to attract the ruthless and hardhearted Pharaoh and his armies.

If Moses were to use Israel as bait, we would call it irresponsible, since his main task would be to deliver the people of Israel from Egypt in the fastest possible way. But for Yahweh to do so, with his pillar of cloud and fire to lead them, it is entirely appropriate. Yahweh is not risking the people, but he has an additional objective: to humble Pharaoh and the gods of Egypt in the process of delivering the Israelites.

Pharaoh Rises to the Bait (Exodus 14:5-9)

As devastated as Egypt has become through the Ten Plagues, Pharaoh can't resist bringing the Israelites back. He and his officials are greedy.

> "The LORD hardened the heart of Pharaoh king of Egypt, so that he pursued the Israelites, who were marching out boldly.[26] The Egyptians – all Pharaoh's horses and chariots, horsemen and troops – pursued the Israelites and overtook them...." (14:8-9)

A chariot army is a terrifying weapon of war in ancient Egypt. While chariots aren't very useful in the Judean hills that the Israelites will eventually claim as their homeland, they are chillingly effective in the flat delta plain of Egypt, as well as the flat coastal plains bordering the Mediterranean.

In a field action, a chariot division usually

Rameses II and chariot at the Battle of Kadesh (1274 BC). Relief inside his Abu Simbel temple, Nubia, Southern Egypt.

---

[25] The basic meaning of *shûb* is "(re)turn." In a theological sense it is used for repentance, "turning one's heart to the Lord." (Victor P. Hamilton, *shûb*, TWOT #2340).

[26] "Boldly"(NIV, NRSV), "with a high hand" (KJV) is an idiom that uses the term *rāmam*, "high," which might refer to arrogance, but here to self-confidence and boldness. The event is recounted later: "The children of Israel went out with an high hand in the sight of all the Egyptians" (Numbers 33:3, KJV).

delivered the first strike, to be followed by infantry advancing to exploit a tactical success. The largest chariot battle ever fought took place about 1274 BC at the Battle of Kadesh in Syria, when Rameses II attacked the Hittites, a battle involving perhaps 5,000 to 6,000 chariots.

An Egyptian light chariot contained one driver and one fighter, usually armed with a bow. The chariot is fast and deadly – all of the fear factor of cavalry, but with the added accuracy of a stable shooting platform, with room to store additional arrows (and short spears when the arrows were exhausted).

Blaming the Leader – Again! (Exodus 14:10-12)

Pharaoh's pairs of horses thundering towards the Israelites threw them into panic.

> "10 As Pharaoh approached, the Israelites looked up, and there were the Egyptians, marching after them. They were terrified and cried out to the LORD.
>
> 11 They said to Moses, 'Was it because there were no graves in Egypt that you brought us to the desert to die? What have you done to us by bringing us out of Egypt? 12 Didn't we say to you in Egypt, "Leave us alone; let us serve the Egyptians"? It would have been better for us to serve the Egyptians than to die in the desert!'" (Exodus 14:10-12)

To their credit, the Israelites "cried out to the LORD" (14:10b) as they had during their oppression in Egypt (2:23-24). But they make the mistake of blaming their leader for the problem – as if Moses is leading on his own, rather than following carefully what the Lord tells him to do. They say:

1.　Since we have to die, we would rather die in Egypt where we were comfortable, rather than in this desolate desert.
2.　We told you to leave us alone, but you wouldn't listen.
3.　It would have been better to remain slaves than die in the desert.

I learned a lesson very early in my ministry, that when people praise me I must understand that they are praising God working within me – and that I must pass that praise onto him, rather than keep it for myself to puff me up. What it has taken me much longer to learn is that, if I am leading for God, people's criticisms of me are actually criticisms of God's leadership through me – and that I must pass that criticism on to him and not keep it for myself to eat at me.

Moses Encourages the People (Exodus 14:13-14)

Moses doesn't waste his time answering their petty criticisms. Instead, he reaffirms to them the Lord's victory and tells them how to respond:

"13 Moses answered the people, 'Do not be afraid. Stand firm and you will see the deliverance the LORD will bring you today. The Egyptians you see today you will never see again. 14 The LORD will fight for you; you need only to be still.'" (Exodus 14:13-14)

This is one of the classic encouragements in the entire Bible! Notice that Moses offers three commands (to direct their activity) and makes three faith assertions (to bolster their faith).

Commands:

1. **Do not be afraid**. Fear is their central weakness. We see this command especially on the lips of angels and Jesus in the Gospels.

2. **Stand firm**.[27] The opposite would be to run from the opposing army's forces. Recall Paul's command:

   "Put on the full armor of God, so that when the day of evil comes, you may be able to **stand your ground**, and after you have done everything, to **stand**. **Stand firm** then...." (Ephesians 6:13-14a)

3. **Be still**.[28] Stop whining!

Faith Assertions:

1. You will see the deliverance[29] the Lord will bring.
2. You won't see the Egyptians ever again.
3. The Lord will fight[30] for you!

Moses' ministry here is one of command and of reassurance – making faith statements in the hearing of the people so they would believe God rather than be panicked by their situation.

Again and again we see this theme: the Lord does battle on behalf of Israel.[31] What is unique here is that the Israelites themselves don't have to fight at all – all the fighting is

---

[27] The verb is *yāṣab*, "stand, set or station oneself, present oneself." In a military sense, it means to take one's position to prepare to battle one's opponent (1 Samuel 17:16; Jeremiah 46:4) (Paul R. Gilchrist, *yāṣab*, TWOT #894).

[28] The verb is *ḥārēsh*, "be silent, speechless, deaf." The basic idea is of non-communication, expressed by either not speaking or not hearing (Leon J. Wood, *ḥārēsh*, TWOT #761).

[29] "Deliverance" (NIV, NRSV), "salvation" (KJV) is *yeshû 'â* (the root of Jesus' given name), from the verb *yāsha '*. "The root meaning in Arabic is 'make wide' or 'make sufficient'; this root is in contrast to *ṣārar*, 'narrow," which means 'be restricted' or 'cause distress.' That which is wide connotes freedom from distress and the ability to pursue one's own objectives. To move from distress to safety requires deliverance" (John E. Harley, *yāsha '*, TWOT #929b). Rather than being boxed in between the Egyptians and the sea, they will soon be free to move where they desire.

[30] "Fight" is *lāḥam*, "fight, do battle" (Walter C. Kaiser, *lāḥam*, TWOT #1104).

[31] Exodus 14:25; Deuteronomy 1:30; 3:22; Joshua 10:14, 42; Jeremiah 21:5; Nehemiah 4:14; 2 Chronicles 20:29.

done by the Lord. In most cases, however, the Israelites fight, but have a power-assist from the Most High God. When the Israelites have crossed the Red Sea, this theme is celebrated in a mighty song, declaring, "Yahweh is a warrior" (Exodus 15:3).

Q3. (Exodus 14:11-14) Why do the people blame Moses for the advancing Egyptian army? What motivates their fear? Who are the people really blaming? How does Moses respond to their blame and fear? Why doesn't Moses defend himself from their unfair criticism? How do the people respond to Moses' words?

http://www.joyfulheart.com/forums/index.php?showtopic=1044

E. Crossing the Red Sea (Exodus 14:15-31)

The People March through the Red Sea (Exodus 14:15-16, 21-22)

After comforting and encouraging the people, Moses has been crying out to God himself in intercessory prayer.

> "15 Then the LORD said to Moses, 'Why are you crying out to me? Tell the Israelites to move on. 16 Raise your staff and stretch out your hand over the sea to divide the water so that the Israelites can go through the sea on dry ground.'" (Exodus 14:15-16)

Dear friends, there is a time a time for everything (Ecclesiastes 3:1-8) – a time to pray and cry out to God, and a time to act decisively in order that the prayer might be answered. A time to take your stand, and a time to move on. This is such a time![32]

---

[32] I've heard about sermons contending that God rebukes Moses for praying when he should be leading. But I don't think that's warranted. Moses has listened to God, moved the people of Israel in accordance with God's direction, and quieted the people. Now he is continuing his ministry of intercessory prayer, waiting for the timing of God's strategy to come to fruition. When it does, God calls Moses from his prayer to a period of action.

James J.0, "The Waters Are Divided" (1896-1902), watercolor, Jewish Museum, New York.

When Moses lifts his staff, an extension of his hand (14:16, 21, 27), God acts by moving the "angel of God" to a position between Israel and her enemies:

> "[19] Then the angel of God, who had been traveling in front of Israel's army, withdrew and went behind them. The pillar of cloud also moved from in front and stood behind them, [20] coming between the armies of Egypt and Israel. Throughout the night the cloud brought darkness to the one side and light to the other side; so neither went near the other all night long." (Exodus 14:19-20)

An unseen angel[33] of God has been protecting them. Notice in verse 19 that the angel is differentiated from the pillar of cloud and fire, though the pillar follows the angel. The pillar effectively separates the two armies during the night, serving as darkness to the Egyptians and light to the Israelites.

At Moses' gesture with his hand (and staff, see verse 16), "a strong east wind," presumably off the desert to the east, divides the water with a wall of water on each side (14:21-22). How a normal wind could make a wall[34] of water to the right and left, we just don't know. Perhaps this is a kind of narrow, directed blast. If these were reedy salt marshes with a soft bottom, the wind would serve to dry them out enough so that the Israelites could cross without sinking into the muck.[35] Like other miracles that are one-

---

[33] The word "angel" is *mal'āk*, "messenger, representative, courtier, angel." These were to carry a message, to perform some other specific commission, and to represent more or less officially the one sending him. The term can be used of both human and supernatural messengers (Andrew Bowling, *mal'āk*, TWOT #1068a).

[34] "Wall" is *hômâ*, the common noun used for the wall of a house or of a city (BDB 327).

[35] "Dry land" is actually a single word in Hebrew, *yabbāshâ*, The primary meaning of the root *yābēsh* is "to be or become dry without moisture from necessary or normal fluids." *Yabbāshâ* is used to describe "dry land" in contrast with a body of water, such as Jonah being vomited up on "dry land," that is, the beach. It also used to describe the miracles of the parting of the Red Sea and of the Jordan River at the Conquest (Joshua 2:10; 4:23; Psalm 74:15; Nehemiah 9:11).

of-a-kind events that God brings about, it's difficult to describe them in terms of things we understand.

Gaining Glory over the Egyptians (Exodus 14:4, 17-18)

One of the themes of this part of Exodus is God "gaining glory" or "getting honor" over the Egyptians. It's a difficult concept for us to grasp, but since it is central here and elsewhere in the Old Testament, let's spend some time to understand it.

> "And I will harden Pharaoh's heart, and he will pursue them. But I will **gain glory** for myself through Pharaoh and all his army, and the Egyptians will know that I am the LORD." (Exodus 14:4)

> "[17] I will harden the hearts of the Egyptians so that they will go in after them. And I will **gain glory** through Pharaoh and all his army, through his chariots and his horsemen. [18] The Egyptians will know that I am the LORD when I **gain glory** through Pharaoh, his chariots and his horsemen." (Exodus 14:17-18)

The Exodus may seem to us to be about delivering a large group of people from slavery. But if that's all we see, we're missing an important theme – the glory of Yahweh. This verb "gain glory" (NIV, NRSV), "get honor" (KJV) is the verb *kābēd*, here in the Niphal stem. The basic meaning of the root is "to be heavy, weighty," extending to the figurative idea of a "weighty" person in society, someone who is honorable, impressive, noteworthy, worthy of respect. Common translations are to be "honorable, honored, glorious, glorified."[36]

Up to the time of Moses, the name Yahweh had been relatively unknown (Exodus 6:2-3). When Moses tells Pharaoh that Yahweh says, "Let my people go," Pharaoh replies, "Who is Yahweh, that I should obey him and let Israel go? I do not know Yahweh and I will not let Israel go." (Exodus 5:2).

According to the Egyptian religion, Pharaoh himself is a god; why should he give any regard to the supposedly inferior God of his slaves? Pharaoh mocked the Lord! His heart was arrogant and hard towards God. But after his army's Red Sea disaster, he mocked no more.

We humans often view the pursuit of glory as vain and unworthy; we must be humble. However, God is divine! He is King of the universe! For a petty Pharaoh to defy the Living God must be answered with power, or God's reputation will not be respected among the nations.

[36] John N. Oswalt, *kābēd*, TWOT #943.

More than that, unless Yahweh soundly defeats the Egyptian oppressors, he cannot gain the full faith and allegiance of his people. They have lived under slavery and oppression for hundreds of years. They have been beaten into submission and have a low view of themselves and their God compared to their respect for Egypt and its gods that seem superior. The revelation of God's glory in defeating Egypt is important for the sake of the Egyptians *and* the Israelites.

But seeing God's glory demands responsible action from the people. Later, when the people of Israel balk at entering the Promised Land, God tells them.

> "²¹ As surely as I live and as surely as the **glory of the LORD** fills the whole earth, ²² not one of the men who **saw my glory** and the miraculous signs I performed in Egypt and in the desert ... will ever see the land I promised on oath to their forefathers. No one who has treated me with contempt will ever see it." (Numbers 14:21-23)

God's awesome glory demands faith and obedience!

Leaders, too, have a responsibility in the face of God's glory. We must not take it for ourselves. Through Isaiah, the Lord says:

> "I am the LORD; that is my name!
> I will not give **my glory** to another
> or my praise to idols." (Isaiah 42:8)

> "For my own sake,
> for my own sake, I do this.
> How can I let myself be defamed?
> I will not yield **my glory** to another." (Isaiah 48:11)

Twice, in Exodus, we see the term "my glory" (Exodus 29:43; 33:22). It is not ours, but God's. When he acts powerfully through our ministries, we must acknowledge that the power is his, not ours.

We ourselves are created to glorify God. That is our purpose.

> "... Everyone who is called by my name,
> whom I created for **my glory**,
> whom I formed and made." (Isaiah 43:7)

> "... in order that we, who were the first to hope in Christ,
> might be **for the praise of his glory**." (Ephesians 1:12)

> "And I, because of their actions and their imaginations,
> am about to come and gather all nations and tongues,
> and they will come and **see my glory**.
> I will set a sign among them,
> and I will send some of those who survive to the nations ...

that have not heard of my fame or **seen my glory**.
They will proclaim **my glory** among the nations." (Isaiah 66:18-19)

"Father, I want those you have given me
to be with me where I am, and to **see my glory**,
the glory you have given me
because you loved me before the creation of the world." (John 17:24)

"What if he did this to make the riches of his glory known to the objects of his mercy,
whom he **prepared in advance for glory**" (Romans 9:23)

Q4. (Exodus 14:4, 17-18) Why is God's glory important in the Exodus? How is recognition of his glory important to faith? To holiness? To reverence? What happens when leaders take for themselves the credit and glory that should go only to God? How can leaders keep themselves from pride?
http://www.joyfulheart.com/forums/index.php?showtopic=1045

James J. Tissot, "The Egyptians Are Destroyed" (1896-1900), watercolor, Jewish Museum, New York.

The Destruction of Pharaoh's Army (Exodus 14:23-30)

Now the Egyptians' stubbornness and hard hearts cause their doom.

"[24] During the last watch of the night the LORD looked down from the pillar of fire and cloud at the Egyptian army and threw it into **confusion**. [25] He made the **wheels of their chariots come off** so that they had difficulty driving. And the Egyptians said, 'Let's get away from the Israelites! The LORD is **fighting** for them against Egypt.'

"[27]... Moses stretched out his hand over the sea, and at daybreak **the sea went back to its place**. The Egyptians were fleeing toward it, and the LORD **swept them into the sea**.... [30] That day the LORD saved Israel from the hands of the Egyptians, and Israel saw the **Egyptians lying dead on the shore**." (Exodus 14:24-25, 27, 30)

Look what result this had on the Israelites:

"And when the Israelites saw the great power the LORD displayed against the Egyptians, the people **feared** the LORD and **put their trust** in him and in Moses his servant." (Exodus 14:31)

Why did the Lord wipe out so many Egyptian soldiers in this operation? Four answers may help us:

1. **Protection.** So long as Pharaoh's army is intact, the Israelites are not safe from attack. God has crushed their enemy.
2. **Glory.** Until now, Pharaoh and the Egyptians had acted disrespectfully towards God. No more. Yahweh is now honored and glorified as a great God who has defeated the gods of Egypt.
3. **Faith.** The people of Israel themselves had believed in the might of Egypt over Yahweh's ability to save them. Now they "feared the LORD and put their trust in him" (Exodus 14:31). The Lord is engaged in nation-building. To have people trust in their God is the first step in making a covenant with him at Mt. Sinai.
4. **Leadership.** Moses, too, benefits from God's visible power. As the Lord's servant, the people trust in him, as well. He is now able to lead more effectively than before.

F. Celebration (Exodus 15:1-21)

The Song of Moses (Exodus 15:1-19)

Chapter 15 begins, "Then Moses and the Israelites sang this song to the LORD...." What follows is a poetic psalm, much like the psalms in our Book of Psalms, that show all the elements of Hebrew poetry.[37] We can't cover it all, but here are the main elements. It begins:

> "I will sing to the LORD,
> for he is highly exalted.[38]
> The horse and its rider[39]
> he has hurled into the sea.
> [2] The LORD is my strength and my song;
> he has become my salvation.
> He is my God, and I will praise him,
> my father's God, and I will exalt him." (15:1-2)

The next stanza praises Yahweh as a great warrior, and recounts his exploits over Egypt's army. What follows is a reflection on this unique, one-of-a-kind God who has given victory:

> "[11] Who among the gods is like you, O LORD?
> Who is like you –
> majestic[40] in holiness,
> awesome[41] in glory,[42]
> working wonders[43]?
>
> [12] You stretched out your right hand
> and the earth swallowed them.

---

[37] For more on Hebrew poetic forms, see my book, *Experiencing the Psalms* (JesusWalk, 2010).

[38] "Highly exalted" (NIV), "triumphed gloriously" (NRSV, KJV) is *gā'â*, "rise up, grow up, be exalted in triumph," with the root idea of "to rise." In the Songs of Moses and of Miriam, the verb is doubled using a Hebrew grammatical idiom where the finite verb preceded by infinitive absolute of the same verb, causing the idea to be intensified. So "to exalt" becomes "to exalt highly or greatly," "to triumph" becomes "to triumph gloriously" (Victor P. Hamilton, TWOT #299).

[39] "Rider" is *rākab*, "to mount and ride, ride." Related words are *rekeb*, "chariot, chariotry" and *rakkāb*, "driver, charioteer," so the song is likely referring to the Egyptians riding the chariots.

[40] "Majestic" (NIV, NRSV), "glorious" (KJV) is *'ādar*, "to be majestic... this root connotes that which is superior to something else, and, therefore, that which is majestic" (Leonard J. Coppes, TWOT #28).

[41] "Awesome" (NIV, NRSV), "fearful" (KJV) is *yārē'*, "fear, be afraid, revere.... The Niphal participle [as here] is frequently used to describe things as 'terrible,' 'awesome,' or 'terrifying.' This is a good example of the gerundive character of the Niphal participle, 'to be feared'" (Andrew Bowling, TWOT #907).

[42] "Glory" (NIV), "splendor" (NRSV), "praises" (KJV) is *tehillâ*, "praise, praiseworthy deeds," from *hālal*, "praise, boast" (the root of our word, "Hallelujah"). This noun represents the results of *hālal* as well as divine acts which merit that activity (Leonard J. Coppes, TWOT #500c).

[43] "Wonders" is *pele'*, "wonders," from *pālā'*, "to be marvelous, wonderful." In the Bible the root *pl'* refers to things that are unusual, beyond human capabilities. As such, it awakens astonishment (*pl'*) in man (Victor P. Hamilton, TWOT #1768a).

[13] In your unfailing love[44]
you will lead the people you have redeemed.[45]
In your strength you will guide[46] them to your holy dwelling." (15:11-13)

The song concludes looking forward to entering the Promised Land and arriving at God's dwelling place. In its final line it praises the Lord who will reign forever as the King of Israel:

"The LORD will reign[47] for ever and ever." (15:18)

The Song of Miriam (Exodus 15:20-21)

The section concludes with a song sung by the women and led by Moses' sister Miriam, who is called "the prophetess" here, recapping the first two lines of the Song of Moses (15:1-2)

James J. Tissot, "The Songs of Joy" (1896-1900), watercolor, Jewish Museum, New York.

[20] Then Miriam the prophetess, Aaron's sister, took a tambourine in her hand, and all the women followed her, with tambourines and dancing. [21] Miriam sang to them:

"Sing to the LORD,
for he is highly exalted.
The horse and its rider he has
hurled into the sea."
(Exodus 15:20-21)

Prayer

Lord, thank you for your amazing triumph at the Red Sea. It defied the power of the most powerful nation on earth and formed a people who would trust and follow you,

---

[44] "Unfailing love" (NIV), "steadfast love" (NRSV), "mercy" (KJV) is *hesed*, "kindness, lovingkindness, mercy." This is more than faithfulness to covenant, as some have claimed. It is the Old Testament equivalent of "God is love" (R. Laird Harris, TWOT #698a).

[45] "Redeemed" is *gā'al*, "redeem, avenge, revenge, ransom, do the part of a kinsman" (R. Laird Harris, TWOT #300). God takes on our case as would a kinsman with a family obligation towards one in trouble.

[46] "Guide/guided" is *nāhal*, "lead with care," the root denoting, "a shepherd's loving concerned leading of his flock" (Leonard J. Coppes, TWOT #1312).

[47] "Reign" is *mālak*, "to reign," that is, to be and exercise functions of a monarch, whether male (king) or female (queen) (Robert D. Culver, TWOT #1199).

even in deserts. Thank you for Moses' steady leadership through intense pressure. Give me that kind of fortitude to lead your people as well. In Jesus' name, I pray. Amen.

4. Grumbling, Conflict, and Delegation (Exodus 15-18)

Moses' leadership has got the people out of Egypt. But now the hardships of leading the people through a desert sojourn will challenge him to his limit. Moses, you remember, was familiar with life in the desert; he had been a shepherd in the Sinai wilderness for 40 years when he served his father-in-law, Jethro. But the people of Israel were used to an agrarian life in the well-watered Nile delta. The desert was new and terrifying to them.

James J. Tissot, "The Gathering of the Manna" (1896-1900), watercolor, Jewish Museum, New York.

A. Grumbling (Exodus 15:22-17:7)

Finding Drinkable Water at Marah (Exodus 15:22-25a)

The first crisis they met in the desert was – predictably – thirst. They found water, but it was bitter – unpalatable to drink – perhaps brackish, alkaline water.

Notice what Moses does. He seeks the Lord, literally, he "cried out" to the Lord. The Hebrew verb suggests an urgency and desperation in Moses' plea.[1] Often leaders see themselves as problem-solvers rather than pray-ers. Moses calls on God and God gives him the solution.

He throws a piece of wood into the water and the water becomes drinkable. There are various theories about how the wood might have reacted chemically with the salts or a pungent wood might cover the mineral taste to make the water palatable. One author suggests that barberry has this effect.[2] But the result was that the people could now

---

[1] Sā'aq, "cry, cry for help, call." The root means, "to call out for help under great distress or to utter an exclamation in great excitement" (John E. Hartley, TWOT #1947).

[2] Cole (Exodus, p. 129) cites S.R. Driver, Exodus (1911) who refers to De Lesseps who mentioned that modern Arabs used the barberry bush. Cole says, "No doubt the need was to find some pungent or aromatic shrub whose flavor would cover the mineral taste and make the water palatable."

drink the water, and this new company of refugees from Egypt was saved from dying of thirst.

Grumbling, Complaining, Murmuring, and Quarreling against Leaders

"So the people grumbled against Moses, saying, 'What are we to drink?'" (Exodus 15:24)

Complaining, quarrelling, fractious people begin to wag their tongues with Moses as the target. This is the first of many such crises that Moses the leader has to meet. But perhaps the greater leadership crisis is the kind of rebellion that surfaces when people are afraid or frustrated. This is the first instance of a Hebrew word that we meet several times in Exodus and Numbers.

"Grumble" (NIV), "complain" (NRSV), "murmur" (KJV) is *lîn*, which means, "to murmur, rebel (against)."[3] Here, the people complained to their leader, "What are we to drink?" In later episodes, they seem to hold Moses responsible for every problem: "You brought us out here, now we'll die! What are you going to do about it?"

This complaining behavior clusters around a number of incidents during the Exodus. Several occur in this week's lesson. We'll consider others in Lesson 8 and Lesson 9.

Scripture	Summary	Motivation
Exodus 5:21	Your demands to Pharaoh have made us a stench to him, demanding bricks without supplying straw.	Fear of punishment
Exodus 14:11-12	You brought us to die in wilderness	Fear of dying in battle
Exodus 15:24	Grumbling. Water is bitter at Marah. "What shall we drink?"	Fear of dying of thirst
Exodus 16:2, 7-9, 12	Grumbling. "We'll Starve to death!" Recalled pots of meat in Egypt.	Fear of dying of starvation

---

[3] *Lîn*, TWOT #1097.

Scripture	Summary	Motivation
Exodus 17:3	At Rephidim, Moses strikes the rock at God's command.	Fear of dying of thirst
Numbers 11:1-6	Complaints[4] about their hardships. Tired of manna, craved other food, instigated by the "rabble."	Dissatisfaction with manna
Numbers 14:2, 27, 29, 36-37; Deuteronomy 1:27 and Psalm 106:25 (*rāgan*[5])	Fear of war in Canaan after the report of the 10 unbelieving spies. "We'll fall by the sword. Our wives and children will be taken as plunder." There is talk of selecting another leader. The 10 spies are struck down by the Lord for spreading a bad, unbelieving report.	Fear of death and slavery
Numbers 16:11, 41; 17:5, 10	Korah rebels against Moses and the God-ordained Aaronic priesthood. Moses is also blamed when the leaders of rebellion are struck down by God.	Envy of Moses' leadership
Numbers 20:1-13	At Kadesh the people "gather in opposition against"[6] and "quarreled"[7] with Moses (also Exodus 17:2). Moses strikes the rock in anger rather than speaking to it as God instructed – and is punished by failing to enter the Promised Land.	Fear of dying of thirst

[4] *'Anan*, "complain, murmur" (BDB 59).

[5] *Rāgan*, "murmur, whisper" is used in two ways in the Old Testament: (1) "murmur (rebelliously)" (Psalm 106:25; Deuteronomy 1:27) and (2) "whisper (maliciously), backbite, slander," used in the Proverbs (BDB 832).

[6] The verb *qāhal* conveys the idea of assembling (without regard to purpose). In the Niphal stem (as here), it carries the reflexive idea of a group assembling themselves (Jack P. Lewis, TWOT #1991). It is used with the preposition *'al*, "against."

[7] "Quarreled" (NIV, NRSV), "chode" (KJV) is *rîb*, "strive, contend." The idea of physical combat is primary, but here has transitioned to verbal combat, "to quarrel, to chide one another" (Robert D. Culver, TWOT #2159).

Scripture	Summary	Motivation
Numbers 21:4-9	Impatience, short-tempered, discouraged.[8] Rebels accuse Moses of bringing them out of Egypt to die of thirst and starvation. They detest manna. Punished by poisonous snakes. Set up of bronze serpent on which they look and live.	Impatience with difficult conditions

As you examine the table of dissent above, you see that one of the chief causes is fear, the root of which is unbelief. Asaph the psalmist lays bare the problem in these excerpts from Psalm 78 that recount Israel's sojourn in the wilderness:

"They **forgot** what he had done,
the wonders he had shown them....

But they continued to sin against him,
rebelling in the desert against the Most High....

When the LORD heard them, he was very angry;
his fire broke out against Jacob,
and his wrath rose against Israel,
for they **did not believe** in God
or **trust** in his deliverance....

In spite of all this, they kept on sinning;
in spite of his wonders,
they **did not believe**." (Psalm 78:11, 17, 21-22, 32)

Christian congregations can be afflicted with unbelief in the twenty-first century just as seriously as were the Israelites in Moses' day. They can also become discouraged with their troubles and get involved in leadership takeovers. Like Israel, churches can become nests of criticism and unbelief. They can be bastions of the status quo and resistant to a journey of faith that takes them into uncharted territory. Paul warns us Christians rather clearly:

"And do not grumble,[9] as some of them did – and were killed by the destroying angel."
(1 Corinthians 10:10)

---

[8] "Become impatient" (NIV, NRSV), "be discouraged" (KJV) is *qāṣar*, "be impatient, vexed, grieved," from a root that means "be short." In some passages the root means "discouragement," "vexation" (Judges 10:16; 16:16; Job 21:4), or "loathing" (Zechariah 11:8) (Jack P. Lewis, TWOT #2061).

[9] "Grumble" (NIV), "complain" (NRSV), "murmur" is Greek *gongyzō*, "to express oneself in low tones of disapprobation, grumble, murmur" (BDAG 204, 1).

It's pretty obvious that Moses was affected by the criticism; he didn't ignore it. The question is: How did he respond to it? Was his response spiritual or unspiritual? We'll be looking carefully at these incidents as we come to them, learning from his wisdom – and from his mistakes.

Q1. (Exodus 15:24) What are the reasons that people grumble and complain? How do fear and faith relate to grumbling? What symptoms of grumbling do you see in your own life? What should you do about it?

http://www.joyfulheart.com/forums/index.php?showtopic=1046

Grumbling shows lack of faith + trust!

None of These Diseases (Exodus 15:26)

At Marah, where the brackish water was made sweet, God makes the people a wonderful promise:

> "If you listen carefully to the voice of the LORD your God and do what is right in his eyes, if you pay attention to his commands and keep all his decrees, I will not bring on you any of the diseases I brought on the Egyptians, for I am the LORD, who heals you." (Exodus 15: 26)

"Diseases" is *maḥalâ*, "disease, sickness," from the root, *ḥālâ*, "to be(come) sick or faint." Often, no distinction need be made between "sick" or "weak," the latter resulting from the former. "To be sick" can come from physical injury or wounding: by beating, from battle wounds, from a fall. It is used in a general sense for illness, regardless of cause, sometimes leading to death.[10]

"Heals" is *rāpāʾ*, "heal, make healthful." The root is used of healing physical conditions and diseases, barrenness, sores and boils, as well as making bad water drinkable and broken pots usable.[11]

So what do the "diseases I brought on the Egyptians" have to do with the undrinkable water at Marah? The plagues upon the Egyptians were literally "blows" upon them,

---

[10] Carl Philip Weber, *ḥālâ*, TWOT #655 b and c.
[11] William White, *rāpāʾ*, TWOT #2196.

that gradually brought the nation to its knees. So probably, the reference here is to the plague of blood that made the Egyptians' water undrinkable.

The promise is wonderful – and conditional. Notice that this promise is not made to individuals (contrary to what teachers sometimes tell us), but to the nation of Israel as a whole. If you Israelites will listen and obey God, he will keep you healthy and make you whole, and keep you from disasters (like the plagues upon Egypt) that will weaken and destroy you.

It's not that I disbelieve promises of healing for today. I do believe in miracles of healing in our time! Certainly gifts of healings are promised in the New Testament (1 Corinthians 12:9, 28, 30), elders are instructed to anoint the sick and pray for healing (James 5:14-16), and we are told to expect signs and wonders to accompany believers in Messiah Jesus – including healing (Mark 16:18). But it is important to understand the healing promises that are given us in their proper context.

Unfortunately, the Israelites did *not* listen and obey, so we are unable to see the fulfillment of this promise in their lives.

Grumbling about Food (Exodus 16:2-3)

By now, the supplies of food they had brought with them from Egypt were exhausted and desert fare was too meager to feed this large a group of people.

> "2 In the desert the whole community grumbled against Moses and Aaron. 3 The Israel-ites said to them, 'If only we had died by the LORD's hand in Egypt! There we sat around pots of meat and ate all the food we wanted, but you have brought us out into this desert to starve this entire assembly to death.'" (Exodus 16:2-3)

They remember the "fleshpots" (NRSV, KJV) or "pots of meat" (NIV)[12] and imagined that in Egypt they had eaten "all the food we wanted" – surely an exaggeration! Strange, how attractive hard bondage seemed when the Israelites faced starvation. They longed for the "good old days." They accused Moses of bringing them into the desert with the purpose "to starve this entire assembly to death."

Grumbling against the Lord, not Moses (Exodus 16:7b-8)

> "'[The Lord] has heard your grumbling against him. Who are we, that you should grumble against us?' Moses also said, 'You will know that it was the LORD when he gives you meat to eat in the evening and all the bread you want in the morning, because

---

[12] "Pot" is *sîrâ*, "one of six kinds of cooking utensils, spoken of pots, pans, cauldrons, or basins. Probably made of bronze or earthenware" ("Fleshpots," ISBE 2:315). "Meat" (NIV), "flesh" (NRSV, KJV) is *bāśār*, "animal musculature" (John N. Oswalt, TWOT #291a).

he has heard your grumbling against him. Who are we? You are not grumbling against us, but against the LORD.'" (Exodus 16:7b-8)

As we saw in Lesson 3 (Exodus 14:11-12), people complaining to the leader about their conditions are really complaining about God's provision for them! Samuel faced the same problem when the people clamored for a king to be over them.

"⁶ When they said, 'Give us a king to lead us,' this displeased Samuel; so he prayed to the LORD. ⁷ And the LORD told him: 'Listen to all that the people are saying to you; it is **not you they have rejected**, but they have **rejected me** as their king. ⁸ As they have done from the day I brought them up out of Egypt until this day, forsaking me and serving other gods, so they are doing to you." (1 Samuel 8:6-8)

Sometimes leaders gather the criticism to themselves without realizing that it is really the Lord that the people are criticizing. Both Moses and Samuel had to learn a simple leadership lesson: It's not about you, it's about God. Jesus himself said,

"He who listens to you listens to me; he who rejects you rejects me; but he who rejects me rejects him who sent me." (Luke 10:16)

"Remember the words I spoke to you: 'No servant is greater than his master.' If they persecuted me, they will persecute you also. If they obeyed my teaching, they will obey yours also." (John 15:20-21)

Q2. (Exodus 16:7-8) Why can grumbling against a leader really be a symptom of grumbling against the Lord? Are there any cases where this might *not* be true? Why do leaders tend to take complaints so personally? What does it take to learn that "it's not about you."

http://www.joyfulheart.com/forums/index.php?showtopic=1047

The Glory of the Lord Revealed (Exodus 16:6-12)

When you complain to God, you face him in all his awesomeness.

"In the morning you will **see the glory of the LORD**, because he has heard your grumbling against him…. While Aaron was speaking to the whole Israelite community, they looked toward the desert, and there was the **glory of the LORD appearing in the cloud**." (Exodus 16:7, 10)

The word "glory" is *kābôd*, from the verb *kābēd*, "to be honorable, glorious," which we discussed in Lesson 3 above at Exodus 14:4, 17-18. The root idea is "to be heavy, weighty." That transitions to a "weighty" person in society, someone who is honorable, impressive, worthy of respect. The word "gravitas" carries this sense.[13]

But the idea of "glory" in both the Old and New Testaments also carries the idea of brilliant shining light.

- **Moses' shining face** is veiled after speaking with the Lord "face to face" (Exodus 34:29-35; 2 Corinthians 3:13).
- At Jesus' transfiguration "**his face shone like the sun** and his clothes became as white as the light" (Matthew 17:22; Mark 9:2-3; Luke 9:29).
- In Revelation the **Son of Man's face "was like the sun shining** in all its brilliance" (Revelation 1:16; cf. 10:1).
- In Revelation's depiction of heaven, "the city has no need of sun or moon to shine on it, for the **glory of God is its light**, and its lamp is the Lamb." (Revelation 21:23; cf. Isaiah 60:19-20).

Thus, "the glory of the LORD appearing in the cloud" (Exodus 16:10) must have been more than the pillar of cloud that had remained with the Israelite camp continuously and which they had gotten used to. Keil sees it as "a flash of light bursting forth from the cloud, and revealing the majesty of God."[14]

This phenomenon of the glory of the Lord appearing happens several times in conjunction with the people's complaints, as it does here. In our passage, the glory of the Lord is to build the people's faith and to emphasize that the Lord can work miracles even in the desert. Often, however, the appearance of God's glory comes with severe judgment:

- When the people accept the bad report of the 10 spies (Numbers 14:10).
- At the rebellion of Korah against Moses' authority (Numbers 16:19, 42).
- At the people's complaint about no water (Numbers 20:6).

God's presence is nothing to be trifled with! Childs comments, "In all the wilderness stories, people complain, men dispute, but finally God himself appears and brings the matter to a halt with a decisive judgment."[15]

Scholars use two words to describe these phenomena:

---

[13] "Gravitas," from Latin, "high seriousness (as in a person's bearing or in the treatment of a subject)" (*Merriam-Webster's 11th Collegiate Dictionary* (1993).

[14] Keil and Delitzsch, *Exodus,* p. 66 (commenting on Exodus 16:10)

[15] Childs, *Exodus,* p. 288.

- **Theophany**[16] is a theological term used to describe a visible manifestation of God, a self-disclosure of the deity.
- **Shekinah**[17] was used by later Jews to describe the glory of God's presence.

God's Provision of Quail and Manna (Exodus 16)

Moses had known this day would come when hunger would overtake them. God knew, too, and was prepared ahead of time with a solution: manna.

> "Then the LORD said to Moses, 'I will rain down **bread from heaven** for you. The people are to go out each day and gather enough for that day.'" (Exodus 16:4)

The giving of manna for food is intricately entwined with God teaching the Israelites to observe the Sabbath, resting on the seventh day, since manna appeared every other day except the seventh day. We're not going to study that aspect here, just observe that God provided food for them – both quail ("meat") and manna ("bread"). The provision of quail took place just twice that we know of – here and Numbers 11:31-32. But the manna continued for forty years until they entered the Promised Land.

> "13 That evening quail came and covered the camp, and in the morning there was a layer of dew around the camp. 14 When the dew was gone, **thin flakes** like frost on the ground appeared on the desert floor. 15 When the Israelites saw it, they said to each other, '**What is it?**' For they did not know what it was. Moses said to them, 'It is the **bread** the LORD has given you to eat.'" (Exodus 16:13-15)

Exactly what was the manna? The word "manna" came from the Israelites' question in verse 15: "What is it?" Hebrew *mān hû'*, from *mâ*, "what" + *hû'*, "it." Below I've compiled the other descriptions of manna given in the Bible:

> "31 The people of Israel called the bread manna. It was **white like coriander seed** and tasted like **wafers made with honey**." (Exodus 16:31)

> "7 The manna was like **coriander seed and looked like resin**. 8 The people went around gathering it, and then ground it in a handmill or crushed it in a mortar. They **cooked it in a pot** or made it into **cakes**. And it tasted like something made with olive oil. 9 When the dew settled on the camp at night, the manna also came down." (Numbers 11:7-9)

Frankly, we don't know any more than that. I've heard speculations that it is linked with "secretions of the tamarisk tree (*Tamarix gallica*) that forms small, yellowish-white balls that are very sweet. The substance melts in the heat of the sun."[18] However, this doesn't

---

[16] From Greek *theos*, "God" + *phanō*, "to appear." R.K. Harrison, *Numbers* (Baker, 1992), p. 212; George A.F. Knight, "Theophany," ISBE 4:827-831; M.F. Rooker, "Theophany," DOTP, pp. 859-864.

[17] From Hebrew *shākan*, "settle, dwell, inhabit."

[18] G. Lloyd Carr, "Manna," ISBE 3:239-240.

jive with the description as flakes, the timing of manna's appearance, or its ability to feed a large number of people in the desert for years on end.

This was clearly a supernatural phenomenon, God's provision for his people that was given as long as they needed it – whether they appreciated it or not – for forty years.

> [35] The Israelites **ate manna forty years**, until they came to a land that was settled; they ate manna until they reached the border of Canaan." (Exodus 16:35)

> "[10] On the evening of the fourteenth day of the month, while camped at Gilgal on the plains of Jericho, the Israelites celebrated the Passover. [11] The day after the Passover, that very day, they ate some of the produce of the land: unleavened bread and roasted grain. [12] **The manna stopped the day after they ate this food from the land**; there was no longer any manna for the Israelites, but that year they ate of the produce of Canaan." (Joshua 5:10-12)

Q3. (Exodus 16) Why did God provide manna for the people? Why did the manna finally cease? Why do you think that the people gradually began to take the manna for granted? What provision of God are you taking for granted?
 http://www.joyfulheart.com/forums/index.php?showtopic=1048

The People Grumble about Water (Exodus 17:1-7)

For people living in the desert, the need for food and water was a continual concern.

> "They camped at Rephidim, but there was no water for the people to drink." (Exodus 17:1b)

Following the pillar of cloud and fire, the people stopped to camp at Rephidim, a waterless place. God was the Leader, not Moses, but they blame Moses for the problem. They are so angry they are ready to murder Moses by stoning. Moses refers them back to the Lord.

> "[2] So they quarreled[19] with Moses and said, 'Give us water to drink.' Moses replied, 'Why do you quarrel with me? Why do you put the LORD to the test[20]?'

---

[19] "Quarreled" (NIV, NRSV), "found fault" (RSV), "did chide" (KJV) is *rîb*, "strive, contend," the root of *merîbâ*, "strife, contention," that became one of the names for this place in verse 7. The idea of physical

> [3] But the people were thirsty for water there, and they grumbled against Moses. They said, 'Why did you bring us up out of Egypt to make us and our children and livestock die of thirst?'" (Exodus 17:2-3)

Here again we see that when people blame and complain to God's leaders about a situation, they are actually questioning the faithfulness of God himself. It is unbelief that we often see in the outspoken, but spiritually immature, people in our congregations. Now Moses does the right thing. He brings the problem to God!

> "Then Moses cried out to the LORD, 'What am I to do with these people? They are almost ready to stone me.'" (Exodus 17:4)

Then God gives Moses specific instructions on how to get water.

> [5] The LORD answered Moses, 'Walk on ahead of the people. Take with you some of the elders of Israel and take in your hand the staff with which you struck the Nile, and go. [6] I will stand there before you by the rock at Horeb.[21] Strike the rock, and water will come out of it for the people to drink.'
>
> So Moses did this in the sight of the elders of Israel. [7] And he called the place Massah and Meribah because the Israelites quarreled and because they tested the LORD saying, 'Is the LORD among us or not?' (Exodus 17:2-7)

The psalmist wrote of these times:

> "He spread out a cloud as a covering,
> and a fire to give light at night.
> They asked, and he brought them quail
> and satisfied them with the bread of heaven.
> He opened the rock, and water gushed out;
> like a river it flowed in the desert." (Psalm 105:39-41)

---

combat is primary with this word, but here it carries the idea of verbal combat, "to quarrel, to chide one another" (Robert D. Culver, TWOT #2159 and #2159c).

[20] "Put to the test" (NIV), "test" (NRSV), "tempt" (KJV) is *nāsâ*, which, "in most contexts ... has the idea of testing or proving the quality of someone or something, often through adversity or hardship." It is the root of *massâ*, which became the other name for the place in verse 7 (Marvin R. Wilson, *nāsâ*, TWOT #1373 and #1373a).

[21] Why "Horeb" appears here is a mystery, since Horeb is usually associated with Mt. Sinai. Rephidim (wherever it was) was the last stop before Mt. Sinai (Exodus 19:1-2; Numbers 33:15; see Exodus 18:5). Perhaps the general area was referred to as Horeb, not just the mountain. We just don't know.

Including the Elders and Officers (Exodus 17:5-7)

Another leadership principle we see in verses 5 and 6 is the importance of working with the existing leadership of the group, here the tribal leaders known as "elders." In the book of Exodus, Moses honors the elders a number of times:

- Reporting God's promises to the Israelite elders in Egypt after God appeared to him (Exodus 3:16, 18; 4:29)
- Passing instructions through the elders concerning the coming Passover (Exodus 12:21)
- Striking the rock at Rephidim (Exodus 17:5-6)
- Eating of the sacrifices with the elders and Jethro (Exodus 18:12)
- Selecting capable men to serve as judges and officers (Exodus 18:21-26)
- Communicating the Lord's words regarding the Covenant at Sinai (Exodus 19:7)
- Climbing Mt. Sinai where they "saw God" and "ate and drank" in his presence (Exodus 24:1-9)

In Numbers:

- The elders receive some of the Spirit that is on Moses and they prophesy (Numbers 11:16-30)
- The elders accompany Moses at the rebellion of Korah when the rebels are to be punished (Numbers 16:25)

Moses is clearly the chief leader, served by lieutenants Aaron and Joshua, but he honors the leaders of the people and tries to act in concert with them. To oust all the existing and accepted leadership and try to lead without them is usually a recipe for disaster.[22]

Double References to Water and Quail Miracles

One factor that complicates interpreting the events of the Exodus is the existence of similar accounts in Numbers. Do they represent the same event or a different, similar one?

---

[22] However, Israel's leaders don't always listen, as in the period after Pharaoh had rebuffed Moses' initial requests. "Moses reported [God's promises] to the Israelites, but they did not listen to him because of their discouragement and cruel bondage" (Exodus 6:9). At the bad report of the 10 spies, the elders don't rally to support Moses and the Lord. As a result the people spend 38 more years in the desert.

Miracle of the Quail	Exodus 16:13	Numbers 11:31-34
	in the Desert of Sin	at Kibroth Hattaavah
Water from the Rock	Exodus 17:1-7	Numbers 20:1-13
	at Rephidim	at Kadesh

If you study the Pentateuch carefully, you can discern the presence of different sources that were pieced together by a final editor to form the first five books of the Bible as we have them today. In the Introduction, I discussed the JEDP Documentary Hypothesis that traces four strands. In recent years this complex theory has been discredited, but that doesn't negate the likelihood that there were various sources that were combined to form the present text.

So are these two separate incidents? I think you'll agree that they are separate as we study their parallels in Lesson 8 and Lesson 9. It doesn't seem unlikely that flocks of quail would find themselves in a desert Israelite camp twice in 40 years. Nor is it unlikely that the people would be desperate for water twice in their sojourn. It's just that nicknames for the locations are the same – Meribah, "quarreling," and Massah, "putting to the test." Notice that the second incident is differentiated from the first by the term Meribah Kadesh (Numbers 27:14; Deuteronomy 32:51).

B. Battle (Exodus 17:8-16)

Fighting the Amalekites (Exodus 17:8-16)

Now Israel sees war. The Amalekites were a nomadic tribe that lived throughout the area. They raided the Israelites while they camped there, trying to drive off these newcomers who were competing with them for water and pasture for their animals.

After the Amalekites attacked, warriors were selected to serve under Joshua's generalship to fight them off. Moses goes to a hilltop with the "staff of God" in his hands.

> "[10] So Joshua fought the Amalekites as Moses had ordered, and Moses, Aaron and Hur went to the top of the hill. [11] As long as Moses held up his hands, the Israelites were winning, but whenever he lowered his hands, the Amalekites were winning.
>
> [12] When Moses' hands grew tired, they took a stone and put it under him and he sat on it. Aaron and Hur held his hands up – one on one side, one on the other – so that his hands remained steady till sunset. [13] So Joshua overcame the Amalekite army with the sword." (Exodus 17:8-11)

John Everett Millais (English Pre-Raphaelite painter, 1829-1896), "Victory, O Lord" (1871), oil on canvas, Manchester City Gallery. It pictures Aaron and Hur holding up Moses' hands until the battle is won.

Just like for the plagues on Egypt, parting the waters of the Red Sea, and bringing water from a rock, the "Rod of God" is used in battle to direct God's power against the enemy. It is a sign of lifting up his hands to God's throne, seeking God's might (Exodus 17:16a).

The leadership lesson is that sometimes we need others to help us as we lead and sustain us as we serve God. Moses allowed Aaron and Hur to keep his hands lifted up throughout the long battle. Rather than being a lonely mission, leadership is better accomplished by a leadership team working towards a single objective.

Yahweh Is My Banner (Exodus 17:15-16a)

Moses' staff serves as a rallying signal to the troops fighting below. The "Staff of God" becomes the name of an altar that Moses builds to commemorate the victory.

"Moses built an altar and called it The LORD is my Banner. He said, 'For hands were lifted up to the throne[23] of the LORD.'" (Exodus 17:15-16a)

Banner is the Hebrew noun *nēs* (*nissi* is the first person possessive, "my banner"). It is apparently derived from a root meaning "raised, displayed, prominent." It means "signal pole, standard, ensign, banner, sign" used in war to signal the troops and rally them in battle.[24] In this instance, perhaps "signal pole" might be a better translation than

---

[23] Childs, *Exodus*, pp. 311-312 argues that in verse 16, "throne" (*kēs*) should be emended to "banner" (*nēs*) due to a probable textual corruption, in order to make better sense of the verse (adopted by the RSV and NRSV). However it is read, it is a difficult verse to understand completely.

[24] Marvin R. Wilson, *nāsas*, TWOT #1379a. "In the Old Testament, *nēs* generally means a rallying point or standard which drew people together for some common action or for the communication of important information. This usually happened on a high or conspicuous place within the camp or community. There,

"banner," because Moses was using his rod as a rallying point for the troops. But since troops in all but the most modern warfare used flags as rallying points, perhaps "banner" conveys the idea effectively to our time.

You may remember the story of Francis Scott Key's national anthem, "The Star Spangled Banner." In the War of 1812, battle raged as a British warship shelled one broadside after another against Fort McHenry defending Baltimore. It wasn't immediately apparent to Francis Scott Key if the American fort had been taken or not, whether or not the colors had been struck. Finally, from the light of battle he could see that the flag still flying:

> ".... And the rockets' red glare, the bombs bursting in air,
> Gave proof through the night that our flag was still there."

It's that kind of sentiment that Moses expressed toward Yahweh himself at the battle with the Amalekites. Of course, Yahweh-nissi was a name given to an altar, not a name used to address God in Scripture. But the name is closely associated with Yahweh, in that it describes one of his characteristics – Yahweh my banner, the one I look to in battle as my rallying point. The staff in Moses' hands, the "rod of God" was that pole or standard lifted high that won the battle for Israel – Yahweh-nissi.

C. Jethro (Exodus 18)

Jethro Learns about Yahweh (Exodus 18:1-12)

Having heard how God had delivered Israel from Egypt, Moses' father-in-law Jethro comes to meet him near Mt. Sinai. Moses tells him the exploits of Yahweh to deliver the people and Jethro comes to faith in Yahweh.

> "¹⁰ He said, 'Praise be to the LORD, who rescued you from the hand of the Egyptians and of Pharaoh, and who rescued the people from the hand of the Egyptians.
>
> ¹¹ Now I know that the LORD is greater than all other gods, for he did this to those who had treated Israel arrogantly.'" (Exodus 18:10-11)

---

a signal pole, sometimes with an ensign attached, could be raised as a point of focus or object of hope.... Realizing that the LORD was the Banner around which Israel had rallied, Moses called the altar Jehovah-nissi (the LORD is my banner)."

Jethro is a spiritual man, a religious man, a priest. But from his son-in-law he learns about Yahweh and acknowledges him as "greater than all other gods." Now Jethro leads Moses, Aaron, and the elders of Israel in a sacrifice and feast.

> "Then Jethro, Moses' father-in-law, brought a burnt offering and other sacrifices to God, and Aaron came with all the elders of Israel to eat bread with Moses' father-in-law in the presence of God." (Exodus 18:12)

Of course, this was before the worship of Yahweh was structured around consecrated priests and worship at the tabernacle and later at the temple. But Jethro, a new convert to Yahweh worship – through Moses' testimony – is the priest here, and he leads the sacrifice.

James J. Tissot, "Jethro and Moses" (1896-1900), watercolor, Jewish Museum, New York.

Jethro Teaches Moses to Delegate Responsibility (Exodus 18:13-27)

Perhaps the most obvious leadership lesson in the Bible is the one Moses learns from his father-in-law Jethro. It begins, as with many of our lessons, by observations on how difficult our task as leaders seems to be. Jethro watches as Moses fulfills his responsibility to bring justice as cases are brought before him as leader.

Why did Moses do this all by himself? Tradition. Acting as judge was a common role that kings performed in many ancient Near Eastern cultures. King David performed this role (2 Samuel 15:2) as did Solomon (1 Kings 3:16-28). Allowing access to the top ruler was a wonderful tradition. But in an unorganized government, it was consuming and draining. Jethro tells him:

> "17b What you are doing is not good. 18 You and these people who come to you will only wear yourselves out. The work is too heavy for you; you cannot handle it alone.

> 19 Listen now to me and I will give you some advice, and may God be with you. You must be the people's representative before God and bring their disputes to him. 20 Teach them the decrees and laws, and show them the way to live and the duties they are to perform." (Exodus 18:17b-20)

He is suggesting a role-change for Moses. Instead of being the main judge, he is to become the top judge in a judicial infrastructure. Moses is to teach the law and train capable people who can then judge run-of-the-mill cases.

> "21 But select capable men from all the people – men who fear God, trustworthy men who hate dishonest gain – and appoint them as officials over thousands, hundreds, fifties and tens. 22 Have them serve as judges for the people at all times, but have them bring every difficult case to you; the simple cases they can decide themselves. That will make your load lighter, because they will share it with you.
>
> 23 If you do this and God so commands, you will be able to stand the strain, and all these people will go home satisfied." (Exodus 18:21-23)

Notice the qualifications in verse 21.

- **Capable**.
- **God-fearing**, that is, those who revere God.
- **Honest**, trustworthy, who not only refuse bribes, but hate the very idea.
- **Accountable**. They share the task with Moses, rather than displacing him. Moses remains the ultimate judge in the system.

Learning to Delegate

It's not uncommon for Christian leaders to have a Messiah-complex and think that they are indispensable. It feels good to the ego to be needed! Such leaders feel they must do everything and make all the decisions. But when they do so, they limit the size of their ministry. A single full-time pastor can care for perhaps 150 members in a small congregation. But for a church to grow beyond that, the pastor must grow beyond being a shepherd, and learn to be a rancher who gets the work done through ranch hands.

To his credit, Moses didn't respond to Jethro, "What makes you think you know everything? You've never had to lead more than a tribe, let alone a nation! Who do you think you are?" Rather, Moses humbled himself and was able to learn – even from his father-in-law.

The role of New Testament leaders is not to *do* the work of ministry all by themselves, but to teach, train, and equip *others* to do the work of the ministry.

> "The gifts he gave were that some would be apostles, some prophets, some evangelists, some pastors and teachers, *to equip the saints for the work of ministry*, for building up the body of Christ...." (Ephesians 4:11-12, NRSV)

It is important, however, in observing this lesson in delegation, to take note that Moses doesn't abdicate his role as leader, nor does he give up his overall authority. He

Humble!

handles the hard cases. Later, when the tabernacle is being built, Moses delegates the day-to-day construction and direction of craftsmen to Bazalel and Oholiab (Exodus 31:1-6). But Moses is the one who received the vision. He is responsible to see that everything is done "exactly like the pattern" that God has shown him on the mountain (Exodus 25:9, 40). At the end of construction he inspects the work to make sure the workmen followed the instructions that he had received from God and passed on to them (Exodus 39:43). Delegation requires accountability.

Delegating to the 70 Elders (Numbers 11:10-30)

While we are on the topic of delegating, let's skip ahead to a later time when Moses is struggling again under the burden of leadership. He has delegated the judicial functions of his office, but not the day-to-day execution of decision-making. He is burned out. He hears the people crying for food and just can't handle it any more. He says to the Lord:

> "14 I cannot carry all these people by myself; the burden is too heavy for me. 15 If this is how you are going to treat me, put me to death right now – if I have found favor in your eyes – and do not let me face my own ruin." (Numbers 11:14-15)

Instead of rebuking him for his petulance, God understands him and lets it pass. He instructs Moses:

> "16 Gather for me seventy of the elders of Israel, whom you know to be the elders of the people and officers over them; bring them to the tent of meeting, and have them take their place there with you. 17 I will come down and talk with you there; and I will take **some of the spirit** that is on you and **put it on them**; and they shall bear the burden of the people along with you so that you will not bear it all by yourself." (Numbers 11:16-17)

Moses' job is to gather accredited leaders from the various tribes – people who are recognized leaders – and gather them together at the tabernacle. God does the rest.

> "Then the LORD came down in the cloud and spoke to him, and took some of the spirit that was on him and put it on the seventy elders; and when **the spirit rested upon them**, they **prophesied**. But they did not do so again." (Numbers 11:25)

God puts his Holy Spirit on the elders to equip them to share Moses' ministry. But observe that their experience of prophecy (a sign of the coming of the Spirit[25]) was not continuous, but only an initial experience. Moses own experience of God as the nation's prophet (Deuteronomy 34:10) was continuous. When Joshua wants to quench the Spirit

---

[25] 1 Samuel 10:5-6, 10; 19:20-24; Joel 2:28-29; Acts 2:17-18; 10:44-45; 19:6.

on a couple of leaders who didn't make it to the meeting, but who were prophesying in the camp, Moses says poignantly,

> "Are you jealous for my sake? I wish that all the LORD's people were prophets and that the LORD would put his Spirit on them!" (Numbers 11:29)

By these words, Moses looks forward to the Day of Pentecost when the Spirit is poured out on all.

The leadership lesson is that we can't do the work of God adequately by just competency and recognition as leaders. We must possess the Spirit of God!

> "While staying with them, [Jesus] ordered them not to leave Jerusalem, but to wait there for the promise of the Father. 'This,' he said, 'is what you have heard from me; for John baptized with water, but you will be baptized with the Holy Spirit not many days from now.'" (Acts 1:4-5; cf. Luke 24:49)

We can learn a lot from studying secular leadership. But there's a limit. Secular leadership relies on human wisdom to make decisions. Christian leadership combines natural wisdom with listening to what the Holy Spirit says. Christian leadership relies on God's direction and his power to accomplish the task. Never forget that!

Q4. (Exodus 18:13-27; Numbers 11:10-30) Why do you think it took Moses so long to delegate his judicial role to others? What were the qualifications of these judges? How is Moses' role similar to the role of leaders in Ephesians 4:11-12? What is the importance of the anointing of the Spirit in Christian leadership?

http://www.joyfulheart.com/forums/index.php?showtopic=1049

Leadership is never easy – and sometimes not much fun at all! The leader must take upon himself the loneliness of office, the criticisms of the people, the responsibility to remain steady during the battle, the care of the people, and the task of training and delegating authority to leaders under him. This is why the author of Hebrews says:

> "Obey your leaders and submit to their authority. They keep watch over you as men who must give an account. Obey them so that their work will be a joy, not a burden, for that would be of no advantage to you." (Hebrews 13:17)

Prayer

Heavenly Father, we come to you with the heavy task of leading your people. We pray for our leaders. Give them wisdom, faith, stamina, and courage. When they are weak, strengthen them. When they are discouraged, bless them with renewed vision and faith. In Jesus' name, we pray. Amen.

5. The Covenant at Mount Sinai (Exodus 19-24)

Moses' task under God wasn't simple. First, he needed to deliver the people of Israel from their bondage in Egypt. But then, he needed to help the Israelites come to know their God and walk in his ways. The first task took physical miracles and bold leadership. The second took spiritual miracles and modeling before the people what it meant to serve the Lord.

At long last, the people of Israel arrive at the very spot where God had met Moses in the burning bush a year or so before.

James J. Tissot, "Moses Forbids the People to Follow Him" (1896-1900), watercolor, Jewish Museum, New York.

"¹ In the third month after the Israelites left Egypt – on the very day – they came to the Desert of Sinai. ² After they set out from Rephidim, they entered the Desert of Sinai, and Israel camped there in the desert in front of the mountain." (Exodus 19:1-2)

A. Invitation to the Covenant (Exodus 19:1-9)

Invitation to a Unique Covenant Relationship (Exodus 19:3-6)

We'll spend quite a bit of time on two verses (verse 5 and 6) filled with themes that echo through the Old and New Testaments, and down to our own day.

"³ Then Moses went up to God, and the LORD called to him from the mountain and said, 'This is what you are to say to the house of Jacob and what you are to tell the people of Israel:

"⁴ You yourselves have seen what I did to Egypt, and how I carried you on eagles' wings¹ and brought you to myself. ⁵ Now if you obey me fully and keep my

---

¹ The eagle referred to is probably the Palestinian vulture (Cole, *Exodus*, p. 144). "Wing" is the "appendage of a bird with which it flies, denoting speed as well as protection." (John N. Oswalt, *kānāp*, TWOT 1003a). Here, the reference seems to be to protection, as in Deut 32:10b-11.

covenant, then out of all nations you will be my **treasured possession**. Although the whole earth is mine, [6] you will be for me a **kingdom of priests** and a **holy nation**."

These are the words you are to speak to the Israelites.'" (Exodus 19:3-6)

Let's look at the key phrases one by one.

Requirement: Keeping the Covenant (Exodus 19:5a)

The covenant is mentioned extensively in Genesis where God makes a covenant with Abraham,[2] renewing it with Isaac and Jacob. This

Traditional area for the location of Mount Sinai, probably either Jebel Musa ("Mountain of Moses") or Jebel Serbal.

patriarchal covenant is referred to in Exodus 2:24 and 6:4-5 as the reason God is delivering the descendants of the patriarchs. But now it is time for the people themselves to make a proper covenant with God.

The word "covenant" is the Hebrew noun *b^erit*. Between nations it is a "treaty, alliance of friendship." Between individuals it is "a pledge or agreement, with obligation between a monarch and subjects: a constitution." Between God and man it is "a covenant accompanied by signs, sacrifices, and a solemn oath that sealed the relationship with promises of blessing for keeping the covenant and curses for breaking it."[3] Here in Exodus, God makes a covenant with his people as a nation, on the pattern of the suzerain-vassal treaties found in the Ancient Near East.

In the Ancient Near East suzerain-vassal treaties were commonplace. A great king (suzerain) would conquer weaker kingdoms and extract pledges of allegiance – and annual tribute – from their kings (vassals). In return, the suzerain had an obligation to protect vassal kingdoms in case they were attacked. The suzerain was known as the king

---

[2] See my study *Discipleship Lessons from the Faith of Abraham* (JesusWalk, 2004), Hchapter 4H.

[3] Elmer B. Smick, *b^erit*, TWOT #282a.

of kings – the king of all the other kings. In the Near East pantheon of gods there would be one that would be seen as superior to the others, the god of gods.

The Old Testament teaches clearly that Yahweh is the true King of Israel.[4] It is no accident then that the giving of the law at Mt. Sinai has clear parallels to a Suzerain-Vassal treaty, by which a powerful monarch sets up a treaty with a less powerful nation, confirmed by written covenants as well as sacrifices, blessings, cursings, etc.[5]

These treaties or covenants typically included elements that seem to appear especially in the fuller account given of these events in Deuteronomy:

1. Preamble (1:1-5)
2. Historical prologue (1:6-4:40)
3. General stipulations (5:1-11:32)
4. Specific stipulations (12:1-26:15)
5. Blessings and curses (27:1-28:68)
6. Witnesses (30:19; 31:19; 32:1-43)[6]

Our account in Exodus truncates this outline, but the historical roots of the covenant are quite clear. As a great king, a suzerain, Yahweh covenants with Israel to be their King and Protector. Yahweh is the high King, the great King, the King of kings and the Lord of lords. In Lesson 7 we'll see that the tabernacle in the wilderness is the portable home of Yahweh in the midst of his people. The courtyard defines the royal precincts, the tent is his abode, and the mercy seat of the Ark of the Covenant is his throne.

Scholars trace a number of covenants in the Bible. When the covenant in our passage is referred to, it is called the Mosaic Covenant (given through Moses) or the Sinaitic Covenant (given at Mt. Sinai), or, when contrasted with the New Covenant through Jesus, it is called the Old Covenant.

In our passage, God tells the people:

"Now if you obey me fully and **keep my covenant**, then…." (Exodus 19:5a)

Keeping covenant obligations is the requirement placed upon the people, and they accept it in the Covenant in Exodus 24:7-8.

---

[4] Numbers 23:21; 1 Samuel 8:7; 12:12; Psalm 24:8-10; 29:10; 74:12; Isaiah 6:5; 33:22; Zephaniah 3:15; Zechariah 14:16-17.

[5] J.A. Thompson, *The Ancient Near Eastern Treaties and the Old Testament* (London: The Tyndale Press, 1964).

[6] G.E. Mendenhall (*Law and Covenant in Israel and the Ancient Near East* (Presbyterian Board of Colportage of Western Pennsylvania, 1955) developed this understanding of Deuteronomy. See Richard A. Taylor, "Form Criticism," DOTP 340. Paul R. Williamson, "Covenant," DOTP 139-155. M.W. Chavalas, "Moses," DOTP 577. Peter C. Craigie (*The Book of Deuteronomy* (New International Commentary on the Old Testament; Eerdmans, 1976), pp. 79-83) sees an Egyptian background to the Deuteronomic covenant.

Here are the steps involved in making this covenant at Sinai, as outlined in Exodus 19-24:

1. Israel arrives at Sinai and encamps (19:1-2)
2. God announces his intention to covenant with Israel and the people agree (19:3-9)
3. Preparations prior to the third day, washing clothes, consecration (19:10-15)
4. Assembly before Mt. Sinai on the third day (19:16-25)
5. Proclamation of the Ten Commandments (20:1-17)
6. Further laws and stipulations of the covenant (20:18-23:19)
7. Promise of the Land (23:20-33)
8. Reading the Book of the Covenant and sprinkling with blood (24:1-11)

God's Treasured Possession, Personal Property, Chosen People (Exodus 19:5)

This is clearly a conditional covenant. But the benefits of the covenant are awe-inspiring!

"Now if you obey me fully and keep my covenant,
then out of all nations you will be my treasured possession." (Exodus 19:5)

"Treasured possession" (NIV, NRSV), "peculiar treasure" (KJV), "personal possession" (New Jerusalem Bible) is a single word: *segullâ*. The basic meaning of this noun is "personal property."[7] Imagine being considered by God as his own very personal and dear possession! The word occurs several other key places in the Old Testament:

"For you are a people holy to the LORD your God.
Out of all the peoples on the face of the earth,
the LORD has chosen you to be his **treasured possession**." (Deuteronomy 14:2)

"And the LORD has declared this day that you are his people,
his **treasured possession** as he promised,
and that you are to keep all his commands." (Deuteronomy 26:18)

"For the LORD has chosen Jacob to be his own,
Israel to be his **treasured possession**." (Psalm 135:4)

"A scroll of remembrance was written in his presence
concerning those who feared the LORD and honored his name.
'They will be mine,' says the LORD Almighty,
'in the day when I make up my **treasured possession**.'"
(Malachi 3:16b-17, KJV "when I make up his jewels")

---

[7] R.D. Patterson, *segullâ*, TWOT #1460a.

The immense privilege of being God's chosen people became a source of national pride for Israel, causing them to despise the Gentiles, rather than becoming a source of humility and awe as intended. In the New Testament, this privilege of being God's special people is opened to all who trust in Jesus the Messiah!

> "... Jesus Christ, who gave himself for us to redeem us from all wickedness and to purify for himself **a people that are his very own**, eager to do what is good." (Titus 2:13b-14)

> "But you are a chosen people, a royal priesthood, a holy nation, **a people belonging to God**,[8] that you may declare the praises of him who called you out of darkness into his wonderful light." (1 Peter 2:9)

Q1. (Exodus 19:5; 1 Peter 2:9) From an emotional standpoint, what does it feel like to take out and look over one of your treasured possessions? How was the idea of "treasured possession" fulfilled in Israel? What does it feel like to be God's treasured possession – as we Christians clearly are according to 1 Peter 2:9?
http://www.joyfulheart.com/forums/index.php?showtopic=1050

A Kingdom of Priests (Exodus 19:6a)

The next phrase we'll examine is "a kingdom of priests."

> "[5b] Although the whole earth is mine, [6] you will be for me a kingdom of priests and a holy nation." (Exodus 19:5b-6)

This phrase "kingdom of priests" (NIV, KJV), "priestly kingdom" (NRSV) is fascinating. What does God mean here? "Kingdom" is *mamlākâ*, "kingdom,"[9] from *melek*, "king." Of course, a kingdom assumes a king, since no other form of government was known in the Ancient Near East. [10] Yahweh is the King, as we'll see in Lesson 7.

---

[8] In both these New Testament passages KJV version famously translates the phrase as "a peculiar people," using "peculiar" in the sense of "special, particular" rather than "eccentric, queer."

[9] *Mamlākâ* occurs about 115 times in the Old Testament, as (1) "kingdom, dominion,"(2) "royal power" or "dignity," (3) "king," and (4) theologically at 2 Chronicles 29:11 (Holladay, *Lexicon*, p. 199); (1) "kingdom, realm" (mainly), then (2) "sovereignty, dominion," and finally (3) "reign" (BDB 575).

[10] Childs (*Exodus*, p. 342) sums up the consensus of the study of the syntax and meaning of this expression: "'Priests' is an attribute of 'kingdom' as 'holy' is an attribute of 'nation'" (citing W.L. Moran, "A Kingdom of Priests," *The Bible in Current Catholic Thought* (New York, 1962), pp. 7-20).

Priests of foreign gods, of course, were known in both Mesopotamia and Egypt. Prior to this in the Pentateuch both Melekizedek (Genesis 14:18) and Jethro (Exodus 3:1; 18:1-2) have been mentioned as priests who worshipped the true God. But there was no group within Israel selected to be priests, as yet. So what does "priest" mean in this context? Cole suggests,

> "Presumably the basic thought is of a group set apart peculiarly for God's possession and service, with free access to His presence. The thought of acting as God's representative for, and to, the other nations of the world cannot be ruled out. Whether realized at the time or not, this was to be the mission of Israel (Genesis 12:3)."[11]

Israel, then, is either (1) a kingdom *consisting of* priests – people, set apart to God (that is "holy"), who relate to God directly and serve him, or (2) "royal priests," a cadre of priests *belonging* to Yahweh the King. Either way, it is a position of great privilege and access.

This idea is echoed in the New Testament, and became the basis of Martin Luther's teaching of the "priesthood of believers."

> "But you are a chosen people, a royal priesthood, a holy nation, a people belonging to God, that you may declare the praises of him who called you out of darkness into his wonderful light." (1 Peter 2:9)

Q2. (Exodus 19:6; 1 Peter 2:9) What did priests do in the Old Testament? In what sense are you a priest? How do you function as a priest? In what sense are you a "royal" priest? In what areas can your personal priestly function improve?
http://www.joyfulheart.com/forums/index.php?showtopic=1051

A Holy Nation (Exodus 19:6b)

Finally, we see the phrase "a holy nation" both in Exodus 19:6b and 1 Peter 2:9. Nation is *gôy*, which is used especially to refer to "specifically defined political, ethnic or territorial groups of people without intending to ascribe a specific religious or moral

---

[11] Cole, *Exodus*, p. 145.

connotation."[12] Only later the *gôyim* are "the nations, the Gentiles." The concept of being "holy" (Hebrew *qādôsh*; Greek *hagios*) is used extensively in both the Old and New Testaments.

> "The adjective *qādôsh* denominates that which is intrinsically sacred or which has been admitted to the sphere of the sacred by divine rite or cultic act. It connotes that which is distinct from the common or profane."[13]

Those who are holy have been set apart from the common or ordinary to be sacred, devoted to, belonging exclusively to the holy God. Because they are holy, they are not to contaminate themselves with worship of other gods or practices that are forbidden by God.

Q3. (Exodus 19:6; 1 Peter 2:9) In what sense is Israel a "holy" nation? What does it mean to be holy? Why do you think that personal holiness is de-emphasized in our time? http://www.joyfulheart.com/forums/index.php?showtopic=1052

Identity Statement (Exodus 19:5-6)

> "[5] Now if you obey me fully and keep my covenant, then out of all nations you will be **my treasured possession**. Although the whole earth is mine, [6] you will be for me a **kingdom of priests** and a **holy nation**." (Exodus 19:5-6)

These descriptors define the covenant people and become for us a kind of identity statement as well as an ideal.

1. God's special, personal possession
2. Priests to God who form the basis of his kingdom
3. Holy nation, set apart for his service exclusively

What a calling! Sadly, the Israelites did not live up to this high calling. That remained for fulfillment under the New Covenant that was to come with Jesus the Messiah.

---

[12] Gerard Van Gronigen, *gwh*, TWOT #326e.
[13] Thomas E. McComiskey, *qādash*, TWOT #1990b.

Initial Agreement to Enter into Covenant (Exodus 19:7-8a)

Moses has apparently ascended Mt. Sinai and received these words from God to speak to Israel. Now he returns.

> "7 So Moses went back and summoned the elders of the people and set before them all the words the LORD had commanded him to speak. 8 The people all responded together, 'We will do everything the LORD has said.'" (Exodus 19:7-8a)

The response is unanimous: "We will do everything the LORD has said," that is, we want to enter into covenant and will obey whatever stipulations the Lord requires.

Moses the Go-Between (Exodus 19:8b-9a)

Moses is acting like the go-between here, a kind of mediator, carrying messages back and forth between the Lord and the people.

> "So Moses brought their answer back to the LORD. 9 The LORD said to Moses, 'I am going to come to you in a dense cloud, so that the people will hear me speaking with you and will always put their trust in you.'" (Exodus 19:8b-9a)

There's a leadership lesson here. People will trust leaders who they believe are talking to God and who hear from God! This can be faked. This can be phony. But I believe that people can smell out the fake and phony. Though a leader's prayer time needs to be private and non-ostentatious, yet there will be an outflow from it that will touch and impact the congregation.

As a ten-year-old boy I can remember my Presbyterian pastor, who would give an invitation to receive Christ at the close of the service each Sunday at our small, tourist-area church. One Sunday, when no one responded to the invitation immediately, he said to us: "This morning God told me that six will come forward. We'll just wait for you." He waited – and the six came. There I was, a young boy seeing a man of God who prays and listens to God. I trusted the pastor because I knew he heard from God.

Leader, are you willing to pay the price Moses paid to hear from God? If you do, God will anoint your leadership with his sign of approval before the people.

B. Preparing for the Covenant (Exodus 19:10-25)

Consecrate the People (Exodus 19:10-11)

> "10 And the LORD said to Moses, 'Go to the people and **consecrate** them today and tomorrow. Have them wash their clothes 11 and be ready by the third day, because on that day the LORD will come down on Mount Sinai in the sight of all the people'

... [14] After Moses had gone down the mountain to the people, he **consecrated** them, and they washed their clothes. [15] Then he said to the people, 'Prepare yourselves for the third day. Abstain from sexual relations.'" (Exodus 19:10-11, 14-15)

The word "consecrate" (NIV, NRSV), "sanctify" (KJV) is *qādash*, "to be holy." In the Piel stem, it has the causative sense, "to make holy, to sanctify, to consecrate."

The idea of holiness is prominent especially in Exodus, Leviticus, Numbers, and Deuteronomy. God is pure, holy, full of glory. To approach God, man must prepare himself. To be a Levite (as we'll see in Lesson 7), a man must live differently. To be a priest, the bar was higher and required a higher level of holy living. To be high priest, the standard was even higher.

In Protestant circles especially, we have blurred the line between the clergy and the laity, and this isn't all bad. Indeed, we are *all* priests. But with this blurred line we have come to believe that spiritual leaders are no different than anyone else, that there are no special qualifications, and that the standard of behavior for leaders is no greater than for the members of the congregation. This is wrong and unscriptural!

> "Here is a trustworthy saying: If anyone sets his heart on being an overseer, he desires a noble task. Now the overseer must be above reproach...." (1 Timothy 3:1-2a)

Here are some of the ways men and women are told to prepare themselves for holy encounters, that is, to be sanctified or consecrated:

- Take off one's shoes (Exodus 3:5; Joshua 5:15)
- Wash one's clothes and sometimes one's body (Exodus 19:10, 14; Leviticus 16:26, 28; Numbers 8:21; 19:7)
- Abstain from food, fast (Leviticus 16:29; 23:27)
- Abstain from sexual relations (Exodus 19:15)
- Offer sacrifices for atonement for sin (Exodus 12:7; Leviticus 1; etc.)
- Confess one's sins (Leviticus 16:21; 26:40)
- Act justly and keep the moral laws (Exodus 20; Micah 6:8)
- Keep the Sabbath
- Keep other rules of ritual purity

Is there anything wrong with food? No. Is there anything wrong with wearing shoes? Of course not. Is it morally wrong to go without a shower?

Do taking these actions actually make you holy? No, but they are gestures of contrition and desire to make oneself right before God. Ultimately, we are helpless to atone for our own sins, but these are signs and symbols of our allegiance to the Lord. Take the Sabbath, for example:

> "... This is a sign between me and you throughout your generations, given in order that you may know that I, the LORD, sanctify you." (Exodus 31:13)

Regardless of our position, we cannot remain passive about our sins. We must recognize who we are before the Lord's holiness and be humble. The New Testament also shows believers taking special steps to sanctify themselves before the Lord (1 Corinthians 7:5; Acts 18:18; 21:23; Matthew 6:16). Nevertheless, we acknowledge the truth that we are accepted before the Lord by his grace, not our works (Ephesians 2:8-10). We hold two truths side by side:

1. **The Lord sanctifies us**: "You shall be for me ... a holy nation."(Exodus 19:6)
2. **We sanctify ourselves**: "Prepare yourselves...." (Exodus 19:15)

The role of the leader is to call people to prepare their hearts and lives before the Lord and to live holy lives – and for the leader to model this lifestyle before the people. The people are to hold high standards of holiness as a community as they live their lives before the Lord and one another.

The People Witness the Lord at the Mountain (Exodus 19:16-21)

> "On the morning of the third day there was thunder and lightning, with a thick cloud over the mountain, and a very loud trumpet blast. Everyone in the camp trembled." (Exodus 19:16)

The purpose of this was to put the fear of God in the people, so that they might not treat God casually – or Moses, his servant.

> "18 When the people saw the thunder and lightning and heard the trumpet and saw the mountain in smoke, they trembled with fear. They stayed at a distance 19 and said to Moses, **'Speak to us yourself and we will listen. But do not have God speak to us or we will die.'**
>
> 20 Moses said to the people, 'Do not be afraid. God has come to test you, so that **the fear of God will be with you to keep you from sinning.'** 21 The people remained at a distance, while Moses approached the thick darkness where God was." (Exodus 20:18-21)

It is sad to observe that, in their fear, the people reject their own role as priests before the Lord (Exodus 19:5-6). Rather they say to Moses:

> "Speak to us yourself and we will listen. But do not have God speak to us or we will die." (Exodus 20:19)

What a tragedy! We must fear God in the sense that we are afraid to displease him by sinful actions. But we are not to let terror rule the relationship. The Apostle John says:

"There is no fear in love. But perfect love drives out fear, because fear has to do with punishment. The one who fears is not made perfect in love." (1 John 4:18)

I believe that a healthy fear of God is a necessary step in a disciple's life. I have a rule when driving: don't mess with large trucks and buses – they are so large they can flatten my car in a split second! Healthy fear is good, but it is not the ultimate step. That step is love. We find that love for God is a much more powerful motivator for keeping from sin than fear ever was.

C. Requirements of the Covenant (Exodus 20-23)

The Ten Commandments and Book of the Covenant (Exodus 20-23)

Moses and Aaron are on the mountain when the Lord gives what are known as the Ten Commandments (Exodus 34:28; Deuteronomy 4:13; 10:4-5). We won't take time to look at each of these here.

But note that these commandments are the core of the covenant being made between God and the people of Israel. They are "the words of the covenant" (Exodus 34:28) and are referred to as "the covenant" itself (Deuteronomy 4:13). When they are eventually written on tablets of stone, they are placed in the ark (Deuteronomy 10:5), which is subsequently known as "the ark of the covenant" (Numbers 10:33; 14:44; Deuteronomy 10:8; 31:9, 25-26).

The Book of the Covenant (Exodus 20-23)

The Ten Commandments are primarily moral principles that form the basis of our actions. In Exodus 21-23 God gives Moses civil and religious laws to govern the nation of Israel.

"³ When Moses went and told the people all the LORD's words and laws, they responded with one voice, **'Everything the LORD has said we will do.'** ⁴ Moses then wrote down everything the LORD had said." (Exodus 24:3-4)

The people formally and unanimously accept these terms of the covenant. Based on that initial acceptance, Moses prepares the covenant documents in writing for a public reading later.

It is strange that some scholars deny that Moses was the author of the five "Books of Moses," the Pentateuch, the Torah. Moses was an educated man, capable of reading and writing, and is clearly described as "writing" God's words down. These commandments were not orally transmitted, only to be recorded generations later (as some historical sections of the Bible probably were), but written down soon after they were given on Mt. Sinai. While the hands of other editors are visible in the Pentateuch, much of it is no doubt Moses' own work, or that of the scribes to whom he personally dictated the material God had given him.

D. Confirming the Covenant (Exodus 24)

The Formal Ratification of the Covenant (Exodus 24:4-8)

The next day, sacrifices are prepared by the "young Israelite men,"[14] both burnt offerings and fellowship offerings:

> "4 He got up early the next morning and built an altar at the foot of the mountain and set up twelve stone pillars representing the twelve tribes of Israel. 5 Then he sent young Israelite men, and they offered burnt offerings and sacrificed young bulls as fellowship offerings to the LORD. 6 Moses took half of the blood and put it in bowls, and the other half he sprinkled on the altar." (Exodus 24:4-6)

Though the significance of the blood is spelled out more clearly in Leviticus 17:11, even here the blood is set apart for a special purpose to consecrate the people. Blood was also shed in ratifying the Abrahamic Covenant (Genesis 15:9-18), as was common in Ancient Near Eastern covenants.

Now Moses reads from the "Book of the Covenant," the Ten Commandments and ordinances that Moses had told the people about previously (Exodus 24:3-4). That was preliminary; this is the formal acceptance of a written covenant.

> "Then he took the Book of the Covenant and read it to the people. They responded, 'We will do everything the LORD has said; we will obey.'" (Exodus 24:7)

The Blood of the Covenant (Exodus 24:8)

> "Moses then took the blood, sprinkled it on the people and said, 'This is **the blood of the covenant** that the LORD has made with you in accordance with all these words.'" (Exodus 24:8)

This significance of the blood in the making of the covenant is mentioned in the New Testament by the writer of Hebrews in chapter 9:

> "18 The first covenant was not put into effect without **blood**.

---

[14] Perhaps these are the "priests" mentioned in Exodus 19:22-24 prior to the ordination of the Aaronic priesthood in Exodus 28-29.

[19] When Moses had proclaimed every commandment of the law to all the people, he took the blood of calves, together with water, scarlet wool and branches of hyssop, and sprinkled the scroll and all the people. [20] He said, 'This is **the blood of the covenant**, which God has commanded you to keep.'

[21] In the same way, he **sprinkled with the blood** both the tabernacle and everything used in its ceremonies. [22] In fact, the law requires that nearly everything be **cleansed with blood**, and without **the shedding of blood** there is no forgiveness." (Hebrews 9:18-22)

Now that we have seen the holiness of the blood of the covenant, how much more special are Jesus' words at the Last Supper when he held up a cup and said to his disciples:

"[27b] Drink from it, all of you. [28] This is **my blood of the covenant**, which is poured out for many for the forgiveness of sins." (Matthew 26:27b-28)

The Old Covenant and the New Covenant

The Old Covenant which God brought through Moses anchored the people of Israel to God for more than 1,200 years. But even while it was in effect, God speaks through his prophet Jeremiah about its replacement in this famous passage:

[31] "'The time is coming,' declares the LORD,
'when I will make a new covenant
with the house of Israel and with the house of Judah.
[32] It will not be like the covenant I made with their forefathers
when I took them by the hand to lead them out of Egypt,
because they broke my covenant,
though I was a husband to them,' declares the LORD.

[33] 'This is the covenant I will make
with the house of Israel after that time,' declares the LORD.
'I will put my law in their minds and write it on their hearts.
I will be their God, and they will be my people.
[34] No longer will a man teach his neighbor, or a man his brother, saying,
"Know the LORD," because they will all know me,
from the least of them to the greatest,' declares the LORD.
'For I will forgive their wickedness
and will remember their sins no more.'" (Jeremiah 31:31-34)

The final covenant, the New Covenant brought in through Jesus, was the fulfillment – not made by "the blood of bulls and goats" (Hebrews 10:4) which is not really adequate to take away sins (Hebrews 10:4), but made by his own blood, "the precious blood of Christ, a lamb without blemish or defect" (1 Peter 1:19).

Q4. (Exodus 24:8; Matthew 26:27-28) What is the function of the "blood of the covenant" in Exodus? What is the "blood of the covenant" in the New Testament? How is the Old Covenant similar to the New Covenant? How are they different?
http://www.joyfulheart.com/forums/index.php?showtopic=1053

Eating and Drinking on the Mountain (Exodus 24:9-11)

Now the future priests (Aaron and his older sons) and the seventy elders of Israel go up on the mountain where they are given a vision of God.

"9 Moses and Aaron, Nadab and Abihu, and the seventy elders of Israel went up 10 and saw the God of Israel. Under his feet was something like a pavement made of sapphire, clear[15] as the sky itself. 11 But God did not raise his hand against these leaders of the Israelites; they saw God, and they ate and drank." (Exodus 24:9-11)

This is a theophany, an appearance of God. Did they see God himself? No, according to Jesus (John 1:18; 6:46). But like others they see a manifestation of God that makes them believers, so they can better lead the people.

There is real significance in eating and drinking together on the mountain. This is a kind of covenant meal with God (the Suzerain) and representatives of the vassal nation: Moses (leader), Aaron and his sons (priests), and the 70 elders.[16]

Moses Ascends the Mountain for Forty Days (Exodus 24:12, 18)

Now Moses goes up the mountain with only Joshua as his companion and assistant.

"12 The LORD said to Moses, 'Come up to me on the mountain and stay here, and I will give you the tablets of stone, with the law and commands I have written for their in-

---

[15] The pavement that was both "made of sapphire" and yet "clear" reminds us somewhat of other revelations (Revelation 21:11, 18, 21). In a word, the vision was indescribable in human terms.

[16] This kind of covenant meal seems to be occurring at Genesis 14:18; Exodus 18:12; and, of course, Passover, and the Lord's Supper.

struction.' [13] Then Moses set out with Joshua his aide, and Moses went up on the mountain of God.

.... [18] Then Moses entered the cloud as he went on up the mountain. And he stayed on the mountain forty days and forty nights." (Exodus 24:12-13, 18)

During this time, God reveals to him the "pattern" for the tabernacle and its furniture and the priests' garments (Exodus 25-30) that we'll look at in Lesson 7. Finally, this long session with God concludes:

"When the LORD finished speaking to Moses on Mount Sinai, he gave him the two tablets of the Testimony, the tablets of stone inscribed by the finger of God." (Exodus 31:18)

This expression, "the finger of God," is very evocative, if not anthropomorphic. We see it in Exodus 8:19 and Luke 11:20 to describe the very work of God himself in a situation.

The Covenant is the basis of Israel's relationship to God, just as the New Covenant is the basis of our relationship to God through Jesus Christ.

Dear friend, have you accepted the Covenant that God wants to make with you? Are you willing to be his personal possession? Are you willing to be his priest? Are you willing to be his holy subject? Are you willing to participate in his cross by eating and drinking of the New Covenant in his body and blood? If this is a new experience for you, Jesus is calling you to follow him on a new pathway that leads to glory.

It is an awesome and solemn privilege to enter into and continue in a relationship with the Living God!

We conclude with a benediction from the Book of Hebrews:

"May the God of peace, who through the **blood of the eternal covenant** brought back from the dead our Lord Jesus, that great Shepherd of the sheep, equip you with everything good for doing his will, and may he work in us what is pleasing to him, through Jesus Christ, to whom be glory for ever and ever. Amen." (Hebrews 13:20-21)

Prayer

Father, thank you for this immense privilege of being called to know you and walk with you as your special and holy emissaries and priests. We are not qualified in ourselves, but you have made us holy and worthy through the blood of the everlasting covenant. In the name of Jesus Christ our Savior and Lord, we thank you. Amen.

6. The Golden Calf and Moses' Intercession (Exodus 32-34)

We go from one of the high points of the Old Testament – the giving of the Covenant – to one of Israel's blackest sins. And from this tragedy we learn some valuable lessons of discipleship and of leadership.

James J. Tissot, detail of "The Golden Calf" (1896-1900), watercolor, The Jewish Museum, New York.

A. Idolatry (Exodus 32)

The Israelites Worship the Golden Calf (Exodus 32:1-6)

When Moses doesn't return soon from up on the mountain, the people become restless.

> "¹ When the people saw that Moses was so long in coming down from the mountain, they gathered around Aaron and said, 'Come, make us gods who will go before us. As for this fellow Moses who brought us up out of Egypt, we don't know what has happened to him.'
>
> ² Aaron answered them, 'Take off the gold earrings that your wives, your sons and your daughters are wearing, and bring them to me.' ³ So all the people took off their earrings and brought them to Aaron." (Exodus 32:1-3)

I'm amazed at Aaron's complicity in this idolatry! He is the delegated leader along with Hur (Exodus 24:14). But instead of rebuking the idolaters, he helps them.

Aaron reminds me of the leadership philosophy that says: Find out where people want to get, then get ahead of them and lead them there. This is a prime example where rule by majority fails to be rule by God. We sometimes see visioning exercises in churches that ask people what they'd like the church to do. Then those various visions are prioritized by votes of the people and the top ones are selected. While voting can help a group find God's will (if that is their heartfelt, prayerful desire), it often falls to the lowest common denominator of people's desires and understandings.

Dear leader, if you are just a facilitator of the desires of your people, are you a real leader under God? Or do you seek God's will on behalf of your people and represent God's interests when they are threatened in your church?

Next, Aaron directs the molding and shaping of the idol:

> "He took what they handed him and made it into an idol cast in the shape of a calf, fashioning it with a tool. Then they said, 'These are your gods, O Israel, who brought you up out of Egypt.'" (Exodus 32:4)

Aaron now confuses worship of the calf with Yahweh worship by combining them into a single festival.

> "[5] When Aaron saw this, he built an altar in front of the calf and announced, 'Tomorrow there will be a festival to the LORD.' [6] So the next day the people rose early and sacrificed burnt offerings and presented fellowship offerings. Afterward they sat down to eat and drink and got up to indulge in revelry."[1] (Exodus 32:5-6)

This practice of combining elements of various religions is called syncretism, a sin that Israel suffered from for many centuries after they entered Canaan. Perhaps Aaron justifies his action in trying to keep Yahweh in the picture, so the heathen worship isn't directed entirely towards other gods, but the damage is severe!

The Israelites had spent 400 years in Egypt, which was rife with many gods that appeared as animals. The Apis Bull and the bull-headed Khnum were comparable objects of worship in Egypt. You can take the Israelites out of Egypt, but it's not so easy to get Egypt out of the Israelites!

---

[1] "Indulge in revelry" (NIV, cf. NRSV), "to play" (KJV) is *ṣāḥaq*, which means "laugh" in the Qal stem and "play, mock" in the Piel stem, as in verse 6. The Piel of *śāḥaq* does, however, progress, where Samson was summoned by the cruel Philistines to "make sport," i.e., entertainment, before them (Judges 16:25); Jeremiah disdained the company of "them that make merry" (Jeremiah 15:17; 1 Kings 4:20). At Sinai their revelry included dancing (J. Barton Payne, *ṣāḥaq*, TWOT #1905). Acts 7:41 refers to it as "a celebration." 1 Corinthians 10:7 refers to it as "pagan revelry," *paizō*, to engage in some activity for the sake of amusement, play, amuse oneself" (BDAG 750). The religious celebration before Baal of Peor (Numbers 25:1-3) near the end of the Exodus involved sexual immorality. Here it included dancing (Exodus 32:19) as well as "running wild ... out of control" (Exodus 32:25).

Q1. (Exodus 32:1-6) Why do you think the people of Israel were so quick to make idols, even after hearing the monotheism of the Ten Commandments that forbade graven images? Why do you think Aaron facilitated their sin? How do you think the golden calf made God feel? What idols do Christian churches allow that lead them away from pure worship of God in our day?

http://www.joyfulheart.com/forums/index.php?showtopic=1054

A Stiff-Necked People (Exodus 32:7, 9)

Up on the mountain, God tells Moses what is going on with the people.

"Go down, because your people, whom you brought up out of Egypt, have become corrupt.... They are a stiff-necked people." (Exodus 32:7, 9)

Stiff-necked" is a reference to a mule or ox which would resist the lead rope and refuse to let its master lead it. Instead it would stiffen its neck against the reins. The Israelites have attributed to an idol what the invisible God has done! It is a terrible sin!

God's Righteous Anger (Exodus 32:10)

Now God says to Moses:

"Leave me alone so that my anger may burn against them and that I may destroy them. Then I will make you into a great nation." (Exodus 32:10)

The people have utterly rebelled against God by substituting idols and attributing God's salvation to them. This is treason against the Monarch, the Suzerain. This is rebellion.

God is angry – "wroth," you might say. Cole calls this

"... a deliberate 'anthropopathism,' [anthropos, "mankind" + pathos, "feelings, passion"] describing God's feelings in human terms, as being more comprehensible to us."[2]

Now, now, some people might chide God. You shouldn't be angry. But God's anger at sin can't be understood apart from his own holiness, his separateness from sin, his nature utterly opposed to injustice, sin, and human degradation. Our sins offend God's

---

[2] Cole, *Exodus*, p. 215.

very character. The Bible contains hundreds of statements about God's anger at sin. We, too, are told, "Let those who love the LORD hate evil" (Psalm 97:10a).

If you can't accept an angry God, then you won't be able to understand him. If God's anger at sin offends you, then you have placed yourself above God as his judge, with no understanding of God's holiness or his mercy. Is God's anger merely an anthropomorphism, a solely human attribute projected upon God? I don't think so. That's too easy a dismissal of a characteristic of God which is enmeshed in our entire revelation of him and his character.

Moses Intercedes for the People (Exodus 32:11-13)

God tells Moses that he will destroy the nation of Israel, and reconstruct the nation from Moses' own offspring: "Then I will make you into a great nation" (Exodus 32:10b). Since Moses himself is a direct descendent of Abraham, Isaac, and Jacob, God's promises to the patriarchs would be fulfilled. God had destroyed mankind once and restarted it with Noah and his descendents (Genesis 6-8); Moses has every reason to believe that God is quite serious.

> "[11] But Moses sought the favor of the LORD his God. 'O LORD,' he said, 'why should your anger burn against **your people**, whom you brought out of Egypt with great power and a mighty hand? [12] **Why should the Egyptians say**, "It was with evil intent that he brought them out, to kill them in the mountains and to wipe them off the face of the earth"? Turn from your fierce anger; relent and do not bring disaster on your people. [13] **Remember** your servants Abraham, Isaac and Israel, to whom **you swore** by your own self: "I will make your descendants as numerous as the stars in the sky and I will give your descendants all this land I promised them, and it will be their inheritance forever."'" (Exodus 32:11-13)

Moses' intercession is a clear example of someone who has taken God's interests into his heart as his own. Even though, in a way, Moses' own family would benefit from God's proposal as the New Patriarchs, Moses appeals to God, boldly interceding for the people of Israel, pleading for mercy rather than condemnation upon them. In the end God relents and responds positively to Moses' prayer.

When I read Moses' intercession, it makes me think of a Prime Minister appealing to the King to alter his decree so that it is in keeping with the concerns of foreign relations, previous treaties, the King's character, and previous decrees. Notice the basis of Moses' appeals:

1. Because the Israelites are God's own people
2. Because of God's reputation among the heathen

3. Because of God's promises

God answers Moses' prayer of intercession.

> "Then the LORD relented[3] and did not bring on his people the disaster he had threatened." (Exodus 32:14)

The leadership lesson here and later in Moses' ministry[4] is that we are to intercede for our people, in spite of their great sins. God is merciful and will keep his promises. The leader stands between God and the people in intercessory prayer.

Moses Breaks the Tablets (Exodus 32:15-16, 19)

God had invited Moses up the mountain and promised him tablets of stone.

> "The LORD said to Moses, "Come up to me on the mountain, and wait there; and I will give you the **tablets of stone**, with the law and the commandment, which I have written for their instruction." (Exodus 24:12)

> "When the LORD finished speaking to Moses on Mount Sinai, he gave him the two **tablets of the Testimony**, the tablets of stone inscribed by the finger of God." (Exodus 31:18)

James J. Tissot, "Moses Destroys the Tables of the Ten Commandments" (1896-1900), watercolor, Jewish Museum, New York

Moses has been given two stone tables (KJV) or tablets (NIV, NRSV), *lûah*, "tablet, plank, board,"[5] fashioned by God and written on or engraved by God himself, by the "finger of God."[6]

---

[3] The word translated "relented" (NIV), "repented" (KJV), and "changed his mind" (NRSV) is the verb *nācham*, "be sorry, repent, regret, be comforted, comfort." In the majority of cases, this verb refers to God's repentance, not man's. When man's repentance is in view, the Hebrew verb *shub* is mainly used (Marvin R. Wilson, *nācham*, TWOT #1344).

[4] Exodus 33:12-17; Numbers 14:13-20; 21:6-7.

[5] *Lûah* can refer to writing surfaces of stone, the wooden planks of the tabernacle, or of a ship, and the metal plates on the bases of the lavers in Solomon's temple (Walter C. Kaiser, TWOT #1091a).

[6] "The finger of God" is figurative, of course, since God is Spirit (John 4:24) and has no fingers. But the term is used elsewhere (Exodus 8:19; Luke 11:20) to indicate the immediate and direct action of God himself.

After God promises mercy on the people, Moses descends from the mountain, carrying the Ten Commandments.

> "[15] Moses turned and went down the mountain with the two tablets of the Testimony in his hands. They were inscribed on both sides, front and back. [16] The tablets were the work of God; the writing was the writing of God, engraved on the tablets…." (Exodus 32:15-16)

They are called here and later in the Pentateuch the "tablets of the Testimony" (NIV, KJV) or "covenant" (NRSV). The word is 'ēdût, "testimony, reminder, warning sign," related to the verb 'ûd, "bear witness, admonish, warn."[7] But now Moses is overcome by anger at what he sees:

> "[19] When Moses approached the camp and saw the calf and the dancing, his anger burned and he threw the tablets out of his hands, breaking them to pieces at the foot of the mountain." (Exodus 32:19)

The tablets didn't *slip* out of Moses' hands; he *threw* them in anger![8] They shattered. The tablets represented God's covenant with Israel. Israel had broken the covenant almost immediately after it was made and were now attributing God's mighty salvation to mere idols.

Moses Destroys the Golden Calf (Exodus 32:20)

Moses is still angry.

> "And he took the calf they had made and burned it in the fire; then he ground it to powder, scattered it on the water and made the Israelites drink it." (Exodus 32:20)

Moses destroys and desecrates this idol. The text says that he "burned it in the fire." But how do you burn a molten image? We don't have a good answer. Some have suggested that it was a gold plating over a wood structure. Perhaps. The point is that Moses took what was left – and ground it up. We also read that centuries later, during Josiah's revival, the king burned idols and then crushed them to powder, "and scatter[ed] the dust over the graves of the common people" (2 Kings 23:6, 15). Perhaps crushing an idol to powder is how one is to "utterly demolish" an idol (Exodus 23:24).

Then Moses made the people drink the water over which he had scattered this gold powder. He "threw the dust into a stream that flowed down the mountain" (Deuteronomy 9:21). In other words, he polluted the people's drinking water with the remnants of

---

[7] Carl Schultz, 'ēdût, TWOT #1576f.

[8] "Threw" (NIV, NRSV), "cast" (KJV) is shālak, "throw, cast, hurl" (Herman J. Austel, shālak, TWOT #2398).

the idol. Why, we just don't understand, but it may have had some kind of symbolic significance.

Moses Reprimands Aaron (Exodus 32:21-24)

Now, Moses confronts his brother Aaron, who is deeply implicated in this.

> "21 He said to Aaron, 'What did these people do to you, that you led them into such great sin?'
>
> 22 'Do not be angry, my lord,' Aaron answered. 'You know how prone these people are to evil. 23 They said to me, "Make us gods who will go before us. As for this fellow Moses who brought us up out of Egypt, we don't know what has happened to him." 24 So I told them, "Whoever has any gold jewelry, take it off." Then they gave me the gold, and I threw it into the fire, and out came this calf!'
>
> 25 Moses saw that the people were running wild and that Aaron had let them get out of control and so become a laughingstock to their enemies." (Exodus 32:21-24)

First, let's examine Aaron's sin.

1. **Bringing idolatry and syncretism** (32:21), in the sense that he not only passively allowed it to occur, but actually led by supervising the fashioning of the golden calf.[9]
2. **Letting people get out of order and control** (32:25) uses a single Hebrew word twice: *pāra'*, "let go, let loose, ignore." Here it has the sense of "to let go, let loose people, that is, remove restraint from them."[10] Instead of stopping this wild worship of idols, he did not restrain the people. It is the job of a godly leader to keep order, even among unruly, disorderly people. To let them run wild with a mere shrug of the shoulders is not an option.

But what is worse is Aaron's false repentance. Instead of being shocked and humbled by the trouble he caused, rather he offers a lame explanation:

> "Then they gave me the gold, and I threw it into the fire, and out came this calf!" (Exodus 32:24)

Recently I had occasion to see this kind of excuse in action, where an officer of the church caused schism by an action completely out of church order, and then claimed no responsibility for the resulting departure of people from the church.

---

[9] "Led into such great sin (NIV), "brought such great sin upon them" (NRSV, KJV) is "bring." Hiphil stem of *bô'* (Elmer A. Martens, *bô'*, TWOT #212).

[10] BDB 829. The word is also used in the sense of cutting or unbraiding one's hair and in the sense of "to let slip through the fingers," that is, "to ignore, reject" advice, disciple, and instruction (Victor P. Hamilton, *pāra'*, TWOT #1824).

I am still amazed that Aaron isn't severely punished for his leadership in idolatry and his refusal to take responsibility for his actions! Moses' sister Miriam receives a clear rebuke from the Lord for her rebellion against Moses' leadership (Numbers 12:1-15), but we don't read of Aaron being punished for leading a rebellion against the Lord!

Nevertheless, God had already told Moses on the mountain that Aaron and his sons will serve as priests in the Tabernacle. God, in his mercy, can see ahead in a way we cannot.

Q2. (Exodus 32:21-24) What was the nature of Aaron's sin with the golden calf? Why do you think he won't take responsibility for his actions? Why do you think he gets off so easily? Why must leaders be accountable for their actions? What is necessary for leaders to be able to learn from their mistakes?

http://www.joyfulheart.com/forums/index.php?showtopic=1055

Levites Slaughter the Idolaters (Exodus 32:26-29)

Perhaps because of the urgency of the situation, Moses can't deal with Aaron at this time. And perhaps Aaron redeems himself by joining the other Levites in putting the idolaters to death. We're not told. But the people are running wild, so Moses takes action:

> "26 So he stood at the entrance to the camp and said, 'Whoever is for the LORD, come to me.' And all the Levites rallied to him." (Exodus 32:26)

Moses says, "If you're for Yahweh, gather around me!" In my mind I hear the echoes of Joshua's challenge a generation later:

> "Choose for yourselves this day whom you will serve.... But as for me and my house-hold, we will serve Yahweh!" (Joshua 24:15)

The Levites, of course, are Moses' and Aaron's kinsmen, the tribe of Levi. Of anyone among the Israelites, they were most likely to be loyal to Moses. So they follow Moses' direction.

> "27 Then he said to them, 'This is what the LORD, the God of Israel, says: "Each man strap a sword to his side. Go back and forth through the camp from one end to the other, each killing his brother and friend and neighbor."'

[28] The Levites did as Moses commanded, and that day about three thousand of the people died." (Exodus 32:27-28)

People object to this slaughter of the idolaters as unloving or unjust. But it is likely that because of the Levites' action – taken at the direct command of the Lord – Israel was spared greater judgment. As it is the Lord blotted the idolaters out of his book (Exodus 32:34), and we read:

"And the LORD struck the people with a plague because of what they did with the calf Aaron had made." (Exodus 32:35)

Verse 29 is difficult for us to understand.

"Then Moses said, 'You have been set apart to the LORD today, for you were against your own sons and brothers, and he has blessed you this day.'" (Exodus 32:29)

Some translators have treated this as a statement, some as a command. The ancient Septuagint and Vulgate translations see this as a *statement*, followed by several modern translations:

"You have been set apart to the LORD today..." (NIV)

"Today you have ordained yourselves for the service of the LORD..." (NRSV)

"Today you have consecrated yourselves to Yahweh..." (NJB)

Others translate it as a *command*, following the Hebrew text itself:

"Today ordain yourselves" (NRSV margin)

"Consecrate yourselves" (KJV)

"Dedicate yourselves today" (NASB)

The verb translated set apart / ordain / consecrate / dedicate is a two-word phrase, an idiom, literally, "fill your hand...." Keil comments, "'To fill the hand for Jehovah' does not mean to offer a sacrifice to the Lord, but to provide something to offer God."[11] So "to fill one's hand (with sacrifices)," means, "to consecrate" one's service.[12]

Cole sees this in the context of *hērem*, or "sacred war," that develops in the Conquest under Joshua. As gruesome as it may seem to us, "The dead were regarded as an 'installation-sacrifice' by which Levi was consecrated to the service of the Lord."[13] The phrase "and he has blessed you this day," refers not to the slaughter, but to the privilege

---

[11] Keil and Delitzsch, *Exodus*, p. 299.

[12] "Consecration was depicted by the idiom 'fill the hands.' Some suggest that the sense of filling means the hands were full and had no time for other business, though others think that 'filling' was with a sacrificial portion since this phrase was predominately used in the commissioning of priests" (Ralph H. Alexander, *yād*, TWOT #844).

[13] Cole, *Exodus*, p. 220.

of serving the Lord in close proximity to his holy things. Later, Phinehas, Aaron's grandson, performs a similar act of zeal for Yahweh and receives the blessing of a perpetual priesthood (Numbers 25:10-13). Cole comments, "It is important to realize that it was not the nature of the vengeance that secured the blessing. It was the wholehearted following of God."[14]

B. Interceding (Exodus 32:30-33:23)

Moses Intercedes for the People – Again (Exodus 32:30-35)

The rebellion against God has been put down and that danger eliminated. But now the danger to the Israelites is from God, for they have flagrantly broken his covenant with them. Moses acts here as a mediator of God to the people, and of the people to God. When you consider it, he takes on an amazing role.

> "[30] The next day Moses said to the people, 'You have committed a great sin. But now I will go up to the LORD; perhaps I can make atonement for your sin.'
>
> [31] So Moses went back to the LORD and said, 'Oh, what a great sin these people have committed! They have made themselves gods of gold. [32] But now, please forgive their sin – but if not, then blot me out of **the book** you have written.'
>
> [33] The LORD replied to Moses, 'Whoever has sinned against me I will blot out of **my book**. [34] Now go, lead the people to the place I spoke of, and my angel will go before you. However, when the time comes for me to punish, I will punish them for their sin.'
>
> [35] And the LORD struck the people with a plague because of what they did with the calf Aaron had made." (Exodus 32:7-35)

Here, the "book you have written" doesn't seem to refer to *eternal* life, as it does in the New Testament (Philippians 4:3; Revelation 3:5), but of *physical* life. God will put to death each of the sinners.

The Lord listens to Moses, but does not answer his request. Each person will be responsible for his sin and bear his punishment, says the Lord. A plague or blow from the Lord strikes the people – but doesn't wipe them all out. However, Moses' intercession is not over.

---

[14] Cole, *Exodus*, p. 220. Joshua 14:8; Numbers 25:11; Psalm 139:21-22.

Repentance and Mourning (Exodus 33:1-6)

"[1] Then the LORD said to Moses, 'Leave this place, you and the people you brought up out of Egypt, and go up to the land I promised on oath to Abraham, Isaac and Jacob, saying, "I will give it to your descendants." [2] **I will send an angel** before you and drive out the Canaanites.... **But I will not go with you**, because you are a stiff-necked people and I might destroy you on the way.' [4] When the people heard these distressing words, they began to mourn and no one put on any ornaments." (Exodus 33:1-4)

The Lord had said to them,

"'Now take off your ornaments[15] and I will decide what to do with you.' So the Israelites stripped off their ornaments at Mount Horeb." (Exodus 33:5b-6)

God calls them to a time of mourning rather than lightness, to repentance rather than celebration – and they respond. They finally are beginning to understand the seriousness of turning away from Yahweh to the gods of Egypt. God is threatening to remove his Presence from their camp.

When we repent, we can avoid discipline, but if we remain adamant in our opposition to God's will, we expose ourselves to God's terrible judgment. Two verses come to mind:

"It is a dreadful thing to fall into the hands of the living God." (Hebrews 10:31)

"But if we judged ourselves, we would not come under judgment. When we are judged by the Lord, we are being disciplined so that we will not be condemned with the world." (1 Corinthians 11:31-32)

Having a healthy fear of God is a good thing – even though it is only a step on the way to maturity (1 John 4:16-18).

Moses Intercedes One More Time (Exodus 33:12-17)

The people had experienced the Presence of the Lord in the pillar of cloud and fire (Exodus 13:21). Now God threatens to substitute a powerful intermediary, an angel, for his own Presence. While the people are humbling themselves before the Lord, Moses intercedes for them. Observe this remarkable dialog between Moses and the Lord.

"[12] Moses said to the LORD, 'You have been telling me, "Lead these people," but you have not let me know whom you will send with me. You have said, "I know you by name and you have found favor with me." [13] If you are pleased with me, teach me your

---

[15] "Ornaments"('adî) is translated by Durham as "festive dress" ... "any ornamental or fancy dress, any attire that might suggest not just joyful life, but even life as normal" (Durham, *Exodus*, p. 435, citing BDB 725-726). 'Adî is from the verb 'ādâ, "to adorn, bedeck oneself."

ways so I may know you and continue to find favor with you. Remember that **this nation is your people.**'

[14] The LORD replied, '**My Presence**[16] will go with you, and I will give you rest.'"[17] (Exodus 33:12-14)

On what bases does Moses appeal to God?

1. God's promise to be with Moses personally (Exodus 3:12), not through an intermediary.
2. God's statement that he has found favor with God.[18]
3. Moses' continued to desire to learn from God and please Him – "teach me your ways."
4. God's declaration that the Israelites are "my treasured possession" (Exodus 19:5). Moses reminds God, "Remember that this nation is your people."

In other words, Moses intercedes on a combination of (1) God's Word and promises and (2) Moses' own personal favor with God.

In the course of my business and ministry, I have developed a large network of contacts, people I know and have worked with. Often, when I need a favor, I call them up, give them my name, which they recognize immediately because of our former relationship, and then ask for what I need. If they didn't know me, they might be guarded in their response, but because we have a relationship, they answer positively if they can.

Moses can ask God for favors based on his personal relationship with him. Moses "hangs out" with God in the "tent of meeting" until his face glows (Exodus 33:7-11; 34:33-35; 2 Corinthians 3:7, 13). The Bible says,

"The LORD would speak to Moses face to face, as a man speaks with his friend." (Exodus 33:11).

And the LORD said to Moses, 'I will do the very thing you have asked, **because I am pleased with you** and I know you by name.'" (Exodus 33:17)

Lessons for Leader-Intercessors

In the text we've studied lie several important leadership lessons:

---

[16] "Presence" is literally "face" (*pânîym*). To "see one's face" means to have a personal interview with him, rather than just through a messenger or representative.

[17] Durham translates this phrase, "Thus I will dispel your anxiety" (*Exodus*, p. 444).

[18] We don't find this statement of favor prior to this in Exodus. God had said it to Moses, but it was unrecorded.

1. Leaders are to intercede for their people, even when their people have not acted in a worthy manner.
2. We intercede on the basis of God's promises. Therefore, we must know the Word. We must know intimately the promises of God.
3. We intercede on the basis of our personal relationship with God, forged in prayer. Yes, in the New Testament, we come in Jesus' name, not our own (John 16:23-26). But there is no substitute for getting to know God in prayer, so that he is a personal friend. Jesus reminds us to develop our own prayer relationship with the Father: "The Father himself loves you because you have loved me" (John 16:27).

So many people approach God only liturgically or at arm's length. But we are to develop a "face-to-face" relationship with God in prayer, an intimacy, like Jesus himself had. Jesus spent hours a day in prayer with the Father, and wouldn't do anything he didn't see the Father doing (John 5:19). He patterns that same intimacy for us, his disciples! Only as we become intimately acquainted with God and his ways can we do our job as leaders when there is a crisis.

Q3. (Exodus 32:11-13, 30-35; 33:12-17) Why is interceding for the people so important in Moses' ministry? Why is this such an important role for pastors and lay leaders today? To intercede effectively before God, why must we know both his character and his promises?

http://www.joyfulheart.com/forums/index.php?showtopic=1056

Teach Me Your Ways (Exodus 33:13)

Notice one other element of Moses' character: a longing to learn from God. He says,

"If you are pleased with me, teach me your ways so I may know you and continue to find favor with you." (Exodus 33:13)

Notice the contrast when this is expressed by the Psalmist:

"He made known his ways to Moses,
his deeds to the people of Israel." (Psalm 103:7)

Yes, this could be only an example of synoptic parallelism common in Hebrew poetry. But I think it reflects more than that. Moses is seeking God himself. "Ways" is *derek*, from *dārak* "to tread, trample." Thus, "it refers first to a path worn by constant walking." While it can be used in a literal sense, here it seems to be used in terms of God's customary way of doing things.[19]

Here is a disciple lesson: seek to learn to know God intimately. The people were afraid of God and didn't want God to talk to them (Exodus 20:19). They only saw God's mighty acts of power. But Moses sought to understand God himself. We followers of Christ can pray with the Psalmists, "Teach me your way, O Lord" (Psalm 25:4; 27:11; 86:11).

God with Us (Exodus 33:15-16)

Observe how important God's Presence is to Moses.

"[15] Then Moses said to him, 'If your Presence does not go with us, do not send us up from here. [16] How will anyone know that you are pleased with me and with your people unless you go with us? What else will distinguish me and your people from all the other people on the face of the earth?'" (Exodus 33:15-16)

Dear friends, our only power and claim to anything is that God's Presence goes with us. That is the only thing that distinguishes us and our churches from the world. Therefore, the prime thing we must do as Christian leaders and congregations is to seek the Presence of the Lord, by praise, by honor, and by repentance when our people have sinned before him. We cannot afford to "grieve the Holy Spirit" by our rebelliousness (Ephesians 4:30). I can't help but think of the wife of one of Eli's corrupt sons:

"She named the [newborn] boy Ichabod, saying, 'The glory has departed from Israel' – because of the capture of the ark of God." (1 Samuel 4:21)

God forbid that "Ichabod" be written over the door of our church because we have not sought the Presence of the Lord and his glory has departed from our assembly!

Moses' "Tent of Meeting" Outside the Camp (Exodus 33:7-11)

Now let's back up just a bit. In Exodus 33:7-11, we're introduced to a special tent where Moses' would meet with God, a tent that preceded the construction of the Tabernacle.

---

[19] Herbert Wolf, *dārak*, TWOT #453a.

"[7] Now Moses used to take a tent and pitch it outside the camp some distance away, calling it the '**tent of meeting**.' Anyone inquiring of the LORD would go to the tent of meeting outside the camp. [8] And whenever Moses went out to the tent, all the people rose and stood at the entrances to their tents, watching Moses until he entered the tent.

[9] As Moses went into the tent, the pillar of cloud would come down and stay at the entrance, while the LORD spoke with Moses. [10] Whenever the people saw the pillar of cloud standing at the entrance to the tent, they all stood and worshiped, each at the entrance to his tent.

[11] The LORD would speak to Moses face to face, as a man speaks with his friend. Then Moses would return to the camp, but his young aide Joshua son of Nun did not leave the tent." (Exodus 33:7-11)

What makes this confusing is that this "tent of meeting" uses the same term that in most places refers to the Tabernacle. Apparently after the construction of the Tabernacle (Exodus 39:32), the term "Tent of Meeting" was transferred to the formal location of God's presence in the center of the camp. However, the differences between the early tent and the later tabernacle are clear:

	Moses' "tent of meeting" (Exodus 33:7-11)	The Tabernacle
Location	Outside the camp	Center of camp (Num 2:2)
Purpose	Inquiring of the Lord and speaking with the Lord face-to-face	Formal worship and sacrifice, and location of the ark of the covenant
Attendants	Joshua	Priests and Levites

This "tent of meeting" is referred to when Moses speaks with the Lord "face to face," that is, intimately.[20]

"[33] When Moses finished speaking to them, he put a veil over his face. [34] But whenever he entered the LORD's presence to speak with him, he removed the veil until he came out. And when he came out and told the Israelites what he had been commanded, [35] they saw that his face was radiant. Then Moses would put the veil back over his face until he went in to speak with the LORD." (Exodus 34:33-35)

After the tabernacle was built, however, Moses would enter there and seek the Lord:

---

[20] Other possible references to this tent of meeting outside the camp can be found in Numbers 11:14-17, 24-30 and Numbers 12:4-5. Richard E. Averbeck ("Tabernacle," DOTP pp. 807-827) believes that the oracular tent of meeting existed even after the tabernacle was dedicated.

"When Moses entered the Tent of Meeting to speak with the LORD, he heard the voice speaking to him from between the two cherubim above the atonement cover on the ark of the Testimony. And he spoke with him." (Numbers 7:89)

Here he would receive additional revelations from the Lord.[21]

One of the secrets of Moses' ministry was his prayer and communion time spent before the Lord in this tent of meeting. Here he came to seek the Lord, and people would come here to inquire of the Lord.

Friend, do you have a place which is your "tent of meeting" with the Lord? If not, why don't you find a place and time where you can meet with the Lord regularly. As you are faithful to do this and to listen – not to fill the time only with your own prayers – you'll find an intimacy develop with the Lord that you've never experienced before.

Q4. (Exodus 33:7-11) Why is Moses' pre-tabernacle "tent of meeting" so important in Moses' ministry? Why is it called the "tent of meeting"? What would it take for you to spend longer periods of intimate time seeking God? How do you think this would affect your ministry?
http://www.joyfulheart.com/forums/index.php?showtopic=1057

Moses Sees God's Glory (Exodus 33:18-23)

Moses has talked to God face-to-face in his "tent of meeting" (Exodus 33:7-11) but he longs for a greater knowledge of and intimacy with God.

"[18] Then Moses said, 'Now show me your glory.' [19] And the LORD said, 'I will cause all my goodness to pass in front of you, and I will proclaim my name, the LORD, in your presence…. [20] But,' he said, 'you cannot see my face, for no one may see me and live.' [21] Then the LORD said, 'There is a place near me where you may stand on a rock. [22] When my glory passes by, I will put you in a cleft in the rock and cover you with my hand until I have passed by. [23] Then I will remove my hand and you will see my back; but my face must not be seen.'" (Exodus 33:18-23)

---

[21] Exodus 40:34-35; Leviticus 1:1; 9:23; Numbers 1:1.

You understand, of course, that all the talk of God's face and his back are symbolic. God is Spirit, not flesh and bones (John 4:24). But the symbolic language speaks of a very great reality, the power of intimacy with the Father! Do you desire it like Moses did when he asked, "Show me your glory"? Or are you content with the relationship you already have?

The discipleship lesson I learn here from Moses is that we must keep pressing into God, not content with a status quo relationship, but always desiring more. Paul shared Moses' heart towards God:

> "I regard everything as loss because of the surpassing value of knowing Christ Jesus my Lord…. **I press on** to make it my own…. This one thing I do: forgetting what lies behind and straining forward to what lies ahead, **I press on** toward the goal for the prize of the heavenly call of God in Christ Jesus." (Philippians 3:8a, 12b, 13b-14)

Dear friend, Moses was an Old Covenant prophet, whose potential intimacy with God was far less than yours (Matthew 11:11). But did Moses love God more than you do?

C. A Second Chance (Exodus 34)

The Second Giving of the 10 Commandments (Exodus 34:1-4)

> "¹ The LORD said to Moses, 'Chisel out two stone tablets like the first ones, and I will write on them the words that were on the first tablets, which you broke. ² Be ready in the morning, and then come up on Mount Sinai….'
>
> ⁴ So Moses chiseled out two stone tablets like the first ones and went up Mount Sinai early in the morning, as the LORD had commanded him; and he carried the two stone tablets in his hands." (Exodus 34:1-2, 4)

The first time, Yahweh had presented Moses with the stone tablets; he didn't have to bring anything to write on. But because Moses had broken what God had written on, this time Moses had to bring his own writing material.

The terms of the covenant are renewed and given again – and Moses faithfully records them, though we won't rehearse them here (Exodus 34:10-27). Moses is in God's presence for a long time, basking in his glory.

> "²⁸ Moses was there with the LORD forty days and forty nights without eating bread or drinking water. And he wrote on the tablets the words of the covenant – the Ten Commandments.

> [29] When Moses came down from Mount Sinai with the two tablets of the Testimony in his hands, he was not aware that his face was radiant because he had spoken with the LORD." (Exodus 34:28-29)

This is an important discipleship lesson. When we spend time in the presence of the Lord, we are changed by it. Others can see it, and though they may not understand it, they are affected by it. Paul wrote:

> "And all of us, with unveiled faces, seeing the glory of the Lord as though reflected in a mirror, are being transformed into the same image from one degree of glory to another; for this comes from the Lord, the Spirit." (2 Corinthians 3:18, NRSV)

Proclamation of the Name of Yahweh (Exodus 34:5-7)

We'll close this lesson with the declaration of Yahweh's name as he reveals his glory to Moses. This is important:

> "[5] Then the LORD came down in the cloud and stood there with him and proclaimed his name, the LORD. [6] And he passed in front of Moses, proclaiming, 'The LORD, the LORD, the compassionate and gracious God, slow to anger, abounding in love and faithfulness, [7] maintaining love to thousands, and forgiving wickedness, rebellion and sin. Yet he does not leave the guilty unpunished....'" (Exodus 34:5-7a)

Notice that when God revealed his glory, he declared his goodness and graciousness. So here on the mountain God reveals his character. This quintessential statement of God's gracious character is reiterated at least twelve times in Scripture.[22]

God is good, God is loving, God is faithful, And God is just – and most of all, God is gracious!

> "May the grace of the Lord Jesus Christ, and the love of God, and the fellowship of the Holy Spirit be with you all." (2 Corinthians 13:14)

Prayer

Father, help us to seek you with all of our hearts, that we may know you with the same intimacy as Moses did. Forgive our prayerlessness. Forgive us for trying to do your work with merely human tools. Help us to lead your people in your ways by your mighty power! In Jesus' name, we pray. Amen.

---

[22] Numbers 14:17-19; Deuteronomy 5:10; Joel 2:13; Jonah 4:2; Nahum 1:7; 2 Chronicles 30:9; and Psalms 86:15; 103:8-13; 111:4; 112:4; 116:5; and 145:8. You can find an exposition of this passage in my book *Names and Titles of God* (JesusWalk, 2010), chapter 10, H"The God of All Grace."

7. The Tabernacle, Priesthood, and Sacrifices (Exodus 20-31, 35-40; Leviticus 1-17; Numbers 6-10)

We've spent considerable time looking at Moses the leader and his role in establishing a covenant relationship with Yahweh on behalf of the people. In this session, we're looking for worship lessons. We'll do a survey of the visible pieces that are the manifestation of this covenant: the law, the tabernacle, the priesthood, and the sacrifices.

There's no way we can do justice to so many chapters from the Bible in just one lesson – even a long one like this – but let's look and then draw some lessons for ourselves. Because of the nature of the material, we'll be skipping around. For example, the laws aren't all grouped together, nor are the descriptions of the tabernacle, priestly garments, and the sacrifices.

Tabernacle model at Timna Park, near Eliat, Israel. Photo: Todd Bolen. Used by permission of BiblePlaces.com

A. The Kingdom of God

The key unifying concept to grasp is that Yahweh is Israel's King. The law, the tabernacle, and the priesthood all relate to worshipping Yahweh as King. Three passages from the Pentateuch make it clear that Israel considers Yahweh its King. First, the Song of Moses after crossing the Red Sea:

"The LORD will **reign** for ever and ever." (Exodus 15:18)

"Reign" is *mālak*, "'to reign,' that is, to be and exercise functions of a monarch."[1] Also:

---

[1] Robert D. Culver, *mālak*, TWOT #1199.

"The LORD their God is with them;
the **shout²** **of the King** is among them." (Numbers 23:21)

"He was **king** over Jeshurun³
when the leaders of the people assembled,
along with the tribes of Israel." (Deuteronomy 33:5)

In Lesson 5, we studied the giving of the Covenant, which has a number of parallels to a Suzerain Vassal Treaty. The Suzerain or Great King or King of kings makes treaties with kingdoms under him, and in return for obedience and subservience, offers protection and aid. But in this particular case, Israel is the King's favorite of all the kingdoms on earth.

"⁵ Now if you obey me fully and keep my covenant, then out of all nations you will be my treasured possession. Although the whole earth is mine, ⁶ you will be for me a kingdom of priests and a holy nation." (Exodus 19:5-6)

Yahweh's Presence in the Midst of His People (Numbers 2:1-3:39)

No other nation has this special relationship. Instead of being an absent Suzerain, this Great King chooses to live in the midst of his special people – in a tabernacle or travelling throne room made to his specifications. In the face of the people's sin, Moses had interceded with God for his forgiveness and grace that God's presence might continue in their midst. Indeed, God in their midst is Israel's only distinctive feature as a nation (Exodus 33:2-3, 12-17, Lesson 6).

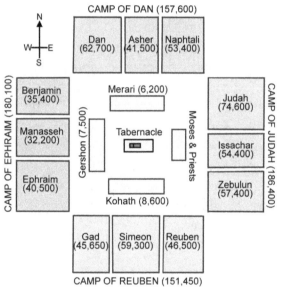

Arrangement of the Camp of Israel
Numbers 2:1-3:39
Copyright 2011, Ralph F. Wilson (pastor@joyfulheart.com)
Permission to reprint granted to all so long as copyright line remains

---

² "Shout" (NIV, KJV), "acclaimed" (NRSV) is *terû'â*, here, "human shout (of joy)" (Ashley, Numbers, P. 479), from *rûa'*, "to raise a noise" by shouting or with an instrument" (William White, TWOT #2135). The idea is that wherever the King goes, his people acclaim him with shouts, such as with English monarchy, the customary shout would be, "Long live the king!"

³ Jeshurun is *yeshurûn*, an honorific title for Israel, meaning something like "upright one" (Thompson, *Deuteronomy*, p. 308). Also used in Deuteronomy 32:15; 33:26; Isaiah 44:2.

The very organization of Israel's camp reflected this truth according to Numbers 2:1-3:39. God's presence dwelt in the tabernacle. The priests and Levites were camped closest. Each clan of Levites had its own responsibilities for the tabernacle and its furniture. Then arrayed around them were the twelve tribes, each in its assigned position and order of march, when the camp got ready to move.

Yahweh's Presence is with his people, in their very center. The same principle should apply to the church today. Christ is not only the theoretical Head of the congregation, he is also to be central in everything we do. Christ in our very midst is what makes the church different from any group of people on earth. At its core, the church is not merely a human organization, but one energized by the Spirit of Christ!

Q1. (Numbers 2:1-3:39) Why was the camp of the Israelites laid out as it was? What did this layout teach the Israelites? Why were the Levites and priests camped closer than the other tribes?
http://www.joyfulheart.com/forums/index.php?showtopic=1058

B. The Laws of the Covenant

Through Moses, Yahweh is also the Lawgiver (James 4:12; Isaiah 33:22). Though it is called "the Law of Moses" or "Mosaic Law," it is clearly God's law given through Moses. Certainly, as the Great Suzerain, Yahweh imposes his own laws upon Israel as part of the terms of the Covenant.

Does this mean that the Mosaic Law is designed for all cultures at all times, that it is the one perfect law of God? That's a question that we New Covenant Christians need to explore.

Jesus came to fulfill the Law, not to abolish it (Matthew 5:17-18). One way to view the Law is as:

1. The *civil law* that governed the nation of Israel,

2. The *religious law* that detailed the sacrifices and temple ceremonies required for the forgiveness of sin, and

3. The *moral law,* underlying principles such as those found in the Ten Commandments.

1. Civil Law

The civil law contained in the Pentateuch describes property rights, civil liability, and inheritance. Obviously most of the laws given in Exodus and Leviticus are designed to outline the way Israel should conduct itself as a theocratic nation, that is, a nation governed by Yahweh (*theos*, "God" + *kratia*, "rule"). However, the writer of Hebrews tells us:

> "By calling this covenant 'new,' he has made the first one obsolete; and what is obsolete and aging will soon disappear." (Hebrews 8:13)

> "They are only a matter of food and drink and various ceremonial washings – external regulations applying until the time of the new order." (Hebrews 9:10)

The theocracy of Israel finally passed away when the last king of Judah was deposed and the nation was taken into exile. Never again was Israel an independent nation, except for a brief period under the Maccabees. When the people returned from exile, they did so as vassals of the Persians, later the Greeks, and still later the Romans. Only for brief periods did Israel exist as an independently governed nation. The Kingdom of God had seemingly come to an end.

But that Kingdom was fulfilled in Jesus himself. When the Jewish leaders rejected King Jesus, the kingdom was removed from Israel. Jesus said,

> "Therefore I tell you that the kingdom of God will be taken away from you and given to a people who will produce its fruit" (Matthew 21:43).

Outside this specific context of the theocracy of Israel, most of the laws don't really apply in other government settings, though many of the principles provide the basis for our tradition of laws in Europe and America.

2. Religious or Ceremonial Law

Exodus and Leviticus describe in great detail the construction of a tabernacle (later, the temple) and the sacrifices required to atone for sin. "Without the shedding of blood there is no forgiveness of sins," we are reminded in Hebrews 9:22b. But the New Testament describes how Jesus, as "the Lamb of God that takes away the sin of the world" (John 1:29), poured out his blood for the forgiveness of sins (Matthew 26:28), once for all and for all time (Hebrews 10:10). The Letter to the Hebrews explains how Jesus is the fulfillment of the Law. So in himself, Jesus fulfilled the religious or ceremonial law.

3. Moral Law

The final kind of law is what we might call the moral law, those moral principles that endure from one age to another. We find them, for example, in the Ten Commandments. "Thou shalt not kill ... thou shalt not commit adultery ... thou shalt not steal ... thou shalt not bear false witness against your neighbor ...." In the *Shema* we read,

> "Hear, O Israel: The Lord our God, the Lord is one. Love the Lord your God with all your heart and with all your soul and with all your strength." (Deuteronomy 6:4-5)

> "Love your neighbor as yourself." (Leviticus 19:18)

Jesus said,

> "All the Law and the Prophets hang on these two commandments." (Matthew 22:40)

More than anything else, Jesus sent us his Holy Spirit to energize our lives. The Spirit makes the law obsolete.

> "By dying to what once bound us, we have been released from the law so that we serve in the new way of the Spirit, and not in the old way of the written code." (Romans 7:6)

> "If you are led by the Spirit, you are not under law." (Galatians 5:18)

Is the Mosaic Law Binding on Christians?

The Moral Law certainly hasn't changed. Of the Ten Commandments, the only one which is not commanded of Christians is Sabbath keeping, though this is disputed by my Seventh Day Adventist brothers and sisters. Certainly, the principle of rest is seen in the life of Jesus. But observance of the Seventh Day was not imposed by the Jerusalem Council on Gentile Christians (Acts 15:23-29). In fact, Paul warns the Colossian church that was having problems with Jewish teachers:

> "Therefore do not let anyone judge you by what you eat or drink, or with regard to a religious festival, a New Moon celebration or a Sabbath day." (Colossians 2:16)

With the exception of the Sabbath commandment, all the rest of the Ten Commandments are reiterated in New Testament lists of sins.[4]

Jesus came to fulfill the Kingdom his Father had established, to fulfill the Law his Father had instituted, and to live out in his life the quality of life to which the Law

---

[4] Mark 7:21-23; Romans 13:9; 1 Corinthians 6:9-10; Galatians 5:19-21; Colossians 3:5-8; 1 Timothy 1:9-10; etc.

aspired. "I didn't come to abolish the Law and the Prophets," Jesus said, "but to fulfill them" (Matthew 5:17). And Jesus did fulfill them all – by his life, by his sacrificial death, by instituting a New Covenant, by his Messiahship to reign under his Father, by his resurrection, and by sending the Spirit.

C. The Tabernacle

While Jesus fulfilled the religious and ceremonial law, when you understand the Jewish institutions and ceremonies, you have a much greater realization of and appreciation for what Christ has done. First, we'll examine the tabernacle.

As we saw in Lesson 5, the first "tent of meeting" was a simple tent that Moses pitched outside the camp, the place where Moses routinely spent time in God's presence, so intensely that his face would glow (Exodus 33:7-11).

But God revealed to Moses on Mount Sinai the details of how the tabernacle of Yahweh was to be constructed under the Covenant that formally recognized Yahweh the Suzerain-Protector of Israel. He was to dwell in their midst in an elaborate tent as might a desert monarch.

The keys to understanding the tabernacle are two-fold:

1. It is the throne-room and precincts of the King's dwelling.
2. Moses received the exact pattern on Mount Sinai to be reproduced by skilled craftsmen, detail by detail.

> "Make this tabernacle and all its furnishings **exactly like the pattern** I will show you." (Exodus 25:9, 40)

The writer of Hebrews makes the point that the Tabernacle in the Wilderness was not the primary place God dwelt, but an earthly representation of God's dwelling in heaven.

> "They serve at a sanctuary that is a copy and shadow of what is in heaven. This is why Moses was warned when he was about to build the tabernacle: 'See to it that you make everything **according to the pattern** shown you on the mountain.'" (Hebrews 8:5)

Craftsmen and Materials

The Holy Spirit came upon two men, Bezalel and Oholiab, with the artistic ability, craftsmanship, and capability to supervise those who built the structures and fashioned the furniture and related utensils (Exodus 31:1-5). The materials were supplied by the offerings of the people.

"Everyone who was willing and whose heart moved him came and brought an offering to the LORD for the work on the Tent of Meeting, for all its service, and for the sacred garments. All who were willing, men and women alike, came and brought gold jewelry of all kinds…. They all presented their gold as a wave offering to the LORD…." (Exodus 35:21-22)

The response was overwhelming! For example, nearly one ton of gold was offered (Exodus 38:24) before Moses called for a halt to the offering (Exodus 36:6-7).

Three Names for the Tabernacle

The Tabernacle in the Wilderness is known by three terms in Scripture, each of which refers to a different aspect of its significance:

1. **Sanctuary** emphasizes the sacredness or holiness of the place. This is the most common designation, *miqdāsh*, "holy place, sanctuary, chapel, hallowed part," from *qādash*, "to be hallowed, holy, sanctified" the state of that which belongs to the sphere of the sacred, distinguished from the common or profane. Later this word is used to describe Solomon's temple.[5]
2. **Tabernacle**, literally, "tent, dwelling," emphasizes the nearness and closeness of God's presence dwelling with the Israelites in the midst of their camp.[6]
3. **Tent of Meeting**, emphasizing that function of being a place of "meeting" between God and his people.[7]

The Tabernacle Itself (Exodus 26-27)

The tent itself was a fairly elaborate affair – compared to modern-day camping tents, at least. It was designed to be grand enough to be the portable earthly dwelling place of Yahweh. Assuming that a cubit (the measurement from the elbow to the finger tips) is about 18 inches, the dimensions of the tabernacle were 45 feet long, 15 feet wide, and 15 feet high (13.7 m. x 4.5 m. x 4.5 m.; Exodus 26:15-30). It was divided into two rooms – the Holy of Holies, where the ark was kept (the inner sanctum, which was a 15 foot cube), and the Holy Place, where the priests tended the table of showbread, the lampstand, and the altar of incense. The tabernacle seems to have been constructed of a series of acacia-

---

[5] Thomas E. McComiskey, *qādash*, TWOT #1990f.

[6] *Mishkān*, "dwelling place, tabernacle," from *shākan*, "to dwell" (Victor P. Hamilton, *shākan*, TWOT #2387c). The term "shekinah" comes from this same root, speaking of the glorious presence of God.

[7] This phrase consists of two words: *Ōhel* is the common word for "dwelling, home, tabernacle, tent," referring originally to the animal skin or goat's hair dwelling of nomadic people (Jack P. Lewis, *ōhel*, TWOT #32a). *Mô ēd* means "appointed place, place of assembly" (Jack P. Lewis, *mô ēd*, TWOT #878b).

wood[8] frames[9] set side by side, covered with gold leaf, set into silver bases. The tabernacle was draped with four separate coverings, made in panels and fastened together with gold and bronze clasps. From the inside out they were:

1. **Tapestry**, beautiful tapestry that decorated the inside of the tabernacle, visible on the ceiling and walls from within:

   "… curtains of finely twisted linen and blue, purple and scarlet yarn, with cherubim worked into them by a skilled craftsman" (Exodus 26:1).

2. **Goat's Hair**, spun and woven goat's hair, the material commonly used for making tents. It was probably nearly black, the first protective covering over the expensive tapestry.

3. **Ram Skins Dyed Red** were next.[10]

4. **Hides**, on the outside of the tabernacle, were apparently from sea cows, dugongs, or dolphins.[11] They provided protection against the sun, rain, and cold.

Cherubim are probably similar to the sphinx or winged bulls or lions found in the Ancient Near East. Striding sphinx. Phoenician, 899–700 B.C. From Nimrud, ivory, 6.9 cm x 7.75 cm. The Trustees of the British Museum.

---

[8] Most probably, Old Testament references to acacia ("shittim," KJV, cf. Hebrew *shittâ*) are to *Acacia seyal*, which grow in the Jordan Valley as well as certain places in the Sinai Peninsula. Though commonly found as shrubs, under favorable conditions they can grow as tall as 25 feet. The orange-brown wood is very durable (R.K. Harrison, "Acacia," ISBE 1:22).

[9] "Frames" (NIV, NRSV), "boards" (KJV) is *qeresh*, "plank" (Holladay, p. 326). Boards or planks indicating a solid construction would mean that the embroidered inner covering would not be able to show through. Also the weight would be prohibitive for a portable structure. Recent commentators see these as frames, in keeping with more recent archaeological discoveries. In the tomb of Queen Hetepheres (mother of Khufu, builder of the great pyramid about 2,600 BC), was found a disassembled portable tent that had once enclosed the queen's bedchamber. It consisted of a gold-covered wooden framework, as did several other Egyptian finds. Texts from Mari and Ugarit describe similar portable tent frames (Kitchen, *Reliability*, pp. 275-279; also Averbeck, DOTP, p. 818-819).

[10] Ram skins dyed red are known from later Arab portable shrines (Averbeck, DOTP, p. 823).

[11] The word is *taḥash*. "Since the badger is rarely if ever seen in Sinai, and since Arabic *tuḥas* "dolphin," seems to be cognate to Hebrew *taḥash*, most recent commentators translate the Hebrew word as "dolphin, porpoise, dugong" or the like. The bottle-nosed dolphin (*Tursiops truncatus*) is found in the eastern

The tapestry featured cherubim (*kerûb*), supernatural winged creatures whose duty was to guard and protect. It is apparently similar to a sphinx, examples of which have been found throughout the Ancient Near East. The Assyrians and Babylonians had large winged bulls and lions to provide protection to the king in grand palaces.[12]

The tabernacle or tent was located in a sacred courtyard measuring 150 feet by 75 feet, separated from the common areas by a 7½ foot high curtain of finely-twisted white linen (Exodus 27:9-19).

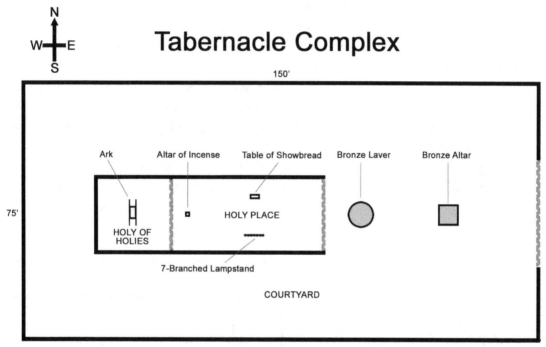

Copyright 2011, Ralph F. Wilson (pastor@joyfulheart.com). Permission to reprint is granted if copyright information is included

Many teachers have been tempted to spiritualize the tabernacle and its materials. Ram skins dyed red covering the tabernacle is too good to pass up; of course, it represents sacrifice, they say. I remember a pastor saying, "Bronze speaks of judgment," but I've looked in vain in Scripture to find a convincing passage. However, the function of the pieces of furniture in the courtyard and tabernacle proper can teach us some important lessons about worship, as we'll see in a moment.

Mediterranean, while the dugong (*Dugong dugong*) is plentiful in the Red Sea and the Gulf of Aqaba, the skin of the latter is still used by Bedouin to make sandals" (Ronald F. Youngblood, *taḥash*, TWOT #2503).
[12] R.K. Harrison, "Cherubim," ISBE 1:642-643.

It is clear that there is a gradation in metals used the closer you get to the ark. While bronze is used in the courtyard area for outside furniture, silver is used in the bases of the tabernacle frames, while gold covers the ark and other furniture within the tent. There is also a gradation of holiness. Common people could be involved in fellowship sacrifices within the courtyard, priests could enter the Holy Place, but only the high priest could enter the Holy of Holies – and even then only once a year.

Tabernacle Furniture (Exodus 25, 27, 30)

Let's look briefly at the tabernacle furniture – all very functional. Each piece was fitted with rings and poles so it could be carried by the Levites when the camp moved. Beginning from the gate of the courtyard:

1. **Altar of Burnt Offering**. The altar was an acacia wood box covered with bronze sheets, about 7½ feet square and 4½ feet high, topped by a grate, filled with earth, with horns at each corner. Here offerings were made to the Lord, both animals and grain.

2. **Bronze Laver or Basin**. This was a basin made of solid bronze set on a bronze stand. It was filled with water for the priests to wash their hands and feet before making an offering or entering the tabernacle. No dimensions are given in the Bible.

3. **Table of Showbread**.
   "The bread of the Presence" (NIV, NRSV), "shewbread" (KJV) is literally "bread before the face."[13] The table made of acacia-wood, plated in gold, measuring 3 feet by 1½ feet and 2¼ feet high. It bore 12 flat loaves of bread, one for each of the tribes, which were refreshed weekly. It symbol-

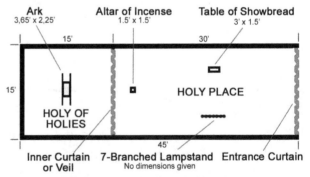

Tabernacle in the Wilderness
Copyright 2011, Ralph F. Wilson (pastor@joyfulheart.com)
Reprint rights granted if copyright information is included

ized providing food for the King in their midst.

---

[13] The face was used to indicate God's presence. When God spoke to Moses "face-to-face" (Exodus 33:11) the idiom indicated intimacy. Aaron's blessing, which we'll study shortly, uses facial metaphors for God's presence and blessing.

4. **7-Branched Lampstand**. The lampstand elevated seven oil lamps high enough to illuminate the entire Holy Place. The lamps were probably open saucers with a wick draped over a lip formed in one end of the vessel burning olive oil. The lamps were to remain lit always. No dimensions are given for the lampstand.

5. **Altar of Incense**. This altar is 1½ feet square and about 3 feet high, with horns on each corner, and made of acacia-wood, plated with gold. It was used to burn sweet-smelling incense in the presence of the Lord, as might be burned in the presence of an earthly monarch.

6. **Ark of the Covenant** (Exodus 25:10-22). The ark in the Holy of Holies was the most holy object of all, a gold-covered acacia-wood chest (dimensions 3¾ by 2¼ feet and 2¼ feet high) that served as the portable throne of Yahweh. The top lid made of pure gold and called the "atonement cover" (NIV), "mercy seat" (NRSV, KJV), is the Hebrew noun *kappōret*, literally, "performance of re-conciliation or atonement"[14] or "place of atonement," from *kāpar*, "make an atonement, make reconciliation."[15] At each end of the cover was a solid gold cherub. These cherubim faced each other with their "wings spread upward, overshadowing the cover" (Exodus 25:20). Kitchen says these were "possibly winged sphinxes, such that the box was base and footstool and the cherubs a throne for the invisible deity."[16] The idea that this was a throne is supported by several verses:

"There, above the cover between the two cherubim that are over the ark of the Testimony, I will meet with you and give you all my commands for the Israel-ites." (Exodus 25:22, cf. Numbers 7:89)

"… The ark of the covenant of the LORD Almighty, who is enthroned[17] between the cherubim." (1 Samuel 4:4 and elsewhere)

The ark contained the tablets of the Ten Commandments called the Testimony or Covenant. At various times it also contained a pot of manna (Exodus 16:33; Hebrews 9:4) and Aaron's rod that budded (Numbers 17:10).

---

[14] *Kappōret*, Holladay, p. 163.

[15] R. Laird Harris, *kappōret*, TWOT #1023c.

[16] Kitchen, *Reliability*, p. 280.

[17] *Yāshab*, "sit" (Holladay, p. 146). This phrase is also found in 2 Samuel 6:2 = 1 Chron. 13:6; 2 Kings 19:15; and Psalm 99:1.

Q2. (Exodus 25:10-22) What is the significance of the Ark in the Holy of Holies? What did it represent? Why was it considered so holy? If no one really sat upon it, why was it so important?
http://www.joyfulheart.com/forums/index.php?showtopic=1059

Completing the Tabernacle (Exodus 39-40)

Exodus provides a great deal of detail about the construction of the tabernacle. When you see the scope of preparing the frames, coverings, tapestries, posts, sockets, furniture, as well as all the necessary incense, anointing oils, priests' garments, and utensils for the service in the tabernacle, you can see how large a task it was.

But when the job was complete, Moses took a careful tour to make sure everything had been done correctly.

> "Moses inspected the work and saw that they had done it just as the LORD had commanded. So Moses blessed them." (Exodus 39:43)

Moses had delegated the specialized work of preparing this desert sanctuary. Now he inspected it. Proper delegation includes accountability at appropriate intervals.

The tabernacle was erected on the first day of the second year of the Israelites' sojourn in the wilderness (Exodus 40:17).

The Cloud and the Glory (Exodus 40:34-38)

As soon as the tabernacle was erected – apparently even before it was dedicated – God entered his dwelling.

> "34 Then the cloud covered the Tent of Meeting, and the glory of the LORD filled the tabernacle. 35 Moses could not enter the Tent of Meeting because the cloud had settled upon it, and the glory of the LORD filled the tabernacle." (Exodus 40:34-35)

Can you imagine what that was like? Whoosh! The cloud of God's direction moves over the tent and the Shekinah glory of God fills the tent in overwhelming Presence – so much that Moses couldn't enter until later (Numbers 7:89).

Dedicating the Tabernacle

The priests (Leviticus 8) and Levites (Numbers 8:5-26) were consecrated. The tabernacle and all its accoutrements are dedicated (Numbers 7), and the ministry in the tabernacle begins for the first time. At the end of the dedication ceremony, we read:

> "Moses and Aaron then went into the Tent of Meeting. When they came out, they blessed the people; and the glory of the LORD appeared to all the people. Fire came out from the presence of the LORD and consumed the burnt offering and the fat portions on the altar. And when all the people saw it, they shouted for joy and fell facedown." (Leviticus 9:23-24)

Flow of Worship in the Tabernacle

As I've thought about the order of objects as one enters the tabernacle complex from its entrance on the east, I see a progression as one approaches the very presence of God, a progression that is typical of Christian worship as well as Old Testament worship. Since the High Priest was the only person who could enter the Holy Place, we'll use him as our example of worship.

Flow of Worship

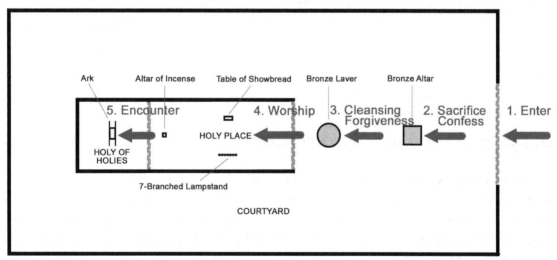

Copyright 2011, Ralph F. Wilson (pastor@joyfulheart.com). Permission to reprint is granted if copyright information is included

1. **Entering.** We enter into prayer to begin to seek God and draw near to him.
2. **Sacrifice and confession of sin** are represented by the bronze altar where sacrifices for sin were made. Christ is our sacrifice since our sin has caused an es-

trangement from God. As we confess our sins in humility and look with faith to his sacrifice for us on the cross, we connect with his grace and atonement.

3. **Cleansing and forgiveness** are represented by the bronze laver or basin. We receive his forgiveness and cleansing by faith with thankfulness.

4. **Worship** is the next step. As the priests tended the lamps, the table, and the altar of incense, we offer regular thanksgiving and praise to God in the Holy Place, as a sweet fragrance before him.

5. **Encounter with God** in the Holy of Holies is the ultimate goal. We hear this in Moses' plea, "Show me your glory" (Exodus 33:18) and in Paul's cry, "that I may know him" (Philippians 3:10). Before him in the Holy of Holies, our words are no longer necessary as we bask in his presence and look forward to the day in the City of God when we shall "see his face" (Revelation 22:4)! Come soon, Lord Jesus!

Q3. What does the arrangement of the furniture, the tabernacle, and the courtyard teach us about worship? Why do you come to the bronze altar and the laver or basin before you reach the tent itself?
http://www.joyfulheart.com/forums/index.php?showtopic=1060

D. The Priests, Levites, and Sacrifices

Prior to Sinai, we've seen a few priests – Melchizedek and Jethro – but for the most part, sacrifices were offered by a patriarch on behalf of his family. However, as the nation of Israel was formed in the wilderness at the foot of Mount Sinai, God set up a specific pattern for atonement from sin, so that the people encamped around him might be cleansed from their sins and remain a holy people.

Priests

Priest in Hebrew is *kōhen*, from which we get the common Jewish surname "Cohen." The etymology of the word is obscure.[18] The priests were charged with ministering to the Lord, first and foremost. Daily they offered sacrifices, burned incense in the Holy Place, and tended the lamps on the lampstand. Weekly they renewed the bread of the Presence and ate the old loaves. Their first focus was on God.

But their second focus was on the people of Israel. The priests attended all of the sacrifices in the tabernacle, catching the blood as the animal died, offering a portion on the altar, and eating the portion assigned to the priests. It was hard work!

Levites

The workers in the tabernacle consisted of two groups: priests and Levites. Levites were all those who were part of the tribe of Levi. The priests were part of the tribe of Levi also, but were in addition descendants of Aaron, Moses' brother. It's confusing. All priests were Levites, but not all Levites were priests.

During the Exodus, the Levites had particular duties in setting up and taking down the tabernacle, preparing it for transport, and actually carrying the ark and other furniture (Numbers 3). It is possible that they had some duties as tabernacle staff as well (Deuteronomy 18:1; 17:9). During the period of the Judges, they may have officiated at other legitimate altars to Yahweh besides the one at Shiloh

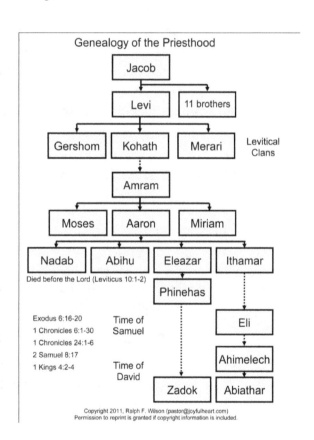

Genealogy of the Priesthood

Copyright 2011, Ralph F. Wilson (pastor@joyfulheart.com)
Permission to reprint is granted if copyright information is included.

---

[18] J. Barton Payne, *kōhen*, TWOT #959a.

(Judges 17-18). We're just not sure.[19] The present-day Jewish surnames "Levi" and "Levine" come from this tribal name.

Tithing

The priests and Levites were to receive no inheritance in the Promised Land; rather they would be supported by the tithes of the people. The Lord told Moses:

> "I give to the Levites all the tithes in Israel as their inheritance in return for the work they do while serving at the Tent of Meeting." (Numbers 18:21)

Then one tenth of their tithe was to be given to the priests to help support their families (Numbers 18:26). In addition, the priests received a portion of the sacrifices and grain offerings for their families to eat (Numbers 18:8-20).

Throughout the history of Israel after this, when the nation's faith was strong, the tithe was available to support the ministry, but when it was weak, revival was necessary to restore the practice of tithing (2 Chronicles 2:2-10). In Malachi's day, the Lord renewed the command – and the accompanying promise:

> "'Bring the whole tithe into the storehouse, **that there may be food in my house**. Test me in this,' says the LORD Almighty, 'and see if I will not throw open the floodgates of heaven and pour out so much blessing that you will not have room enough for it." (Malachi 3:10)

Jesus certainly paid tithes. And while he said little about tithing (Luke 11:42), Paul applied the principle to New Testament ministers:

> "Don't you know that those who work in the temple get their food from the temple, and those who serve at the altar share in what is offered on the altar? In the same way, the Lord has commanded that those who preach the gospel should receive their living from the gospel." (1 Corinthians 9:13-14)

Priestly Garments (Exodus 28 and 39, Leviticus 8:7-9)

The priests wore special garments[20] that distinguished them from the people, "to give them dignity and honor" (Exodus 28:40). Here they are, working from the outside in:

---

[19] D.A. Garrett, "Levi, Levites," DOTP, pp. 519-522. See also Wayne O. McCready, "Priests and Levites," ISBE 3:965-970.

[20] Cornelius Van Dam, "Priestly Clothing," DOTP, pp. 643-646.

	High Priest	Regular Priests
Sacred crown of gold, engraved with the words: "Holy to the Lord."[21]	High priest only	None
Turban of linen, different types	*Miṣnepet*[22]	*Migbā 'â*[23]
Breastpiece, colorful, like the ephod, with 12 stones representing the 12 tribes, plus a pocket in which to put the Urim and Thummim, which seem to be lots used to seek God's will.	High priest only	None
Ephod, "a sleeveless linen waist-coat"[24] worn over the robe.[25]	Ephod made with gold; blue, purple and scarlet yarn; and finely-twisted linen.	Plain linen ephod,[26] at least in David's time.
Robe[27] of the ephod, made of blue cloth, the hem with alternating embroidered pomegranates and gold bells.	High priest only	None
Sash[28]	Embroidered sash	Regular sash

[21] "Diadem" (NIV), "crown" (NRSV, KJV) is *nēzer*, "separation, consecration crown," from *nāzar*, "separate, consecrate (oneself)" (Thomas E. McComiskey, *nāzar*, TWOT #1340a).

[22] *Miṣnepet*, "turban" (KJV "mitre"), the distinctive headgear of the high priest, from *ṣānap* "to wrap around" (Charles L. Feinberg, *ṣānap*, TWOT #1940a).

[23] "Turban, headgear" (KJV "bonnet"), perhaps convex in shape. Related words are translated "hill," "cup, bowl," and "bud." Use only of the priests' headgear (Victor P. Hamilton, TWOT #309c). "Head-band" (Holladay, p. 181).

[24] Leona Glidden Running, "Garments," ISBE 2:405, VII, B.

[25] Leviticus 8:7.

[26] 1 Samuel 2:18; 22:18.

[27] *Me'îl*, "robe, cloak, mantle." Like a shawl there was a hole in the middle, hence to be pulled over the head. It was also worn by men of repute (Victor P. Hamilton, TWOT #1230b).

[28] "Sash" (NIV, NRSV), "girdle" (KJV) is *'abnēṭ*. "Josephus affords some details of the girdle as used in his day. It was wrapped around the chest and after a number of twinings it was tied, hanging freely to the

	High Priest	Regular Priests
Tunic, linen, ankle-length[29]	Perhaps checkered.[30]	Plain white linen
Breeches, linen	Fine-twisted linen	Regular linen
Footwear	None	None

The Aaronic Blessing (Numbers 6:22-27)

One of the ministries of the priests was to bless the people of Israel with these words:

"The LORD bless you and keep[31] you;
the LORD make his face shine upon you
and be gracious[32] to you;
the LORD turn his face toward you
and give you peace." (Numbers 6:24-26)

This blessing uses the idea of "face" twice. In the Ancient Near East to see one's face was to experience a person's immediate presence. To make one's face "shine" indicates metaphorically "a cheerful face expressing good will."[33] May God smile upon you. "To lift up one's face" or countenance towards a person meant to give them full attention and, presumably, grant them what they ask.

God explains through Moses, "So they will put[34] my name on the Israelites, and I will bless them" (Numbers 6:27). Speaking the divine name of Yahweh over the people will have the effect of conferring his authority and blessings upon them. This gives us some idea of the power of the Name. Similarly, in the New Testament:

---

ankles. Such was the girdle which the high priest wore while performing no service. While he was offering sacrifices, in order to allow greater freedom of movement, he threw the sash to the left and wore it over his shoulder" (Josephus, *Antiquities* 3.7.2). (Charles L. Feinberg, TWOT #256a).

[29] *Kuttōnet*, "tunic, a long shirtlike garment, usually of linen." From Akkadian *kitinnu* or *kitintu*, "a linen garment made from *kitū* linen" (TWOT #1058a).

[30] Exodus 28:4 the tunic is described with the word *tashbēs*, "woven work," from *shābās*, "to weave in checkered or plaited work" (TWOT #2320c). Perhaps "checkered work" (Holladay, p. 396).

[31] "Keep" is *shāmar*, "keep, guard, observe, give heed," with the root idea of "to exercise great care over." Here it has the idea of "to guard, take care of" (TWOT #2414).

[32] *Hānan*, "depicts a heartfelt response by someone who has something to give to one who has a need," "an action from a superior to an inferior who has no real claim for gracious treatment" (Edwin Yamauchi, TWOT #694).

[33] Herbert Wolf, *'ôr*, TWOT #52.

[34] "Put" is *śûm*, "put, place something somewhere" (Gary G. Cohen, TWOT #2243).

"Therefore God exalted him to the highest place and gave him the name that is above every name, that **at the name of Jesus** every knee should bow, in heaven and on earth and under the earth." (Philippians 2:9-10).

What a privilege we have of speaking the Name over people and blessing them!

The Sacrifices

Much of Leviticus involves a detailed explanation of the various sacrifices offered in the tabernacle. We see five major kinds of offerings:[35]

1. **Burnt Offering** (Leviticus 1; 6:8-13). In all the other offerings only a portion was offered and the rest was eaten by the priests as part of the atonement. But in the burnt offering, the entire sacrifice is consumed on the altar, not just a part. This offering is designed to make atonement for the offerer's sin. We'll look at it in detail below.
2. **Grain Offering** (Leviticus 2; 6:14-23). It is an offering or gift to God from one's crops. A portion is kept by the priests for their share.
3. **Peace or Fellowship Offering** (Leviticus 3; 7:11-34). This offering was accompanied by the communal celebration of the worshippers who shared in the meat of the offering. There are three sub-types:
   a. A **thank offering** was an expression of thanks for deliverance or blessings granted.
   b. A **votive sacrifice** was offered to give thanks for a blessing or deliverance following a vow.
   c. The **freewill sacrifice** was joyously and willingly presented to express a general thankfulness to God, with no specific deliverance in mind.
4. **Sin (Purification) Offering** (Leviticus 4:1-5:1; 6:24-30). The sin offering and guilt offering are very similar. The primary purpose of the sin offering is to purify people from an unwitting sin. The priest must partake of this offering as part of the atonement (Leviticus 10:17).
5. **Guilt (Reparation) Offering** (Leviticus 5:14-6:7). The guilt offering differs in that a restitution is required – either to God or to another person – in addition to the sacrifice. The primary purpose was to make atonement for desecration or mishandling of sacred things.

---

[35] Richard E. Averbeck, "Sacrifices and Offerings," DOTP, pp. 706-733. Eugene E. Carpenter, "Sacrifices and Offerings in the OT," ISBE 4:260-273.

Repentance Is Necessary

It's important to realize that the sacrifices were more than bare ritual; they were God's means of atonement for sin. But to be effectual, they must be accompanied by a sincere repentance. Sacrifice without real repentance has always been repugnant to God; just as Christians who sin flagrantly because they know God will forgive them is a travesty of grace. The Lord spoke through the prophet Isaiah:

> "'The multitude of your sacrifices
> – what are they to me?' says the LORD.
> 'I have more than enough of burnt offerings,
> of rams and the fat of fattened animals;
> I have no pleasure
> in the blood of bulls and lambs and goats....
> Stop bringing meaningless offerings!....
>
> Your hands are full of blood;
> wash and make yourselves clean.
> Take your evil deeds out of my sight!
> Stop doing wrong, learn to do right!
> Seek justice, encourage the oppressed.
> Defend the cause of the fatherless,
> plead the case of the widow.'" (Isaiah 1:11,13, 15b-17)

God calls us to be a holy people for whom holiness becomes a new way of life, rather than rebellion and sin as the norm. The sacrifice of Christ for our sins is designed to do what we cannot do – cleanse ourselves from sin. But he expects us to repent and cooperate with the Holy Spirit to change our hearts – and our behavior! Yes, his forgiveness is always there for us when we sin, but he calls us to a far better way of life! The apostle John wrote:

> "My dear children, I write this to you so that you will not sin. But if anybody does sin, we have one who speaks to the Father in our defense – Jesus Christ, the Righteous One. He is the atoning sacrifice for our sins, and not only for ours but also for the sins of the whole world." (1 John 2:1-2)

Special Sacrifices

It is important to be aware of three special types of sacrifices – though, of course, there are many details we must skip for lack of time and space.

1. **Morning and Evening Sacrifices** (Exodus 28:38-39; Numbers 28:1-8). One lamb to be offered as a burnt offering in the morning, another at twilight. There were also Sabbath offerings and monthly offerings.

2. **Passover** offerings were a special kind of fellowship offering, in which the family ate the lamb that was sacrificed (Exodus 12; Numbers 9; Deuteronomy 16). You'll find more details on the Passover in Lesson 3.

William Holman Hunt (English Pre-Raphaelite painter, 1827-1910), "The Scapegoat" (1854), oil on canvas, Lady Lever Art Gallery, Merseyside, UK.

3. **Day of Atonement** (Yom Kippur, Leviticus 16) is the day each year when the high priest seeks atonement for the sins of the whole nation. First, he sacrifices a bull to make atonement for his own sins. Then from two goats, one is selected to be a sin offering for the nation. The blood of both the bull and the goat is sprinkled on the mercy seat of the ark in the Holy of Holies. Then the high priest turns to the scapegoat.

> "He is to lay both hands on the head of the live goat and confess over it all the wickedness and rebellion of the Israelites – all their sins – and put them on the goat's head. He shall send the goat away into the desert in the care of a man appointed for the task. The goat will carry on itself all their sins to a solitary place; and the man shall release it in the desert." (Leviticus 16:21-22)

This mission of carrying on oneself the sins of the people is fulfilled in Jesus. Christ is our scapegoat.

> "He himself bore our sins in his body on the tree, so that we might die to sins and live for righteousness; by his wounds you have been healed." (1 Peter 2:24)

Steps in a Burnt Offering (Leviticus 1:3-9)

I think it is useful to study briefly a typical burnt offering to atone for a person's sins. The details concerning this offering are found in Leviticus 1:3-9. Notice these steps:

1. **Sacrifice is without defect** (verse 3). We can't pawn off on God a substandard animal; it must be perfect. And because it is without defect, it is expensive for the worshipper. Sin is costly – that's one of the messages of sacrifice. Of course, Christ is the ultimate sacrifice. We have been redeemed "with the precious blood of Christ, a lamb without blemish or defect" (1 Peter 1:19).

2. **Offerer lays his hand on head of animal** (verse 4). Laying on of hands is accompanied by confession (as in Leviticus 16:21), and involves imparting one's sins to the animal that God has accepted as a substitute. This is the basis of the concept of Substitutionary Atonement. In this case, God accepts from us the death of a lesser being for a greater. But the sacrifice that God provides for us is the Greater (that is, Jesus the Son of God) for the lesser (us).

3. **Offerer slaughters the animal** (verse 5a). The priest doesn't do the killing here; it is at the hands of the sinner himself – a graphic reminder of the appropriate penalty for our sin and rebellion against God.

4. **Priest collects the blood and sprinkles it against the altar** (verse 5b). While the animal is being killed by slitting its throat, a priest holds a basin to collect the blood, then sprinkles it against the altar to make atonement.

   "For the life of a creature is in the blood, and I have given it to you to make atonement for yourselves on the altar; it is the blood that makes atonement for one's life." (Leviticus 17:11)

5. **Offerer skins and cuts the sacrifice in pieces** (verse 6). Offering a sacrifice involves the sinner in getting up close and personal with the process. It isn't pretty!

6. **Priest puts the pieces of the sacrifice on the altar** (verses 7-8). The priest arranges the wood and the sacrifice on the wood.

7. **Sacrifice is completely consumed on the altar** (verse 9). None of this burnt offering goes to the priest[36] – it is all offered to the Lord on behalf of the sinner.

When I've taught about sacrifice, I've found it useful to ask for a volunteer from the class, get him down on all fours, and demonstrate the steps involved. It makes it more real when I get out my pocketknife and a bowl to collect his blood!

---

[36] The hide, however, goes to the priest (Leviticus 7:8).

Q4. (Leviticus 1:3-9) In the burnt offering for an individual's sin: What is the significance of the offerer laying his hand on the animal's head? Why do you think the offerer is to slay the sacrifice rather than having the priest do it? How is the animal's blood significant in sacrifice? In what ways does Jesus' sacrifice on the cross fulfill all of this? http://www.joyfulheart.com/forums/index.php?showtopic=1061

Priests Participate in the Sacrifice (Leviticus 10)

One of the sad incidents that relates to the tabernacle was the death of Aaron's older sons, Nadab and Abihu, who "offered unauthorized fire before the LORD, contrary to his command" (Leviticus 10:1). They both died before the Lord for the sacrilege, possibly committed when they were drunk (Leviticus 10:9).[37] Moses cites the importance of recognizing God's holiness – especially for those who approach God as priests!

> "Among those who approach me
> I will show myself holy;
> in the sight of all the people
> I will be honored.[38]" (Leviticus 10:3)

Aaron and his remaining sons, Eleazar and Ithamar, are in shock following the deaths. They neglect the remainder of the procedures for offering sacrifice, in particular, partaking of a part of the sacrifice, which was their obligation as priests. Moses rebukes Aaron's sons for this infraction of the rules God had given through him for conducting the sacrifice:

> "Why didn't you **eat the sin offering** in the sanctuary area? It is most holy; it was given to you to take away the guilt of the community by **making atonement for them** before the LORD. Since its blood was not taken into the Holy Place, you should have eaten the goat in the sanctuary area, as I commanded." (Leviticus 10:17-18)

Moses doesn't want more deaths to occur because the remaining priests aren't careful to keep God's commandments. But Aaron replies:

---

[37] An analysis of the nature of their sin can be found in Harrison, *Leviticus*, pp. 108-111.
[38] *Kābēd*, "glorified" (KJV, NRSV).

"Today they sacrificed their sin offering and their burnt offering before the LORD, but such things as this have happened to me. Would the LORD have been pleased if I had eaten the sin offering today?" (Leviticus 10:19)

Aaron bares his humanity – his hurt and anger and bitterness over his two sons who had lost their lives. Just keeping the rules while struggling with a bitter heart would not have pleased God, he says.

The Scripture records: "When Moses heard this, he was satisfied" (Leviticus 10:20). Moses acknowledges the truth of Aaron's words and doesn't insist further.

As I reflect on this story, several lessons occur to me.

1. **God demands holiness and obedience from his servants**. In our day we have little understanding of God's holiness, and might even accuse people who contend for holiness as judgmental. Much of the Book of Leviticus involves learning and appreciating God's holiness.

   > "I am the LORD your God; consecrate yourselves and be holy, because I am holy.... I am the LORD who brought you up out of Egypt to be your God; therefore be holy, because I am holy." (Leviticus 11:44-45)

2. **God demands a pure heart from those who make offerings to him**. Aaron understood this, to his credit – and Moses accepted it. We see the same principle in Jesus' teaching:

   > "If you are offering your gift at the altar and there remember that your brother has something against you, leave your gift there in front of the altar. First go and be reconciled to your brother; then come and offer your gift." (Matthew 5:23-24; cf. Mark 11:25)

3. **God shows mercy when he sees in us a desire to please him**, even if we haven't kept all the rules – but we mustn't presume upon his mercy. Moses recognized this and didn't trouble Aaron further about his transgression.

4. **The priests are partakers of the altar – as part of the atonement**. We see an echo of this with reference to the Lord's Supper in the context of eating food offered to idols:

   > "Is not the cup of thanksgiving for which we give thanks a **participation**[39] in **the blood of Christ**? And is not the bread that we break a **participation in the body of Christ**? ... Consider the people of Israel: Do not those who **eat the sacrifices participate in the altar**?" (1 Corinthians 10:16, 18)

---

[39] "Participation" (NIV), "sharing" (NRSV), "communion" (KJV) is *koinōnia*, "participation, sharing" in something (BDAG 553, 4), "the share which one has in anything, participation" (Thayer, p. 352, 1), from *koinos*, "common."

Dear friends, this passage reminds us that when we partake of the Lord's Supper, we are one with Christ's sacrifice for us on the cross!

There is so much more that could be said about the tabernacle, the priesthood, and the sacrifices, but hopefully this lesson has given you an overview of the worship in the wilderness, and later, in the temple.

The Cloud above the Tabernacle (Numbers 9:15-23)

The tabernacle in the midst of Israel's camp reflected the Presence of Yahweh in their midst – displayed by the presence of the pillar of cloud by day and the pillar of fire by night.

> "15 On the day the tabernacle was set up, the cloud covered the tabernacle, the tent of the covenant; and from evening until morning it was over the tabernacle, having the appearance of fire. 16 It was always so: the cloud covered it by day and the appearance of fire by night. 17 Whenever the cloud lifted from over the tent, then the Israelites would set out; and in the place where the cloud settled down, there the Israelites would camp." (Numbers 9:15-17)

The pillar of cloud – God's presence – guided them on their journey – as you and I seek him to guide us today. We don't know the next leg of the journey, but we are secure as we obediently follow the Lord where he leads us.

The Israelites spent a year camped at Mt. Sinai as Moses received the laws from God, the people entered into covenant with Yahweh, and actually built the tabernacle he had prescribed for his dwelling. Now it was time to leave Sinai and continue the journey toward the Promised Land – and the cloud lifted.

> "In the second year, in the second month, on the twentieth day of the month, the cloud lifted from over the tabernacle of the covenant. Then the Israelites set out by stages from the wilderness of Sinai, and the cloud settled down in the wilderness of Paran." (Numbers 10:11-12)

Scripture records:

> Whenever the ark set out, Moses would say,
>
> "Arise, O LORD, let your enemies be scattered,
> and your foes flee before you."
>
> And whenever it came to rest, he would say,
>
> 'Return, O LORD
> of the ten thousand thousands of Israel.'" (Numbers 10:35-36)

The nation of Israel had been formed under God. And Yahweh went with them – led them – on their journey. The tabernacle was his dwelling in their midst. The priests tended the holy things, and offered sacrifices to seek forgiveness and maintain the nation as a holy people that could continue in God's presence.

All these things – tabernacle, priests, and sacrifices – were types and shadows of the true reality that God would bring through Christ, who is both our high priest and our sacrifice.

> "The Holy Spirit was showing by this that the way into the Most Holy Place had not yet been disclosed as long as the first tabernacle was still standing….
>
> When Christ came as high priest of the good things that are already here, he went through the greater and more perfect tabernacle that is not man-made, that is to say, not a part of this creation. He did not enter by means of the blood of goats and calves; but he entered the Most Holy Place once for all by his own blood, having obtained eternal redemption." (Hebrews 9:8, 11-12)

Prayer

Lord, in the tabernacle we learn a great deal about holiness, atonement, and worship. Help us to love you so much that we will live holy lives before you. Give us a hunger to seek your presence and worship you in the beauty of your holiness. Change our lives! Fill us with yourself, we pray, in Jesus' name. Amen.

8. Rebellion against Moses' Leadership (Numbers 11-17)

The Israelite camp is on the move again, and with this advance new challenges emerge.

Moses had met challenges before, but it seems like later in his ministry he meets rebellion in several forms: from his kinsmen, from his sister, and from the people as a whole. Let's see what we can learn.

James J. Tissot, "The Grapes of Canaan" (1896-1900), watercolor, Jewish Museum, New York

A. Demand for Other Food (Numbers 11)

Complaints and Fire at Taberah (Numbers 11)

Before long, people started complaining again.

> "Now the people complained about their hardships in the hearing of the LORD, and when he heard them his anger was aroused." (Numbers 11:1)

God punished their complaining with fire at Taberah, but that didn't seem to stop them.

The next complaints were about manna and began with some of the non-Israelites who had left Egypt with them (Exodus 12:38; Leviticus 24:10-11), referred to here as "rabble."[1]

> "[4] The rabble with them began to crave other food, and again the Israelites started wailing and said, 'If only we had meat to eat! [5] We remember the fish we ate in Egypt at no

---

[1] "Rabble" (NIV, NRSV), "mixt multitude" (KJV) is *ʾasapsup*, "collection, rabble," the motley collection of people who followed Israel from Egypt, from *ʾāsap*, "gather." (Charles L. Feinberg, TWOT #140f).

cost – also the cucumbers, melons, leeks, onions and garlic. 6 But now we have lost our appetite; we never see anything but this manna!'" (Numbers 11:4-6)

They start salivating when they remember all the tasty variety of foods they had in Egypt. It's interesting that even a few complainers in a group can spread the complaining spirit to others. It is a general dissatisfaction with one's condition, but often the general dissatisfaction latches onto some specific issue – in this case, manna, boring manna. The complaints of a few had infected the camp.

"Moses heard the people of every family wailing, each at the entrance to his tent. The LORD became exceedingly angry, and Moses was troubled." (Numbers 11:10)

Moses' Complaint to the Lord (Numbers 11:11-15)

Now Moses brings the problems to the Lord in a kind of petulant way.

"11 He asked the LORD, 'Why have you brought this trouble on your servant? What have I done to displease you that you put **the burden of all these people** on me? 12 Did I conceive all these people? Did I give them birth? **Why do you tell me to carry them in my arms, as a nurse carries an infant**, to the land you promised on oath to their forefathers? 13 **Where can I get meat** for all these people? They keep wailing to me, 'Give us meat to eat!' 14 I cannot carry all these people by myself; **the burden is too heavy for me.** 15 If this is how you are going to treat me, put me to death right now – if I have found favor in your eyes – and **do not let me face my own ruin.**'" (Numbers 11:11-15)

This is not one of Moses' greatest leadership moments. He blames God for the problems. They're *your* problem, he tells God. Why do I have to deal with *your* problem people? At the root of Moses' misery, however, are two elements:

1. The burden of leadership is too heavy for him.
2. He knows he is inadequate to supply what the people are demanding.

Moses is at his wits end. Unless God backs him up, he can't "face [his] own ruin." God answers Moses in two ways:

1. God puts some of his Spirit on 70 of Israel's elders (which we examined in Lesson 4, Numbers 11:24-30)
2. God promises abundant meat (Numbers 11:31-34)

God's promise of a month's supply of meat is so huge even Moses can't believe it. (Numbers 11:21-22). Moses' vision of God is too small! Then God rebukes Moses and tells him to tell the people what he said, even if he can't envision it!

"The LORD answered Moses, '**Is the LORD's arm too short?** You will now see whether or not what I say will come true for you.' So Moses went out and told the people what the LORD had said." (Numbers 11:23-24a)

Q1. (Numbers 11:11-15) Why do you think Moses is so frustrated in his prayer? What do you think is going on in him emotionally and physically at this point? Does he have any grounds for his complaints? Do you think this is designed to be a model prayer? Why are we shown this prayer? How did God answer him?
http://www.joyfulheart.com/forums/index.php?showtopic=1062

The Quail and Plague at Kibroth Hattaavah (Numbers 11:31-34)

For God, providing meat wasn't a problem.

"Now a wind went out from the LORD and drove quail in from the sea. It brought them down all around the camp to about three feet above the ground, as far as a day's walk in any direction." (Numbers 11:31)

These people who had demanded "other food" in their unbelief, now have much more than they can even eat. It begins to spoil, and many of them die from food poisoning, a "severe plague" from the Lord.[2]

B. Handling Criticism (Numbers 12)

Miriam's and Aaron's Criticism and Punishment (Numbers 12:1-15)

Now his own brother and sister begin to criticize Moses.

"[1] Miriam and Aaron began to talk against Moses because of his Cushite wife, for he had married a Cushite.

[2] 'Has the LORD spoken only through Moses?' they asked. 'Hasn't he also spoken through us?' And the LORD heard this. [3] (Now Moses was a very humble man, more humble than anyone else on the face of the earth.)" (Numbers 12:1-3)

Who is this Cushite wife? Zipporah or some new wife? We're not sure. Cush (kûsh) can refer to (1) Nubia, the area along the Nile south of Egypt,[3] (2) a people in Mesopotamia,[4] or (3) just possibly, Midian.[5]

---

[2] In Lesson 4 above we consider the double stories of the quail and note the distinct differences between these two incidents.

If Cush here refers to an area near Midian, then perhaps the wife Miriam is criticizing is Zipporah herself, who wasn't an Israelite. But why would Miriam wait so long to bring this up? If this wife is Nubian, then she wouldn't be Zipporah, but a second wife, perhaps one of the "mixed multitude" or "rabble" that left Egypt with the Israelites. If she were Nubian, some have speculated that she was discriminated against because of her race. She would have had a very dark complexion, but "the people living along the southern border of Egypt were not distinctively Negroid" in their features.[6]

Power Struggles and Pride

However, Moses' wife only seems to be a smokescreen for the real issue: a challenge by Miriam and Aaron to Moses' role as God's authoritative spokesman.

> "Has the LORD spoken only through Moses?' they asked. 'Hasn't he also spoken through us?" (Numbers 12:2)

We see power struggles throughout the Bible: Saul's paranoid fear of David, the disciples' argument about which of them was the greatest, and Simon Magnus who wants to merchandise the Holy Spirit (Acts 8:9-25).

It's not uncommon in churches for people to challenge the authority of the senior pastor. Sometimes the challenge is from an associate pastor, sometimes from a long-time member of the church who struggles to retain power in the church and can't submit to the pastor's authority. Richard Foster observes:

> "Power can destroy or create. The power that destroys demands ascendancy; it demands total control. It destroys relationships; it destroys trust; it destroys dialogue; it destroys integrity."[7]

Pride is at the root of many struggles for power. "I'm better than you." "I deserve this." "I want to be perceived as Number One." The lust for power can become all-consuming.

---

[3] E.g., Ezekiel 29:10; 2 Kings 19:9; Esther 1:1; Isaiah 18:1. This was Nubia, not Abyssinia (William Sanford LaSor, "Cush," ISBE 1:839.

[4] A Kassite, LaSor, ISBE 1:838-839. E.g., Genesis 2:13; 10:8,

[5] An inhabitant of Cushan (*kûshān*), which is used in parallel with Midian in Habakkuk 3:7 (Ashley, *Numbers*, pp. 223-224). David W. Baker ("Cushan," ABD 1:1219-1220) says, "Cushan could be either an alternative name for the Midianites, or a subgroup of them."

[6] Harrison, *Numbers*, p. 194. LaSor (ISBE 1:838-839) notes that nowhere in the Bible is there any evidence that Ham's descendants are negroid. "Both the Ethiopians and Nubians lack the physical characteristics, other than skin pigmentation, that are used anthropologically to define the negroid peoples."

[7] Richard J. Foster, *Money, Sex, and Power* (Harper Row, 1985; republished under the name, *The Challenge of the Disciplined Life*, 1989), p. 175.

Moses, the Humble (Numbers 12:3)

The narrator tells us parenthetically,

> "Now Moses was a very humble[8] man, more humble than anyone else on the face of the earth." (Numbers 12:3)

Moses is the meekest man in all the earth because he does not seek power – or even want it! God has afflicted him with leadership of a disobedient people, and he seeks to be relieved from it (Numbers 11:11-15). He remains in leadership out of obedience, not because of his need for self-aggrandizement.

Jesus taught us to be meek.

> "Blessed are the meek, for they will inherit the earth." (Matthew 5:5)

> "Take my yoke upon you and learn from me, for I am gentle (KJV 'meek') and humble in heart, and you will find rest for your souls." (Matthew 11:29)

The Greek word used is *praus*, "pertaining to not being overly impressed by a sense of one's self-importance, gentle, humble, considerate, meek," in the older favorable sense.[9]

The disciples were incensed at James and John seeking to be seated at Jesus' right and left hand in his Kingdom. Jesus used this as a teaching moment to instruct his disciples on leadership conducted with true humility.

> "Jesus called them together and said, 'You know that those who are regarded as rulers of the Gentiles lord it over them, and their high officials exercise authority over them. Not so with you. Instead, whoever wants to become great among you must be your servant, and whoever wants to be first must be slave of all. For even the Son of Man did not come to be served, but to serve, and to give his life as a ransom for many.'" (Mark 10:42-45)

It is healthy to have a good sense and acceptance of who you are, what psychologists call "ego strength." But when we are compelled to continually assert our self-importance, it is usually a sign of weakness and neediness, rather than of strength. Could it be said of you that you are the humblest leader in your city or region? If not, why not?

---

[8] "Humble" (NIV, NRSV), "meek" (KJV) is the adjective 'ânâv, which "stresses the moral and spiritual condition of the godly as the goal of affliction implying that this state is joined with a suffering life rather than with one of worldly happiness and abundance" from 'ānâ, "afflict, oppress, humble" (Leonard J. Coppes, 'ānâ, TWOT #1652a).

[9] *Praus*, BDAG 863.

Aaron and Miriam Rebuked for Speaking Against Moses (Numbers 12:4-9)

The Lord called for Moses, Aaron, and Miriam to come to the Tent of Meeting and met them in a pillar of cloud. He contrasts a prophet's revelation in visions and dreams with Moses' experience of God:

> "⁷ᵇ [Moses] is faithful in all my house. ⁸ With him I speak face to face, clearly and not in riddles; he sees the form[10] of the LORD. Why then were you not afraid to speak against my servant Moses?" (Numbers 12:7-8)

"Faithful" is 'āman. The root idea is firmness or certainty, as we might describe a person as a "solid" leader. The Niphal participle here means "to be faithful, sure, dependable."[11] God can count on Moses – unlike Aaron who vacillated when Moses was on the mountain and caused great harm to the nation. Aaron and Miriam knew *about* God; Moses knew God *personally!*

Now the Lord asks why Aaron and Miriam weren't afraid to speak against Moses, since he is the Lord's personal servant. Earlier Aaron had seen God's glory on Moses' face.

> "When Aaron and all the Israelites saw Moses, his face was radiant, and they were afraid to come near him." (Exodus 34:30)

God watches out for his servants. Of Abraham, Isaac, and Jacob, God says through the psalmist:

> "Do not touch my anointed ones;
> do my prophets no harm." (Psalm 105:15; 2 Chronicles 16:22)

David feared God so much that he would not raise his hand against the Lord's anointed – king Saul – even though Saul was evil and corrupt.[12]

Miriam's Punishment (Numbers 12:10-15)

When the cloud lifts, Miriam has leprosy. Aaron pleads for mercy from Moses, confessing his and Miriam's sins.

> "Please, my lord, do not hold against us the sin we have so foolishly committed. ¹² Do not let her be like a stillborn infant coming from its mother's womb with its flesh half eaten away." (Numbers 12:11b-12)

Moses asks God to heal her, but God says:

---

[10] "Form" (NIV, NRSV), "similitude" (KJV) is temûnâ, "likeness, form" (Walter C. Kaiser, TWOT #1191b).
[11] Jack B. Scott, 'āman, TWOT #116. We get the word "Amen" from this verb.
[12] 1 Samuel 24:10; 26:9, 11, 16, 23; 2 Samuel 1:14.

"If her father had spit in her face, would she not have been in disgrace for seven days? Confine her outside the camp for seven days; after that she can be brought back." (Numbers 12:14)

If a daughter had been disciplined by her father (Deuteronomy 25:9; Isaiah 50:6), the Lord says, she would have been held in a state of public humiliation for seven days. So then Miriam will spend seven days[13] outside the camp, which is to be holy. Only then can she be restored to her status as a leader.

When leaders commit serious sin in our congregations, after they repent we are sometimes too quick to restore them to leadership. It is appropriate sometimes for leaders to be rebuked publically and be removed from their leadership roles for a period "so that the rest also may stand in fear" (1 Timothy 5:20). Good order requires a consequence for rebellion.

Q2. (Numbers 12) What was Miriam's and Aaron's motivation for speaking against Moses? Why do people seeking power feel a need to discredit the existing leader? How did Moses handle this provocation? How might he have handled it if he were a proud man? How did the Lord handle it?
http://www.joyfulheart.com/forums/index.php?showtopic=1063

C. Faltering at the Edge of Canaan (Numbers 13-14)

Miriam's and Aaron's rebellion was minor compared to what happened next. Their rebellion only affected them and their followers. But the rebellion that occurred on the border of Canaan altered the history of the nation.

Spying Out the Land (Numbers 13:1-25)

The Israelites are encamped at Kadesh-Barnea (Numbers 13:26), a desert town to the south of Canaan. From there Moses commissions an expedition.

---

[13] Leviticus 13 and 14 prescribe 7-day periods for the detection of and the cleansing from leprosy.

"[1] The LORD said to Moses, [2] 'Send some men to explore the land of Canaan, which I am giving to the Israelites. From each ancestral tribe send one of its leaders.' [3] So at the LORD's command Moses sent them out from the Desert of Paran. All of them were leaders of the Israelites." (Numbers 13:1-3)

Of the twelve, only the names of Caleb (tribe of Judah) and Joshua (tribe of Benjamin) are familiar to us today. Their instructions are to conduct surveillance to determine:

1. Character of the land and its fruitfulness
2. Strength and numbers of the populations
3. Fortification of towns and cities
4. Forestation

So they travelled the land from south to north,[14] a distance of about 250 miles each way and were gone 40 days. On the way back they harvested a massive cluster of grapes in the Valley of Eschol and carried it home on a pole between two people.[15]

Here was their report:

"[27] We went into the land to which you sent us, and it does flow with milk and honey! Here is its fruit. [28] But the people who live there are powerful, and the cities are fortified and very large. We even saw descendants of Anak there. [29] The Amalekites live in the Negev; the Hittites, Jebusites and Amorites live in the hill country; and the Canaanites live near the sea and along the Jordan." (Numbers 13:27-29)

They all agreed on the *facts* of the report. It was at the point of *interpretation* that they differed. Caleb (with Joshua) looked with eyes of faith:

"We should go up and take possession of the land, for **we can certainly do it**." (Numbers 13:31)

But the ten other spies looked with eyes of unbelief and "spread among the Israelites a bad report about the land they had explored."

"[31] We can't attack those people; **they are stronger** than we are…. [32] The land we explored devours those living in it. All the people we saw there are of great size. [33] We saw the Nephilim there (the descendants of Anak come from the Nephilim). We seemed like grasshoppers in our own eyes, and we looked the same to them." (Numbers 13:31-33)

[14] "Rehob, toward Lebo Hamath" (Numbers 13:21) is at the northern border of the Promised Land (Numbers 34:8), near Mount Hor.

[15] "Eschol" means "cluster." Though the location is unknown, it is presumably near Hebron, which is still a grape-growing region (Wenham, *Numbers*, p. 118).

Fear and Unbelief Spread (Numbers 14:1-9)

The report of the unbelieving spies spread throughout the camp sparking fear, angry grumbling, and weeping. Again they blamed Moses and Aaron – and the Lord – for bringing them out of Egypt. Their only prospect was fed by their fears:

- Men would "fall by the sword"
- Women and children would be "taken as plunder"

Their conclusion was all-out rebellion:

> "We should choose a leader and go back to Egypt." (Numbers 14:4b)

Not only were the people prepared to select another leader. They talked of stoning Moses and Aaron (14:10), that is, killing them! They were serious!

Joshua and Caleb, the believing spies, pleaded with the people, seeking to build their faith:

> "The land we passed through and explored is **exceedingly good.** 8 If the LORD is pleased with us, **he will lead us into that land**, a land flowing with milk and honey, and will give it to us. 9 Only **do not rebel** against the LORD. And **do not be afraid** of the people of the land, because **we will swallow them up. Their protection is gone**, but the **LORD is with us.** Do not be afraid of them." (Numbers 14:7b-9)

Observe their positive faith:

1. **The Lord will lead us into the land.** This is Yahweh's promise and he will fulfill it.[16]
2. **We will consume the people.** "We will swallow them up" (NIV), "they are no more than bread for us" (NRSV, cf. KJV)
3. **Their protection has been removed.**[17] Their fortifications and weaponry are not sufficient.
4. **The Lord is with us.** This theme ricochets throughout the Old and New Testaments.[18]

Observe also their warnings:

1. Do not **rebel.**[19]

---

[16] "Lead" (NIV) "bring" (NRSV, KJV) is *bô'*, the fourth most common verb in the Old Testament. Here in the Hiphil stem it means "to bring" (Elmer A. Martens, *bô'*, TWOT #212).

[17] "Protection" (NIV, NRSV), "defense" (KJV) is *ṣēl* (from *ṣālal*, "to grow dark"), literally "shadow," conveying the ideas of "shade, shelter, protection, defense" (Genesis 19:8; Isaiah 30:2-3; Ezekiel 17:23) (John E. Hartley, *ṣālal*, TWOT #1921a).

[18] Genesis 39:2, 21; Exodus 3:12; 33:14; Joshua 1:5; Deuteronomy 31:23; Psalms 46:7, 11; Matthew 1:23; 18:20; 28:20; 2 Timothy 4:17; Hebrews 13:5b.

2.   Do not **be afraid** of the people of the land.

It is important to see the close relationship between unbelief, fear, and rebellion. When we believe our circumstances more than we believe God's promises, then we are afraid to follow God, and, indeed, rebel against him and go our own way.

Christian leaders will do well to minister to people's fears with faith, if they desire to lead them forward to God's plan for them and for a local congregation. In this case, however, Joshua and Caleb were not able to stem the tide of fear, and it swept across the people.

The Glory and Wrath of Yahweh (Numbers 14:10-12)

Though the people were preparing to stone Moses and Aaron, God's servants were protected by a show of force by Yahweh that paralyzed them:

> "Then the glory of the LORD appeared at the Tent of Meeting to all the Israelites." (Numbers 14:10b)

As we saw in Exodus 16: 7, 10 in Lesson 4, an appearance of the glory of the Lord was often accompanied by God's judgment. Yahweh says to Moses:

> "[11] How long will these people treat me with contempt? How long will they refuse to believe in me, in spite of all the miraculous signs I have performed among them? [12] I will strike them down with a plague and destroy them, but I will make you into a nation greater and stronger than they." (Numbers 14:11-12)

God is disgusted with the people's contempt,[20] And not only their fear, but their steadfast unbelief in the face of many miracles God had performed for them. God says to Moses that he will destroy the Israelites, and from Moses' descendants raise up an even greater nation. This solution would keep Yahweh's covenant with Abraham to raise up descendants and give them the land.

---

[19] "Rebel" is *mārad*, "be rebellious, rebel, revolt." Hamilton says, "If *mārad* in an international political context refers to disloyalty and disunity among nations in covenant, then it is only natural to assume that it is in this context, i.e., the context of a broken covenant, that the term refers to man's rebellion against God (the five passages in Joshua 22 for example)" (Victor P. Hamilton, *mārad*, TWOT #1240).

[20] "Treat with contempt" (NIV), "despise" (NRSV), "provoke" (KJV) is *nāʾas*, "despise, abhor.... The action or attitude whereby the former recipient of favorable disposition and/or service is consciously viewed and/or treated with disdain" (Leonard J. Coppes, TWOT #1274).

Moses Intercedes Again (Numbers 14:13-20)

Moses had interceded for the people with God three times after the golden calf incident at Sinai.[21] Now he intercedes once again. Moses appeals to the Lord on several grounds:

1. **God's glory**. The Egyptians and Canaanites will hear about it, and God's previous reputation will be hurt. It would be claimed that since he couldn't bring the people into the land, he killed them (14:13-16).

2. **God's character**. God's character had been spoken to Moses when the glory of God came before him in the cleft of the rock: He both loves and forgives sin and rebellion (Exodus 34:5-7). Moses recites God's words back to him.

God answered Moses according to the statement of character Moses had claimed before him.

1. **Forgiveness**. God forgives the people, that is, he will allow the people of Israel, not just the descendants of Moses, to be the heirs of the promise. He will not hold the sin against the people as a whole.

2. **Punishment**. The 10 leaders who brought the bad report that precipitated the general unbelief were punished with sudden death.

   "These men responsible for spreading the bad report about the land were struck down and died of a plague before the LORD." (Numbers 14:37)

   The whole generation of unbelievers, the parents, are punished by not being allowed to enter the Promised Land.

   "In this desert your bodies will fall – every one of you twenty years old or more who was counted in the census and who has grumbled against me. Not one of you will enter the land I swore with uplifted hand to make your home... For forty years – one year for each of the forty days you explored the land – you will suffer for your sins and know what it is like to have me against you."(Numbers 14:29-30)

3. **Visiting the sins of fathers on the children**. Though their children will ultimately enter the Promised Land, they must suffer for their parents' sins. "Your children will be shepherds here for forty years, suffering for your unfaithfulness, until the last of your bodies lies in the desert." (Numbers 14:33-34)

Israel's sins keep them from entering the Promised Land (14:22-23):

1. Disobedience
2. Testing God

---

[21] Exodus 32:11-13; 30-35; 33:12-17; Lesson 6.

3. Treating God with contempt

Caleb's Faith (Numbers 14:24)

The exceptions are Caleb and Joshua:

> "But because my servant Caleb has a different spirit and follows me wholeheartedly, I will bring him into the land he went to, and his descendants will inherit it." (Numbers 14:24)

"Wholeheartedly" (NIV, NRSV) is the Piel stem of *mālēʾ*, "be full, to fill, literally "to be after fully" (KJV). This phrase "to follow wholeheartedly" is mentioned alongside Caleb thereafter. He becomes known as the man who followed the Lord fully.[22] What a wonderful legacy!

The Command to Leave Kadesh-Barnea (Numbers 14:25)

Now the people are commanded:

> "Since the Amalekites and Canaanites are living in the valleys, turn back tomorrow and set out toward the desert along the route to the Red Sea." (Numbers 14:25)

They were to leave Kadesh-Barnea. Wenham makes a striking observation.

> "*Geographically*, this probably means they were to head southeast from Kadesh towards the Gulf of Aqabah, one of the recognized north-south routes across the Sinai Peninsula.

> But *theologically*, 'the way to the Red Sea' suggests they are returning to Egypt. Typical of the irony of this story, their punishment is made to fit the crime. They wanted to die in the wilderness and return to Egypt [Numbers 14:2-4]: in a way rather different from the one they intended, God grants their request."[23]

The Israelites Presume to Enter the Land Anyway (Numbers 14:39-45)

The people receive the news that they will never enter Canaan with anguish: "they mourned bitterly" (14:39). Then in unbelief of God's word of judgment, they disobey yet again and compound the tragedy.

> "Early the next morning they went up toward the high hill country. 'We have sinned,' they said. 'We will go up to the place the LORD promised' … In their presumption[24] they went up toward the high hill country…. Then the Amalekites and Canaanites who

---

[22] Numbers 26:65; 32:12; Deuteronomy 1:36; Joshua 14:6-15.

[23] Wenham, *Numbers*, p. 123.

[24] "Presumption" (NIV), "presumed" (NRSV, KJV) is *ʿāpal*, related to an Arabic word, *ǧafala*, "to be heedless, neglectful, inadvertent." It is used only once in the OT, except perhaps in Habakkuk 2:4 (TWOT #1663). "Have the audacity to" (Holladay, p. 279).

lived in that hill country came down and attacked[25] them and beat them down[26] all the way to Hormah." (Numbers 14:40, 44-45)

Discipleship and Leadership Lessons

As I ponder this refusal of the people to enter Canaan, one of the turning points of the Exodus, I see a number of lessons for us, both as followers of God and as leaders of his people.

1. **Godly leaders must possess faith, not just influence.** Each of the 12 spies was a recognized leader in his tribe. Each saw the same surveillance data, but they came to different conclusions as they analyzed the data. Joshua and Caleb saw the data through the faith-lens of God's promises. The remaining 10 saw the data through the unbelief-blinders that inspired fear.

   Perhaps you've been in congregations that select their leaders by whatever warm bodies can be found to fill the positions required by the bylaws. What a huge mistake! The leaders must be people of faith or the result may be tragic for the congregation! Leaders need to be "full of the Holy Spirit and of wisdom" (Acts 6:3) and, like Barnabas, "full of the Holy Spirit and faith" (Acts 11:24).

2. **The majority doesn't necessarily discern God's will.** Though the surveillance team's "vote" was 10-2 in favor of abandoning the conquest, the majority was wrong. We must seek God for his will, not just count heads!

3. **Leaders have a strong influence on the people who respect them.** Here, the influence of the ten prevailed not only on their tribes, but on an entire nation to its detriment. Influence doesn't always work positively.

4. **Fear opposes faith.** The fear propagated by the ten spread like wildfire throughout the camp and panicked the people. Fear is the opposite of faith. When we allow ourselves – either personally or as a body – to be led by fear rather than faith, we'll go wrong every time. Fear is one of the most powerful tools Satan uses against God's people, since it negates faith and renders people weak (2 Timothy 1:7).

---

[25] "Attacked" (NIV), "defeated" (NRSV), "smote" (KJV) is *nākâ*, "smite, strike, hit, beat, slay, kill" (TWOT #1364), which we saw previously in Exodus 2:12 in Lesson 1.

[26] "Beat down" (NIV), "pursuing" (NRSV), "discomfited" (KJV) is the Hiphil stem of *kātat*, "crush to pieces, crush fine" (TWOT #1062). "Beat, crush by beating" (BDB 510).

5. **Leaders calm fearful people with faith statements.** Though it was not effective on this occasion, both Caleb and Joshua combated fear through words of faith.

6. **Rebellion against authority can be spawned by fear.** Sometimes rebellion is caused by envy or by a lust for power. But it can also be caused by fear – an extremely powerful emotion.

7. **Leaders must intercede on behalf of their people's sins.** Here again, Moses intercedes fervently for the people of Israel, based on God's word – his glory and his character. Too seldom do pastors actually intercede for their congregations before God. They take corporate sin and unbelief too lightly. They usually approach God in complaint instead of in intercessory prayer.

8. **God can forgive the congregation while punishing the offenders.** While the sin of leaders can cripple a congregation's future, God can still bless the congregation, though it takes time. But God will hold leaders accountable for how they "build on this foundation using gold, silver, costly stones, wood, hay or straw" (1 Corinthians 3:12-15).

9. **The sins of the congregation's fathers are visited upon future generations.** How we build is crucial, since it will affect the whole shape of the church, even years after we are gone. What we sow, our "children" will reap – unless God is gracious to bring a revival to transform a crippled congregation.

10. **Some decisions cannot be undone.** When the people heard of their punishment to die in the wilderness for their unbelief, they tried to undo their former decision and enter the land – but without God's blessing and presence. One of the sad lessons of the Bible is that we must obey God when he speaks to us. It is sometimes too late to obey later. The writer of Hebrews reminds us:

    "See that no one … is godless like Esau, who for a single meal sold his inheritance rights as the oldest son. Afterward, as you know, when he wanted to inherit this blessing, he was rejected. He could bring about no change of mind, though he sought the blessing with tears." (Hebrews 12:16-17)

11. **We must follow the Lord wholeheartedly.** Caleb is held up for us as one who followed the Lord fully. And he was eventually rewarded by not only entering the Promised Land, but also possessing the city of Hebron, the home of the giants who had inspired so much fear in the camp of Israel (Joshua 14:6-15).

> Q3. (Numbers 14) Why is this failure to enter the Promised Land so serious? What did it represent on the people's part? What did it represent on the Lord's part? In your opinion, was the punishment too severe? Why or why not? If the people had moved in faith, how long would their trip from Egypt to Canaan have taken?
> http://www.joyfulheart.com/forums/index.php?showtopic=1064

D. Authority Challenged (Numbers 16)

The final leadership challenge of this troubled period in Moses' ministry came from members of his own tribe and from a coalition of leaders from many tribes.

Korah's Rebellion (Numbers 16)

"¹ Korah … the son of Levi, and certain Reubenites … became insolent ² and rose up against Moses. With them were 250 Israelite men, well-known community leaders who had been appointed members of the council.

³ They came as a group to oppose Moses and Aaron and said to them, 'You have gone too far! The whole community is holy, every one of them, and the LORD is with them. Why then do you set yourselves above the LORD's assembly?'" (Numbers 16:1-3)

The issue was who could serve as priests. Korah and his clan members were Levites, but not priests. The Levites had various duties that they fulfilled regarding the tabernacle. For example, as a Kohathite, descendents of Levi's son Kohath, Korah's clan was

"… Responsible for the care of the sanctuary…. for the care of the ark, the table, the lampstand, the altars, the articles of the sanctuary used in ministering, the curtain, and everything related to their use." (Numbers 3:28, 31)

When it came time for the camp to move, this clan packed and carried the most holy things.

But now the Levites, whom Korah represented, wanted to have the status of priests, to offer sacrifices as was only permitted to the priests, the sons of Aaron (who himself was a descendant of Levi). Moses says,

"Now listen, you Levites! 9 Isn't it enough for you that the God of Israel has separated you from the rest of the Israelite community and brought you near himself to do the work at the LORD's tabernacle and to stand before the community and minister to them? 10 He has brought you and all your fellow Levites near himself, but now you are trying to get the priesthood too." (Numbers 16:8b-10)

Korah and his coalition

"... came as a group to oppose Moses and Aaron and said to them, 'You have gone too far! The whole community is holy, every one of them, and the LORD is with them. Why then do you set yourselves above the LORD's assembly?'" (Numbers 16:3)

Moses and Aaron are being accused of pride, of setting themselves above[27] the people. Furthermore, Korah and his followers are questioning Moses' statements that only the priests are permitted to minister with regard to the most holy things – offering sacrifices and burning incense before the Lord. Korah argued.

"The whole community is holy, every one of them, and the LORD is with them." (Numbers 16:3)

What Korah asserted was true, so far as it went. Indeed, the Lord had declared the whole people set apart to him.

"You will be for me a kingdom of priests and a holy nation." (Exodus 19:6a)

And the promise of the Lord's presence was made for the entire people as well (Exodus 33:14).

The problem was that Korah was quoting the selected passages that made his point, but was ignoring the detailed instructions that the Lord had spoken through Moses regarding the distinctions between the priests and Levites (Exodus 29:8-9, 41, 44; Leviticus 8). He was questioning that Moses had actually spoken God's words accurately. But, since Moses *had* written God's words accurately, Korah and his coalition were questioning God himself. This was rebellion against God!

Moses realizes that Korah's company is speaking blasphemy against God – and would bring a terrible judgment on many. Moses fell facedown to humble himself before the Lord in the face of judgment. Then he said to Korah:

"It is against the LORD that you and all your followers have banded together. Who is Aaron that you should grumble against him?" (Numbers 16:11)

When Moses summons the Reubenite leaders of the coalition, Dathan and Abiram, they refuse to come. Perhaps their motive was that they felt slighted in leadership, even

[27] The verb is the Hithpael stem of *nāśā'*, "lift up," here, "be ambitious" as in 1 Kings 1:5 (Holladay, p. 247).

though Reuben had been Jacob's firstborn (Genesis 49:3-4). They may have wanted a greater role in leadership, we're just not sure. Nevertheless, they accuse Moses of:

1. Seeking to kill the people in the desert.
2. Lording it over the people.[28]
3. Failing to lead the people into the abundance of Canaan.
4. Punishing rebellion with torture (Numbers 16:13-14).

Moses commands each of 250 rebels in the coalition to bring a censer with fire and incense to present before the Lord in the morning.

> "When Korah had gathered all his followers in opposition to them at the entrance to the Tent of Meeting, the glory of the LORD appeared to the entire assembly." (Numbers 16:20)

Moses and Aaron immediately prostrate themselves before the Lord and intercede loudly for the people of Israel to avert judgment upon all:

> "O God, God of the spirits of all mankind, will you be angry with the entire assembly when only one man sins?" (Numbers 16:22)

The earth then splits apart and swallows Korah and all his men – with their households – and then closes over them. The 250 leaders who are offering incense before the Lord are struck with "fire from the Lord" and consumed.

The Israelites flee in terror, but the next day the whole Israelite community grumbles against Moses and Aaron and accuses them: "You have killed the LORD's people" (Numbers 16:41). The rebellion that had begun with Korah and 250 leaders had now infected the entire people. The glory of the Lord appears again, and with it, impending judgment.

Moses Intercedes Once More (Numbers 16:42-50)

God threatens to kill the entire assembly of rebels. Again, Moses and Aaron fall prostrate to seek God's mercy. Moses tells Aaron to take fire from the altar with his censer and make atonement for the people's sins. "Wrath has come out from the LORD," he tells Aaron. "The plague has started" (16:46).

> "[47] So Aaron did as Moses said, and ran into the midst of the assembly. The plague had already started among the people, but Aaron offered the incense and made atonement[29]

---

[28] "Lord it over" (NIV, NRSV), "make yourself a prince over" (KJV) is *śārar*, "rule, reign, act as a prince, govern" (Gary G. Cohen, TWOT #2295). In the Hitpael stem it means, "lord it over someone" (Holladay 355). This echoes the charge made of Moses at age 40 using the related noun: "Who made you ruler and judge over us?" (Exodus 2:14).

for them. [48] He stood between the living and the dead, and the plague stopped." (Numbers 16:47-48)

Even so, 14,700 people died before the plague had ceased. The people as a whole had begun to rebel against Moses and Aaron, and the people suffered a great punishment!

Aaron's Rod that Budded (Numbers 17)

Because the whole assembly had become involved in this rebellion – and Moses was accused of killing the people previously when the Lord had brought judgment, one final miracle is necessary to settle the matter. The Lord said, "I will rid myself of this constant grumbling against you by the Israelites" (Numbers 17:5).

The leader of each of the 12 tribes is asked to bring the leader's staff and inscribe his name on it. These are placed before the Tent of Meeting in front of the ark of the covenant. The next day, the rods were the same as before except for Aaron's, which "had not only sprouted but had budded, blossomed and produced almonds" (Numbers 17:8). Aaron's rod was kept in front of the ark "as a sign to the rebellious." The Lord said:

> "This will put an end to their grumbling against me, so that they will not die." (Numbers 17:10)

God has made his point: Aaron and his sons are his choice to be the ones to represent the people before the Lord – and no others! Others who attempt to approach God in the tabernacle will die. At long last, the Israelites come to possess appropriate fear of usurping the authority of Moses and the priests and thus offending God; but the cost in lives has been great (Numbers 17:12-13).

Q4. (Numbers 17) What was the root cause of Korah's rebellion? Which of their accusations were true or partially true? Why is challenging the authority of a spiritual leader so dangerous to the challengers? How is intercession for a sinful people such an important part of a leader's job?

http://www.joyfulheart.com/forums/index.php?showtopic=1065

---

[29] "Make atonement" is *kāpar*, "to ransom, to atone by offering a substitute." Apparently it does *not* mean "to cover" as was once thought, based on an Arabic cognate (R. Laird Harris, TWOT #1023).

This has been a discouraging chapter – as it was a discouraging chapter in Moses' life. But some periods of our lives are like that. It seems like one thing after another, one setback after another. Sometimes we can't look far ahead, but must take it day by day. Nevertheless, through it all, God is present in our lives. And though our route to the Promised Land may seem long and sometimes delayed, God will keep his promises to us and to his people, of that we can be sure!

This lesson reminds me of Andraé Crouch's song, "Through It All":

I've had many tears and sorrows,
I've had questions for tomorrow,
There've been times I didn't know right from wrong.
But in every situation, God gave me blessed consolation,
That my trials come to only make me strong.

Through it all, through it all,
I've learned to trust in Jesus,
I've learned to trust in God.
Through it all, through it all,
I've learned to depend upon His Word.[30]

Prayer

Thank you, Lord, for your presence with us in our trials and times of high stress and difficulty. Teach us to lead your people through those periods as well as through the easy days. And help us to know you better as we walk with you. In Jesus' name, we pray. Amen.

---

[30] By Andraé Crouch, "Through It All" (© 1971, Manna Music, Inc.).

9. Conquering the Transjordan and Moses' Death (Numbers 20-27; Deuteronomy 32, 34)

Nearly 40 years have elapsed since Moses had sent out the spies from Kadesh and the ten had come back with a bad report. Now the Israelites are at Kadesh again at the end of many years of desert wanderings following the Lord's judgment that the entire unbelieving generation would die in the wilderness. At Kadesh they began their wandering, and at Kadesh they will conclude it, for their next stop is at Mount Hor in the plains of Moab in the fortieth year after leaving Egypt (Numbers 33:36-38).[1] Here in Kadesh, Miriam herself dies (Numbers 20:1), one of the last of the old generation.

James J. Tissot, "Moses Strikes the Rock" (1896-1900), watercolor, Jewish Museum, New York.

A. Moses and Aaron Displease the Lord (Numbers 20)

Moses Strikes the Rock at Kadesh and Is Disciplined (Numbers 20:1-13)

Before at Kadesh, there had been plenty of water due to the strong springs there. But this time when they arrive, the water has dried up. This precipitates a now-familiar crisis, this time with the children of those who had crossed the Red Sea some 40 years previously.

"2 Now there was no water for the community, and the people gathered in opposition to Moses and Aaron. 3 They quarreled with Moses and said, 'If only we had died when our

---

[1] Ashley, *Numbers*, p. 380.

brothers fell dead before the LORD! [4] Why did you bring the LORD's community into this desert, that we and our livestock should die here? [5] Why did you bring us up out of Egypt to this terrible place? It has no grain or figs, grapevines or pomegranates. And there is no water to drink!'" (Numbers 20:2-5)

The glory of the Lord appears to Moses and Aaron, a sign of the Lord's anger as before (Numbers 12:5; 14:10; 16:19, 42). The Lord gives Moses very clear instructions.

"[8] Take the staff, and you and your brother Aaron gather the assembly together. **Speak to that rock** before their eyes and it will pour out its water." (Numbers 20:8a)

Early in the Exodus, Moses had brought water from a rock before by striking it in the presence of the elders (Exodus 17:6). But this time, the Lord tells him to *speak* to it, rod in hand. Normally, Moses is careful to do exactly what the Lord tells him, but this time he is angry at the people gathered to watch.

"[10] He and Aaron gathered the assembly together in front of the rock and Moses said to them, 'Listen, you rebels, must we bring you water out of this rock?' [11] Then Moses raised his arm and struck the rock twice with his staff. Water gushed out, and the community and their livestock drank." (Numbers 20:10-11)

The Lord doesn't shame Moses and Aaron before the people; he honors their leadership publicly. Privately, however, the Lord rebukes them:

"Because you did not **trust in me** enough to **honor me as holy**[2] in the sight of the Israelites, you will not bring this community into the land I give them." (Numbers 20:12)

Later in Numbers we read:

"Both of you **rebelled** against (*mārâ*) my command at the waters of Meribah." (Numbers 20:24)

"Both of you **disobeyed** (*mārâ*) my command to honor me as holy before their eyes." (Numbers 27:14)

"Disobeyed" (NIV), "rebelled" (KJV, NRSV) is *mārâ*, "be rebellious against, disobedient towards."[3] The psalmist wrote about this incident, as well:

"By the waters of Meribah they angered the LORD,
and trouble came to Moses because of them;

---

[2] "Honor as holy" (NIV), "show my holiness" (NRSV), "sanctify" (KJV) is *qādash* in the Hiphil stem, "regard, or treat, as sacred, hallow" (BDB 872).

[3] Victor P. Hamilton, *mārâ*, TWOT #1242. Both Numbers 20:24 and 27:14 are in the Qal stem.

for they rebelled against the Spirit of God,
and **rash words**[4] came from Moses' lips." (Psalm 106:32-33)

What did Moses and Aaron do so wrong that they were denied entrance to the Promised Land? The nature of Moses' and Aaron's sin is two-fold:

1. **Disobedience.** They disobeyed God's instructions to *speak to the rock*. Instead they *struck* the rock and *spoke to the people*, as though they possessed the power to produce water from the rock.
2. **Not sanctifying God.** When Moses and Aaron used the word "we" (Numbers 20:10), rather than giving God glory by declaring God's act of power, it had the effect of compromising divine holiness, which was an unpardonable act of insubordination.[5]

How did this disobedience count as unbelief? Certainly, Moses' striking the rock was an act of faith in God's power on his behalf, even though it was arrogant. Nevertheless, while obedience shows faith and trust, disobedience shows disregard for God's word and is an act of rebellion, of breaking faith with God. We are so quick to justify our own rebellion against God's commands that it is hard to understand Moses' sins.

The leadership lesson is that if we are to lead God's people, we must learn to obey exactly what God says – no more and no less. We are not independent leaders, but lead on God's behalf. When we err, we must immediately repent and seek God's forgiveness and mercy – something that we don't read that Moses or Aaron did. When we leaders walk in arrogance, we are on shaky ground with God!

Q1. (Numbers 20:1-13) What did God tell Moses to do to bring water out of the rock? What did Moses actually do? In what way did he sin? What emotions and attitudes were behind his sin, do you think? What must leaders do when they sin in these ways? http://www.joyfulheart.com/forums/index.php?showtopic=1066

---

[4] "Rash words" (NIV, NRSV), "spake unadvisedly" is *bāṭā'*, "speak rashly, thoughtlessly" (Proverbs 12:18; Leviticus 5:4; BDB 104).

[5] Harrison, *Numbers*, p. 267, citing P.J. Budd, *Numbers*, pp. 218-219; L.J. Dubois, *Beacon Bible Commentary*, p. 458. Since, in the Bible the rock is a symbol of God himself (Psalm 18:2; 31:3; 42:9; 1 Corinthians 10:4), so some think that striking it may indicate sacrilege (Wenham, *Numbers*, p. 151, citing J. de Vaulx, *Les Nombres* (Sources Bibliques, 1972) p. 223).

B. Conflict with the People of the Land (Numbers 20-25)

Conflicts with Edom and Arad (Numbers 20:14-21:3)

Now it is time to leave Kadesh, which has served as a base for the Israelites for many years in their desert wanderings. They are now moving to position themselves to enter the Promised Land. But the kingdom of Edom lies in their path along the King's Highway, the main north-south road east of the Dead Sea and the Jordan River.

> "[14] Moses sent messengers from Kadesh to the king of Edom, saying: 'This is what your brother Israel says: You know about all the hardships that have come upon us.... Now we are here at Kadesh, a town on the edge of your territory. [17] **Please let us pass through** your country. We will not go through any field or vineyard, or drink water from any well. We will travel along the king's highway and not turn to the right or to the left until we have passed through your territory." (Numbers 20:14-17)

But the king of Edom refuses them permission and sends his army to challenge them. Moses decides it prudent not to take this route. Nevertheless, the Israelites leave Kadesh and move to Mount Hor,[6] very close to Edom. Here Aaron dies and Eleazar his son takes his place as high priest (Numbers 20:22-29).

From Mount Hor, the Israelites continue east where they are attacked by the king of Arad, an ancient Canaanite city identified with Tell Arad. The Israelites destroy Arad's army and their towns (Numbers 21:1-3).

Vipers Attack the Israelites (Numbers 21:4-9)

The journey continues as the Israelites swing to the south to avoid entering Edomite territory. But as they encounter difficulties, they begin to complain, sounding just like their fathers before them. The problem is familiar: lack of water and manna, which they've grown to hate (as in Numbers 11:6):

> "[4b] But the people grew impatient[7] on the way; [5] they spoke against God and against Moses, and said, 'Why have you brought us up out of Egypt to die in the desert? There is no bread! There is no water! And we detest this miserable[8] food!'" (Numbers 21:4b-5)

---

[6] The actual location of Mount Hor is unknown, but was considered in Edomite territory. Josephus identified Mount Edom as Jebel Nebi Harim near Petra. But a more likely location might be Jebel Madura, about 15 miles northeast of Kadesh at the edge of Edom's territory (Harrison, *Numbers*, p. 272).

[7] "Impatient" (NIV, NRSV), "discouraged" (KJV) is *qāṣar*, "be short, impatient, vexed, grieved." The root designates something that is short (Jack P. Lewis, TWOT #2061).

[8] "Miserable" (NIV), "loath" (KJV) is *qûṣ* (which we saw in Exodus 1:12, Lesson 1, footnote 2), "feel a loathing, abhorrence, sickening dread" (BDB 880), "feel a disgust for" (Holladay, pp. 316-317).

This time, however, they complain openly about God and criticize his provision of food, rather than blame their problems on Moses only. Moses doesn't answer them. But God punishes their rebelliousness with poisonous snakes that strike terror into the multitude.

James J. Tissot, detail of "The Brazen Serpent" (1896-1900), watercolor, The Jewish Museum, New York City.

> "[6] Then the LORD sent venomous snakes[9] among them; they bit the people and many Israelites died. [7] The people came to Moses and said, 'We sinned when we spoke against the LORD and against you. Pray that the LORD will take the snakes away from us.' So Moses prayed for the people." (Numbers 21:6-7)

The people complain against both Moses and the Lord, but when they're in trouble, they confess their sins and they turn to Moses to intercede with the Lord on their behalf.[10] God gives Moses a curious instruction to stimulate the people's faith.[11]

> "[8] The LORD said to Moses, 'Make a snake and put it up on a pole; anyone who is bitten can look at it and live.' [9] So Moses made a bronze snake and put it up on a pole.[12] Then when anyone was bitten by a snake and looked at the bronze snake, he lived. (Numbers 21:8-9)

Keil comments,

> "The Lord helped them, in such a way, however, that the reception of help was made to depend on the faith of the people.... Whoever then of the persons bitten by the poisonous serpents looked at the brazen serpent with faith in the promise of God, lived, that is,

---

[9] "Venomous" (NIV), "poisonous" (NRSV), "fiery" (KJV) is *śārāp*, from *śārap*, "to burn" ... "The fire of these serpents was in the burning pain of the injected venom and the flying [Isaiah 14:29; 30:6] is doubtless a reference to the incredibly swift strike of the snake (NIV 'darting snakes')" (R. Laird Harris, TWOT #2292a). Of the 25 species of snakes in Palestine and Syria, four have a deadly bite, but it's difficult to know which species is indicated here (A.E. Day and G.D. Jordan, "Serpent," ISBE 4:417-418).

[10] See Numbers 11:2; 12:11-13; 14:40.

[11] Rather than continuing to be an object to stimulate faith, in times of apostasy the bronze serpent was worshipped as a god and was destroyed during Hezekiah's revival (2 Kings 18:4).

[12] *Nēs*, "standard, ensign, signal, sign," then "standard," as pole. (BDB 652, 2). This "standard-bearing pole," is literally the word for "sign" both in the Masoretic text and in the Septuagint (Raymond F. Brown, *Gospel of John* (Anchor Bible; Doubleday, 1966) 1:133).

> recovered from the serpent's bite.... It was ... intended as a figurative representation of the poisonous serpents, rendered harmless by the mercy of God."[13]

Jesus compared the snake lifted up in the wilderness to himself being lifted up on the cross – that those who look on him with faith live.

> "Just as Moses lifted up the snake in the desert, so the Son of Man must be lifted up, that everyone who believes in him may have eternal life." (John 3:14-15)

Q2. (Numbers 21:4-9; John 3:14-15) What precipitated the plague of snakes? Is being impatient with God's provision a sin? Why or why not? What are the points of comparison between the bronze snake in the desert and Christ on the cross?
http://www.joyfulheart.com/forums/index.php?showtopic=1067

---

[13] Keil and Delitzsch, Vol. 1, *Numbers*, pp. 139-140.

Conquering Kingdoms East of the Jordan (Numbers 21:10-35)

Now the Israelites travelled east of the King's Highway in order to avoid a conflict with Edom, then headed north into Moabite territory. Moses sends messengers to Sihon, king of the Amorites, to assure him of their peaceful intentions, but Sihon musters his army against Israel and fights them at Jahez. Israel is victorious.

> "24 Israel, however, put him to the sword and took over his land from the Arnon to the Jabbok.... 25 Israel captured all the cities of the Amorites and occupied them, including Heshbon and all its surrounding settlements. 26 Heshbon was the city of Sihon king of the Amorites, who had fought against the former king of Moab and had taken from him all his land as far as the Arnon.... 31 So Israel settled in the land of the Amorites." (Numbers 20:24-25, 31)

Next the Israelite army travels north towards Bashan, the present-day Golan Heights area, east of the Sea of Galilee. Og, king of Bashan, meets them for battle at Edrei. They, too, are defeated, leaving the Israelites in control of all the land north of the Arnon River, east of the Jordan. The Israelites now camp at the plains of Moab along the Jordan River, across from Jericho.

Balak Hires Balaam to Curse Israel (Numbers 22-24)

The Moabites who live east of the Dead Sea are terrified of such a huge number of people. They say to their Midianite allies,

> "This horde is going to lick up everything around us, as an ox licks up the grass of the field." (Numbers 22:4)

Conquest of the Transjordan

To curse the Israelites, Balak, king of Moab, summons a prophet-for-hire named Balaam, who lives near the Euphrates River. Balaam hears from God, from Yahweh, though he is not obedient from the heart. Though God has told him that he must not curse them, eventually he goes to Moab to see if he can earn a handsome fee.

As he goes, Balaam's ass sees the angel of the Lord standing in the road with a drawn sword, but Balaam is so spiritually blind that he cannot see it himself, and beats his donkey. Finally that ass speaks to him; only then can Balaam see the danger.

When he finally arrives in Moab, Balak takes him to various vista points where he can see the Israelite camp and curse them. But each time, instead of cursing, Balaam blesses the Israelites. Balaam finally returns home.

Israelite Men Sin with Moabite Women (Numbers 25)

Though he would not curse Israel, however, Balaam's counsel brings its own kind of curse to God's people. We read in the Book of Revelation:

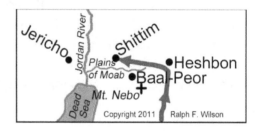

"You have people there who hold to the teaching of Balaam, who taught Balak to entice the Israelites to sin by eating food sacrificed to idols and by committing sexual immorality." (Revelation 2:14)

Peor is a town near to Shittim on the plain of Moab where the Israelites are encamped.

> [1] While Israel was staying in Shittim, the men began to indulge in sexual immorality with Moabite women, [2] who invited them to the sacrifices to their gods. The people ate and bowed down before these gods. [3] So Israel joined in worshiping the Baal of Peor. And the LORD's anger burned against them." (Numbers 25:1-3)

A plague from the Lord strikes Israel. But the sinners act so brazenly that an Israelite brings a Midianite woman into his tent in full sight of Moses.

> "[7] When Phinehas son of Eleazar, the son of Aaron, the priest, saw this, he left the assembly, took a spear in his hand [8] and followed the Israelite into the tent. He drove the spear through both of them – through the Israelite and into the woman's body. Then the plague against the Israelites was stopped; [9] but those who died in the plague numbered 24,000." (Numbers 25:7-9)

Phinehas is rewarded for his zeal to honor the Lord by "a covenant of a lasting priesthood" (Numbers 25:13). Psalm 106 commemorates this act to defend Yahweh's honor.

"They yoked themselves to the Baal of Peor
and ate sacrifices offered to lifeless gods;
They provoked the LORD to anger by their wicked deeds,
and a plague broke out among them.
But Phinehas stood up and intervened,
and the plague was checked.
This was credited to him as righteousness
for endless generations to come." (Psalm 106:28-30)

Israel then goes to war against the Midianites who "deceived you in the affair of Peor" (Numbers 25:18).

Q3. (Numbers 25; Revelation 2:14) Though Balaam wouldn't prophesy evil against Israel, he was willing to counsel the Moabites how to hurt Israel. How did Balaam's counsel lead Israel into sin? Why was Aaron's grandson Phinehas so honored for his action? What was his reward? Why are we so often zealous to defend the rights of God's enemies and so slow to defend God's honor?

http://www.joyfulheart.com/forums/index.php?showtopic=1068

The Census (Numbers 26)

Now Moses and Eleazar, Aaron's son and successor as high priest, take a census of the nation (except for the Levites), counting 601,730 males over 20. The Scripture records the evaluation.

"⁶⁴ Not one of them was among those counted by Moses and Aaron the priest when they counted the Israelites in the Desert of Sinai. ⁶⁵ For the LORD had told those Israelites they would surely die in the desert, and not one of them was left except Caleb son of Jephunneh and Joshua son of Nun." (Numbers 26:64-65)

God's prophecy at Kadesh has been fulfilled. Now the people are ready to enter the Promised Land – all except Moses. His final acts are to commission his successor and to remind the people about the Covenant.

C. Succession (Numbers 27; Deuteronomy 32, 34)

Commissioning of Joshua (Numbers 27:12-18)

Moses says to the Lord,

> [16] "May the LORD, the God of the spirits of all mankind, appoint a man over this community [17] to go out and come in before them, one who will lead them out and bring them in, so the LORD's people will not be like sheep without a shepherd." (Numbers 27:16)

So the Lord directs him to publicly lay his hands on and commission his longtime aide, Joshua, "a man in whom is the Spirit" (Numbers 27:18).

The Song of Moses, Blessings, and Death (Deuteronomy 32)

Now Moses recounts before the assembled people the Covenant and its laws, which comprises most of the book of Deuteronomy. Finally, he recites for them a song, the Song of Moses, recounting their past and future in measured Hebrew poetic form. It is a long psalm, but here are a few excerpts, beginning with praise of Yahweh:

> "[3] I will proclaim the name of the LORD.
> Oh, praise the greatness of our God!
> [4] He is the Rock, his works are perfect,
> and all his ways are just.
> A faithful God who does no wrong,
> upright and just is he." (Deuteronomy 32:3-4)

Then Moses recounts Israel's apostasy.

> "[5] They have acted corruptly toward him;
> to their shame they are no longer his children,
> but a warped and crooked generation.
> [6] Is this the way you repay the LORD,
> O foolish and unwise people?
> Is he not your Father, your Creator,
> who made you and formed you?" (32:5-6)

He reminds them of his tender care for Israel.

> "In a desert land he found him,
> in a barren and howling waste.
> He shielded him and cared for him;
> he guarded him as the apple of his eye,
> like an eagle that stirs up its nest
> and hovers over its young,

> that spreads its wings to catch them
> and carries them on its pinions.
>
> The LORD alone led him;
> no foreign god was with him." (32:10-12)

Now he warns them prophetically of future apostasy.

> "Jeshurun grew fat and kicked;
> filled with food, he became heavy and sleek.
> He abandoned the God who made him
> and rejected the Rock his Savior.
> They made him jealous with their foreign gods
> and angered him with their detestable idols.
> They sacrificed to demons, which are not God–
> gods they had not known,
> gods that recently appeared,
> gods your fathers did not fear." (32:15-17)

After a sad time of turning to other gods, the Lord will again take them up and fight against their enemies.

> "The LORD will judge his people
> and have compassion on his servants
> when he sees their strength is gone
> and no one is left, slave or free." (32:36)

> "See now that I myself am He!
> There is no god besides me.
> I put to death and I bring to life,
> I have wounded and I will heal,
> and no one can deliver out of my hand." (32:39)
> "Rejoice, O nations, with his people,
> for he will avenge the blood of his servants;
> he will take vengeance on his enemies
> and make atonement for his land and people." (32:43)

Jesus Christ, a descendent of the tribe of Judah, is the one whom God sends to make this atonement!

Moses concludes with a charge to the people.

> "Take to heart all the words I have solemnly declared to you this day, so that you may command your children to obey carefully all the words of this law. [47] They are not just idle words for you – they are your life. By them you will live long in the land you are crossing the Jordan to possess." (32:46-48)

The Death of Moses

When Moses' speech and song before the people were completed – on the same day – God tells him how he will die on Mount Nebo, within sight of Canaan, but never to enter it,

> "51 because … you broke faith with me in the presence of the Israelites at the waters of Meribah Kadesh in the Desert of Zin and because you did not uphold my holiness among the Israelites. 52 Therefore, you will see the land only from a distance; you will not enter the land I am giving to the people of Israel." (Deuteronomy 32:51-52)

So Moses climbs Mount Nebo, to the top of the Pisgah range. The Lord shows him the whole land and says:

> "This is the land I promised on oath to Abraham, Isaac and Jacob when I said, 'I will give it to your descendants.' I have let you see it with your eyes, but you will not cross over into it." (Deuteronomy 35:4)

God shows Moses the promise of the land that he has had a part in fulfilling for God. Moses has done his part in God's great plan, and then he dies. And that,

James J. Tissot, "Moses Sees the Promised Land from Afar" (1896-1900), watercolor, Jewish Museum, New York.

dear friends, concludes the story of Moses, the reluctant leader. The scripture records:

> "And **Moses the servant of the LORD** died there in Moab, as the LORD had said. He buried him in Moab, in the valley opposite Beth Peor, but to this day no one knows where his grave is. 7 Moses was a hundred and twenty years old when he died, yet his eyes were not weak nor his strength gone." (Deuteronomy 34:5-6)

Moses didn't want to lead Israel, but God chose him. Moses wasn't a perfect man. His anger got him in trouble more than once. But God selected him to serve, because God chooses imperfect men and women to serve him. He gives them his strength as they lean on him. He gives them his direction as they listen for his voice. And they make a difference in the lives of countless of God's children, because, though perhaps they are reluctant, yet they are obedient to serve.

May Moses' simple epitaph be ours when we die and are taken on to glory:

Moses, the servant of the Lord!

Q4. What about Moses' strengths have inspired you? What about his weaknesses have been a warning to you? If there is one primary thing God has taught you from Moses' life that you seek to apply to yours, what is it?
http://www.joyfulheart.com/forums/index.php?showtopic=1069

Prayer

Thank you, Lord, for the privilege of studying Moses, your reluctant leader. I've been reluctant at times. Forgive me, Lord. Sometimes I've gone ahead in my own "wisdom" and "strength" and fallen on my face. Teach me, Lord. May my ears hunger to hear your voice. May I be patient enough to wait upon you until you show me the way you are leading me and your people. Glorify yourself through me and my brothers and sisters who have been studying with me. In Jesus' name, I pray. Amen.

Epilogue: Moses' Leadership Legacy

Moses is revered in both the Old and New Testaments as prophet, lawgiver, and deliverer of Israel – and rightly so. When I try to assess his secret from a leadership viewpoint, I see two things in particular:

1. He was chosen by God for this particular mission.
2. Moses listened carefully and then obeyed what God told him to do.

On the first point, there isn't much we can do about God's calling. That is His business, and we have but to understand it, accept it, and obey.

It's on the second point, however, that I want to reflect.

Moses: Leadership by Listening and Obeying

Moses practiced leadership by listening and obeying. In this he was unique in the Old Testament. When Miriam and Aaron began to speak against Moses, the Lord said:

J. H. Hartley, "Moses Praying on Mt. Pisgah" (1922), in James Bailie and J H Hartley (illustrator), *The Bible Story, a connected narrative retold from Holy Scripture* (A & C Black Ltd., London, 1923).

> "When a prophet of the LORD is among you,
> I reveal myself to him in visions,
> I speak to him in dreams.
> But this is not true of my servant Moses;
> he is faithful in all my house.
> **With him I speak face to face**,
> clearly and not in riddles;
> he sees the form of the LORD.
> (Numbers 12:6-8)

At the conclusion of the Pentateuch we find similar words about Moses' uniqueness.

> "Since then, no prophet has risen in Israel like **Moses, whom the LORD knew face to face,** who did all those miraculous signs and wonders the LORD sent him to do in Egypt – to Pharaoh and to all his officials and to his whole land. For no one has ever shown the

mighty power or performed the awesome deeds that Moses did in the sight of all Israel." (Deuteronomy 34:10-12)

The Prophet Who Was to Come (Deuteronomy 18:15, 18-19)

But is Moses' leadership style truly unique? God, speaking through Moses, pointed to a successor.

> "[15] The LORD your God will raise up for you a prophet like me from among your own brothers. You must listen to him…. **I will raise up for them a prophet like you from among their brothers**; I will put my words in his mouth, and he will tell them everything I command him. If anyone does not listen to my words that the prophet speaks in my name, I myself will call him to account." (Deuteronomy 18:15, 18-19)

Joshua was a great leader, but he wasn't the fulfillment of this prophecy, nor was any of the Old Testament prophets. The prophet God speaks of is Jesus himself,[1] as Peter testified (Acts 3:22-23).

Jesus: Leadership by Listening and Obeying

When we look at Jesus' leadership style, we see the same underlying pattern that we saw in Moses – though I don't want to oversimplify Jesus' leadership. We see a clear, unapologetic dependence upon the Father.

> "I tell you the truth, the Son can do nothing by himself; he can do only what he sees his Father doing, because whatever the Father does the Son also does. For the Father loves the Son and shows him all he does…." (John 5:19-20a)

The source of Jesus' leadership was a close relationship with the Father nurtured by hours in prayer. Moses had his Tent of Meeting (Exodus 33:7-11); Jesus had the hills where he would lose himself to be with the Father.

> "Very early in the morning, while it was still dark, Jesus got up, left the house and went off to a solitary place, where he prayed." (Mark 1:35 = Luke 4:42)

> "And he withdrew himself into the wilderness, and prayed." (Luke 5:16)

> "One of those days Jesus went out to a mountainside to pray, and spent the night praying to God." (Luke 6:12)

> "Once when Jesus was praying in private and his disciples were with him, he asked them, 'Who do the crowds say I am?'" (Luke 9:18)

---

[1] See also Luke 24:44; John 1:45; 5:46; 26:22; 28:23.

"About eight days after Jesus said this, he took Peter, John and James with him and went up onto a mountain to pray. As he was praying, the appearance of his face changed, and his clothes became as bright as a flash of lightning." (Luke 9:28-29)

"One day Jesus was praying in a certain place. When he finished, one of his disciples said to him, 'Lord, teach us to pray, just as John taught his disciples.'" (Luke 11:1)

"After he had dismissed them, he went up on a mountainside by himself to pray. When evening came, he was there alone." (Matthew 14:23 = Mark 6:46 = John 6:15)

"He withdrew about a stone's throw beyond them, knelt down and prayed." (Luke 22:41)

Can This Leadership Pattern Be Replicated?

Can Moses' and Jesus' pattern of listening and obeying be replicated today? Yes! Of course, Moses was unique among Old Testament prophets and Jesus was uniquely divine. But Jesus' ministry was clearly due to the power and anointing of the Holy Spirit upon him, not just his divinity, for he said to his disciples:

"I tell you the truth, anyone who has faith in me will do what I have been doing. He will do even greater things than these, because I am going to the Father." (John 14:12)

What does Jesus' going to the Father have to do with it? Because then the Spirit will come!

"I tell you the truth: It is for your good that I am going away. Unless I go away, the Counselor will not come to you; but if I go, I will send him to you." (John 16:7)

The same prophetic Spirit that was on Moses (Numbers 11:17, 25), was poured out at Pentecost upon the whole church. When the Holy Spirit comes to dwell within us as individuals and as congregations, then nothing is impossible to us. One of my favorite verses is found near the beginning of 1 Corinthians.

"The man without the Spirit does not accept the things that come from the Spirit of God, for they are foolishness to him, and he cannot understand them, because they are spiritually discerned. The spiritual man makes judgments about all things, but he himself is not subject to any man's judgment:

'For who has known the mind of the Lord that he may instruct him?'

But we have the mind of Christ." (1 Corinthians 2:14-16)

The same Holy Spirit that searches the deep things of God (1 Corinthians 2:10), also flows within us to reveal to us the thoughts of God (verse 11), if we will quiet our hearts and listen. This doesn't mean that God reveals everything to us. Nor does it mean that all of us have the same free-flow of communication that Moses experienced. I've found that you must *learn* to hear the Lord's voice; it is a privilege of all Christians. Of course, God bestows on some a special gift of prophecy that allows them to have a much greater flow of prophetic revelation for the benefit of the body, Christ's church.[2]

Jesus Modeled Spirit-led Leadership

I submit to you, my dear friends, that Jesus himself modeled for his disciples the same sort of leadership pattern that Moses followed more than 1,000 years previously: listen and then obey what God tells you to do.

No one said this leadership pattern is easy. It takes patience, a willingness to seek God, a desire for personal holiness, and a willingness to obey when God does speak. But the resulting power is much greater than any leadership model known to man. Nothing is impossible to the person who obeys what God tells him or her to do. As we conclude this study, I invite you to join me in a truly Spirit-led life.

Prayer

Thank you, Father, for the gift of your Holy Spirit. For too long we have taken your precious Gift for granted and ignored your voice. Teach each of us how to listen and obey. Raise up a generation of leaders who lead by the Spirit like Moses, who walk in Jesus' own steps. In His holy name, I pray. Amen.

[2] 1 Corinthians 12:10, 28-29; chapter 14; Ephesians 4:11-12.

Appendix 1. Participant Handouts for Classes & Groups

If you're working with a class or small group, feel free to duplicate the following handouts in this appendix at no additional charge. If you'd like to print 8-1/2" x 11" sheets, you can download the free Participant Guide handout sheets at: **www.jesuswalk.com/moses/moses-lesson-handouts.pdf**

Discussion Questions

You'll find 4 questions for each lesson. Each question may include several sub-questions. These are designed to get group members engaged in discussion of the key points of the passage. If you're running short of time, feel free to skip questions or portions of questions.

Introduction to the Moses and the Exodus

1. The Birth and Call of Moses (Exodus 1-4)
2. Finding Courage to Stand (Exodus 5-11)
3. Passover and Crossing the Red Sea (Exodus 12-15)
4. Grumbling, Conflict, and Delegation (Exodus 15-18)
5. The Covenant at Mount Sinai (Exodus 19-24)
6. The Golden Calf and Moses' Intercession (Exodus 32-34)
7. The Tabernacle, Priesthood, and Sacrifices (Exodus 20-31, 35-40; Leviticus 1-17; Numbers 6-10)
8. Rebellion against Moses' Leadership (Numbers 11-17)
9. Conquering the Transjordan and Moses' Death (Numbers 20-27; Deuteronomy 32, 24)

Introduction to the Moses and the Exodus

Dating of the Exodus

There are two popular theories of the date of the Exodus:

- Early date, about 1470 BC, end of the Middle Bronze Age
- Late date, about 1250 BC, Late Bronze Age IIB

This is not a matter of liberals vs. conservatives, but a matter of weighing the evidence carefully. Here are some of the dating factors:

- Store Cities of Rameses and Pithom (Exodus 1:11; 12:37)
- Pharaohs Seti I (1294-1279 BC), Rameses II (1279-1213 BC)
- Merneptah Stela (about 1220 and 1207 BC) mentions Israelites in Palestine
- Armana Letters (1390-1352 BC) don't mention Israelites
- Conquest of Canaanite cites, archaeological evidence
- Reference in 1 Kings 6:1 of 480 years from Exodus to the fourth year of Solomon's reign

This study assumes the late date for the Exodus, but we don't know for sure.

Who Wrote the Books of Moses?

- "Seams" between narratives
- Voice is "third person"
- Moses was educated and wrote ((Exodus 17:14; 24:4, 12; 34:27; etc.)
- Discredited Wellhausen "Documentary Hypothesis," JEDP theory

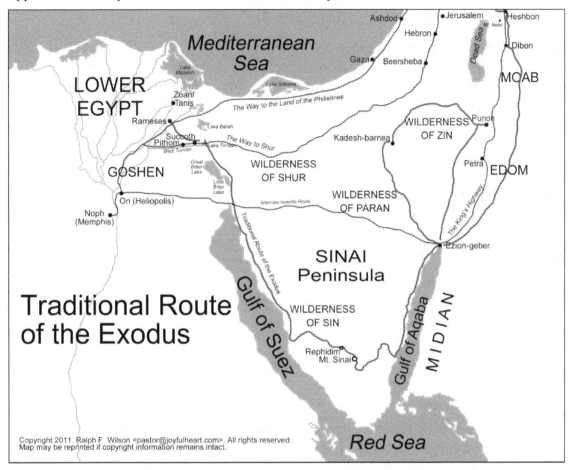

1. The Birth and Call of Moses (Exodus 1-4)

Oppressing the Israelites (Exodus 1:11-14)

1. Construction projects supply depot cities at Pithom and Rameses.
2. Brick making (Exodus 5:7)
3. Field labor.

Birth of Moses

"When he was placed outside, Pharaoh's daughter took him and brought him up as her own son. Moses was educated in all the wisdom of the Egyptians and was powerful in speech and action." (Acts 7:21-22)

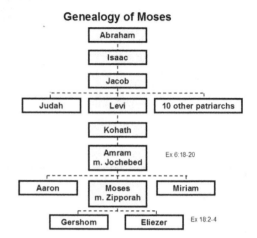

Genealogy of Moses

Moses Commits Murder (Exodus 2:11-15a)

1. He identifies himself as a Hebrew.
2. He has a strong sense of basic justice.
3. He is a man of action.
4. He is physically strong.
5. No sense yet of acting for God.

Leadership Is Influence

Q1. (Exodus 2:11-15a) What do we learn about Moses' motivations, character, and leadership ability from the incident of him killing the cruel Egyptian taskmaster? What positive things do you see in his character? What negative things do you discern?

Moses Flees to Midian and Delivers Jethro's Daughters (Exodus 2:15-17)

Midian is probably east of the Gulf of Aqaba or in the eastern Sinai peninsula. The Call of Moses (Exodus 2:23-4:17)

Three periods in Moses' life

1. Prince of Egypt   Proud in man's knowledge and status   40 yrs
2. Shepherd in Midian   Humbled and molded by God   40 yrs
3. Leader   Obedient servant   40 yrs

The Burning Bush (Exodus 3:1-9)

1. **Seeing.** I have seen my people's misery and oppression.
2. **Hearing.** I have heard their cries and prayers.

3. **Rescuing**. I will rescue them.
4. **Giving**. I will bring them into a land that I will give them.

Q2. (Exodus 3:10-12) Does Moses' response to God's call reflect a low self image, true humility, or lack of faith? How does God reassure him? How does God reassure us when we are called to impossible situations?

God Reveals Himself as Yahweh (Exodus 3:13-15)

'I AM WHO I AM... "I AM has sent me to you." (Exodus 3:13-14). See Hebrews 13:8; Revelation 1:8

Excuses and "what ifs"

1. Who am I? (3:11-12)
2. What if they ask your Name? (3:13-15)
3. What if they don't believe me? (4:1-9)
4. But I'm not eloquent (4:10-12)
5. People will kill me (4:19)

Q3. (Exodus 4:13-14a) Why is God angry with Moses? What is Moses' basic sin? Unbelief, fear, or disobedience? Do you think the Lord has ever been angry with you? How did Moses appease God's anger?

Moses Returns to Egypt (Exodus 4:18-31)

Q4. Why are we so afraid to obey God when he puts on our heart to do something decisive? How are we to deal with fear when we feel it? What is the relationship of fear to courage? Why is courage required in leaders and disciples?

2. Finding Courage to Stand (Exodus 5-11)

A. Moses' Early Failure (Exodus 5:1-3)

1. Come with God's word. "Thus saith the LORD" (KJV). "This is what the LORD says" (NIV). See Isaiah 55:11

2. Patient persistence (Hebrews 6:11-12)

3. Courage, "mental or moral strength to venture, persevere, and withstand danger, fear, or difficulty." (Deuteronomy 31:8)

Brick Making

The sun-dried mud bricks the Israelites were making were commonly used to build houses, palaces, and temples. Bricks were made of soil and water mixed with chopped straw that gave the bricks additional strength. The mud mixture was poured into a frame-like mold. The rectangular mud brick was then tapped from the frame and left to dry in the sun.

The Lord Encourages Moses (Exodus 6:6)

"Redeem" is gā'al, "redeem, avenge, revenge, ransom, do the part of a kinsman." It refers to the responsibilities of a next of kin to rescue family members from difficulty, redeem them from slavery, avenge them when they have been mistreated, etc.

Q1. (Exodus 7:6-7) Why did Moses blame God for his troubles? Why do you think Moses and Aaron are so stubborn? Was it fear? Was it unbelief? Or both, perhaps? Why does God have to command Moses and Aaron?

I Will Harden Pharaoh's Heart (Exodus 7:1-6)

1. Yahweh hardens Pharaoh's heart (active) – Exodus 4:21; 7:3, 13; 9:12; 10:1, 20, 27; 11:10, 14:4, 8, (17)

2. Pharaoh's heart is hardened (passive) – Exodus 7:13, 14, 22; 8:19; 9:7, 35

3. Pharaoh hardens his own heart (reflexive) – Exodus 8:15, 32; 9:34

Pharaoh is an unrepentant sinner from the start. See Romans 1:24, 26.

The Plagues upon Egypt (Exodus 7:8-11:9)

"Plague" is maggēpâ, "blow, pestilence," from nāgap, "to strike."

1. The Egyptians saw the God of the Israelites as the cause of the judgments.

2. The plagues did not fall on the Israelites, only on the Egyptians.

3. The timing was exquisite.

1. **Blood** (7:14-24). The blood of the plague makes the Nile's water undrinkable and kills the fish (7:21) – a major industry along the Nile.
2. **Frogs** (8:1-15). Frogs in Egypt were associated with the god Hopi and the goddess Heqt, who assisted at childbirth, and were thus a fertility symbol. For all the frogs to die and rot must have been seen as a defeat of the Egyptian gods.
3. **Gnats** (8:16-19). "Gnats" (NIV, NRSV), "lice" (KJV) is Hebrew *kēn*. We don't really know what kind of insect is intended by the word. "Fleas" or "sandflies" have been suggested, but more likely it refers to "mosquitoes."
4. **Flies** (8:20-32). "Swarm [of flies]" in verse 20 is literally *'ārōb*, "swarm" ("mixture," from incessant involved motion). Perhaps flies attracted by the decaying frogs. The Septuagint translates the word as *kynomuia*, "dog-fly," perhaps our modern gadfly or Monarch fly, with a painful bite. This plague it is described as a "severe swarm."
5. **Livestock** (9:1-7). Since "livestock" (NIV), "cattle" (KJV) were considered sacred animals by the Egyptians, this plague was a direct blow against Egypt's gods.
6. **Boils** (9:8-12). "Ashes of the furnace" that Moses and Aaron threw into the air would be black and fine like soot. "Festering boils" (NIV, NRSV) consists of two words, perhaps, "boils breaking out into pustules."
7. **Hail** (9:13-35). Hailstones have been measured as large as 8 inches in diameter. Here destroyed crops in the fields and trees, as well as livestock left in the open.
8. **Locusts** (10:1-20). Amos 7:1-3; Joel 1:1-7 seen a terrible figure of God's judgment. Devoured all that was left after the hail (10:15a).
9. **Darkness** (10:21-29). This darkness is so intense that it can be "felt."
10. **Firstborn** (11:1-10; 12:29-32)

Leadership Lessons

1. The Leader Must Confront When Necessary

    Q2. Why is it so difficult for some church leaders to confront people? What fears in this regard does a leader face? How can confrontation and rebuke be a good thing? What happens when we refuse to confront when we should?

2. The Leader Must Deal with Criticism and Pressure
3. The Leader Must Know When to Compromise – and When Not To

    Q3. Why didn't Moses accept Pharaoh's compromises? In what instances should church leaders accept compromise? In what instances is it wrong for church leaders to compromise?

4. The Leader Must Know that the Battle Is the Lord's. Ephesians 6:12.
    *   Moses: Exodus 14:14

- David to Goliath and the Philistines: 1 Samuel 17:47
- Jahaziel: 2 Chronicles 20:14
- Zechariah: Zechariah 4:6

Q4. Why do we tend to fight our battles "in the flesh" rather than using spiritual weapons? Why do we so often mistake the human enemy for the spiritual enemy? When will God fight our battles – and when won't he?

3. Passover and Crossing the Red Sea (Exodus 12-15)

"Then they are to take some of the blood and put it on the sides and tops of the doorframes of the houses where they eat the lambs.... The blood will be a sign for you on the houses where you are; and when I see the blood, I will **pass over** you." (Exodus 12:7, 13)

The word "Passover" is found in Exodus 12:11, 21, 26, 43, 48; 34:25. What does it mean? The word is *pesah*, is traditionally derived from *pāsah*, "to pass over," and interpreted as "the merciful passing over of a destructive power."

- Paul: "Christ, our **Passover lamb**, has been sacrificed." (1 Corinthians 5:7)
- John the Baptist: "Look, the **Lamb of God**, who takes away the sin of the world." (John 1:29)
- Peter: "You were redeemed ... with the **precious blood of Christ, a lamb** without blemish or defect." (1 Peter 1:18-19)

Q1. (1 Corinthians 5:7; John 1:29; 1 Peter 1:18-19) In what sense is Christ our Passover Lamb? In what sense are we marked with his blood? In what sense does God's judgment pass over us because of Christ's blood?

Commemorating the Passover (Exodus 12:14-20)

1. Passover Lamb.
2. Unleavened Bread. Exodus 12:14-20, 34
3. Bitter Herbs. Exodus 1:14

Plundering the Egyptians (Exodus 12:35-36)

Genesis 15:13-14; Exodus 3:21-22.God had a use for the gold and silver: the tabernacle

The Israelites Begin Their Journey (Exodus 12:37-40)

1. Route. From store-city of Rameses to Succoth.
2. Number of Israelites. 600,000 men, plus women and children.
3. Time in Egypt. This completed 430 years from the time Jacob entered Egypt, see also Genesis 15:13.
4. God's army, divisions, hosts. Exodus 13:18.
5. Heterogeneous group. "Rabble," Numbers 11:4; Leviticus 24:10-11.
6. Night Watch. The Lord Brought the Israelites Out of Egypt (Exodus 12:50-51)

The people's deliverance is founded on two elements mentioned in verse 50:

1. Moses and Aaron obeyed what God had commanded them.
2. The people obeyed what Moses and Aaron commanded them.

Q2. (Exodus 12:50) Why was obedience so important to the people's deliverance? Why is obedience so important to our deliverance from "sin, the flesh, and the devil"? Is there any discipleship without obedience? Does a person who says he believes in Jesus but doesn't obey him have real faith?

The Desert Route (Exodus 13:17-18a)

Road to the Philistines had two drawbacks:

1. The presence of military garrisons.
2. Nation-building time needed.

Location of the Red Sea

The Hebrew phrase *yām sûp*, "Reed Sea" is a term used in the Old Testament to identify a number of different bodies of water. Here it is probably some body of water east of the Nile delta, probably either at Lake Timsah or at the Great Bitter Lake, both of which lie along the present route of the Suez Canal.

Chariots

An Egyptian light chariot contained one driver and one fighter, usually armed with a bow. The chariot is fast and deadly – all of the fear factor of cavalry, but with the added accuracy of a stable shooting platform, with room to store additional arrows (and short spears when the arrows were exhausted).

Proposed route of the Exodus from Rameses to the Red Sea.

Moses Encourages the People (Exodus 14:13-14)

Commands:

1. **Do not be afraid**. Fear is their central weakness.
2. **Stand firm**. The opposite would be to run from the opposing army's forces. Ephesians 6:13-14a
3. **Be still**. Stop whining!

Faith Assertions:

1. You will see the deliverance the Lord will bring.
2. You won't see the Egyptians ever again.
3. The Lord will fight for you! Exodus 15:3.

Q3. (Exodus 14:11-14) Why do the people blame Moses for the advancing Egyptian army? What motivates their fear? Who are the people really blaming? How does Moses respond to their blame and fear? Why doesn't Moses defend himself from their unfair criticism? How do the people respond to Moses' words?

Gaining Glory over the Egyptians (Exodus 14:4, 17-18)

"Gain glory" (NIV, NRSV), "get honor" (KJV) is the verb *kābēd*, here in the Niphal stem. The basic meaning of the root is "to be heavy, weighty," extending to the figurative idea of a "weighty" person in society, someone who is honorable, impressive, noteworthy, worthy of respect. Common translations are to be "honorable, honored, glorious, glorified." Numbers 14:20-23; Isaiah 42:8; 48:11; 43:7; Ephesians 1:12; Isaiah 66:18-19; John 17:24; Romans 9:23

Q4. (Exodus 14:4, 17-18) Why is God's glory important in the Exodus? How is recognition of his glory important to faith? To holiness? To reverence? What happens when leaders take for themselves the credit and glory that should go only to God? How can leaders keep themselves from pride?

Reasons for the Destruction of Pharaoh's Army (Exodus 14:23-30)
1. Protection.
2. Glory.
3. Faith. Exodus 14:31
4. Leadership

4. Grumbling, Conflict, and Delegation (Exodus 15-18)

A. Grumbling (Exodus 15:22-17:7)

Finding Drinkable Water at Marah (Exodus 15:22-25a)

The first crisis they met in the desert was – predictably – thirst. They found water, but it was bitter – unpalatable to drink – perhaps brackish, alkaline water.

Grumbling, Complaining, Murmuring, and Quarreling against Leaders

"Grumble" (NIV), "complain" (NRSV), "murmur" (KJV) is *lîn*, which means, "to murmur, rebel (against)."

Scripture	Summary	Motivation
Exodus 5:21	Your demands to Pharaoh have made us a stench to him, demanding bricks without supplying straw.	Fear of punishment
Exodus 14:11-12	You brought us to die in wilderness	Fear of dying in battle
Exodus 15:24	Grumbling. Water is bitter at Marah. "What shall we drink?"	Fear of dying of thirst
Exodus 16:2, 7-9, 12	Grumbling. "We'll Starve to death!" Recalled pots of meat in Egypt.	Fear of dying of starvation
Exodus 17:3	At Rephidim, Moses strikes the rock at God's command.	Fear of dying of thirst
Numbers 11:1-6	Complaints about their hardships. Tired of manna, craved other food, instigated by the "rabble."	Dissatisfaction with manna
Numbers 14:2, 27, 29, 36-37; Deut 1:27 and Ps 106:25	Fear of war in Canaan after the report of the 10 unbelieving spies. "We'll fall by the sword. Our wives and children will be taken as plunder." There is talk of selecting another leader.	Fear of death and slavery

Scripture	Summary	Motivation
Numbers 16:11, 41; 17:5, 10	Korah rebels against Moses and the God-ordained Aaronic priesthood. Moses is also blamed when the leaders of rebellion are struck down by God.	Envy of Moses' leadership
Numbers 20:1-13	At Kadesh the people "gather in opposition against" and "quarreled" with Moses (also Exodus 17:2). Moses strikes the rock in anger rather than speaking to it as God instructed – and is punished by failing to enter the Promised Land.	Fear of dying of thirst
Numbers 21:4-9	Impatience, short-tempered, discouraged. Rebels accuse Moses of bringing them out of Egypt to die of thirst and starvation. They detest manna. Punished by poisonous snakes. Set up of bronze serpent on which they look and live.	Impatience with difficult conditions

Psalm 78:11, 17, 21-22, 32; 1 Corinthians 10:10.

Q1. (Exodus 15:24) What are the reasons that people grumble and complain? How do fear and faith relate to grumbling? What symptoms of grumbling do you see in your own life? What should you do about it?

Grumbling against the Lord, not Moses (Exodus 16:7b-8)

Exodus 14:11-12; 1 Samuel 8:6-8; Luke 10:16; John 15:20-21.

Q2. (Exodus 16:7-8) Why can grumbling against a leader really be a symptom of grumbling against the Lord? Are there any cases where this might *not* be true? Why do leaders tend to take complaints so personally? What does it take to learn that "it's not about you."

The Glory of the Lord Revealed (Exodus 16:6-12)

The word "glory" is *kābôd*, from the verb *kābēd*, "to be honorable, glorious," "to be heavy, weighty," someone who is honorable, impressive, worthy of respect, "gravitas." Carries the idea of brilliant shining light.

- **Moses' shining face**. Exodus 34:29-35; 2 Corinthians 3:13).
- Jesus: "**his face shone like the sun** and his clothes became as white as the light" (Matthew 17:22; Mark 9:2-3; Luke 9:29)
- **Son of Man's face "was like the sun shining** in all its brilliance" (Revelation 1:16; cf. 10:1).
- "The city has no need of sun or moon to shine on it, for the **glory of God is its light**, and its lamp is the Lamb." (Revelation 21:23; cf. Isaiah 60:19-20).

Often, however, the appearance of God's glory comes with severe judgment:

- When the people accept the bad report of the 10 spies (Numbers 14:10).
- At the rebellion of Korah against Moses authority (Numbers 16:19, 42).
- At the people's complaint about no water (Numbers 20:6).

Two related words:

1. **Theophany** is a theological term used to describe a visible manifestation of God, a self-disclosure of the deity.
2. **Shekinah** was used by later Jews to describe the glory of God's presence.

God's Provision of Quail and Manna (Exodus 16)

The word "manna" came from the Israelites' question in verse 15: "What is it?" Hebrew *mān hû'*, from *mâ*, "what" + *hû'*, "it."

"The people of Israel called the bread manna. It was **white like coriander seed** and tasted like **wafers made with honey**." (Exodus 16:31)

"The manna was like **coriander seed and looked like resin**. The people went around gathering it, and then ground it in a handmill or crushed it in a mortar. They **cooked it in a pot** or made it into **cakes**. And it tasted like something made with olive oil. When the dew settled on the camp at night, the manna also came down." (Numbers 11:7-9)

"The Israelites **ate manna forty years**, until they came to a land that was settled; they ate manna until they reached the border of Canaan." (Exodus 16:35; cf. Joshua 5:10-12)

Q3. (Exodus 16) Why did God provide manna for the people? Why did the manna finally cease? Why do you think that the people gradually began to take the manna for granted? What provision of God are you taking for granted?

The People Grumble about Water (Exodus 17:1-7)

Moses goes to God. Exodus 17:4

Psalm 105:39-41

Jethro Teaches Moses to Delegate Responsibility (Exodus 18:13-27)

Tradition of judgment: 2 Samuel 15:2; 1 Kings 3:16-28)

Qualifications of judges:

1. Capable.
2. God-fearing, that is, those who revere God.
3. Honest, trustworthy, who not only refuse bribes, but hate the very idea.
4. Accountable. They share the task with Moses.

Ephesians 4:11-12. Equipping role.

Delegating to the 70 Elders (Numbers 11:10-30)

Q4. (Exodus 18:13-27; Numbers 11:10-30) Why do you think it took Moses so long to delegate his judicial role to others? What were the qualifications of these judges? How is Moses' role similar to the role of leaders in Ephesians 4:11-12? What is the importance of the anointing of the Spirit in Christian leadership?

5. The Covenant at Mount Sinai (Exodus 19-24)

Invitation to a Unique Covenant Relationship (Exodus 19:3-6)

" ⁴ You yourselves have seen what I did to Egypt, and how I carried you on eagles' wings and brought you to myself. ⁵ Now if you obey me fully and keep my **covenant**, then out of all nations you will be my **treasured possession**. Although the whole earth is mine, ⁶ you will be for me a **kingdom of priests** and a **holy nation**." (Exodus 19:4-6)

Requirement: Keeping the Covenant (Exodus 19:5a)

The word "covenant" is the Hebrew noun *bᵉrit*. Between nations it is a "treaty, alliance of friendship." Between individuals it is "a pledge or agreement, with obligation between a monarch and subjects: a constitution." Between God and man it is "a covenant accompanied by signs, sacrifices, and a solemn oath that sealed the relationship with promises of blessing for keeping the covenant and curses for breaking it."

Ancient Near East suzerain-vassal treaties were commonplace. A great king (suzerain) would conquer weaker kingdoms and extract pledges of allegiance – and annual tribute – from their kings (vassals). In return, the suzerain had an obligation to protect vassal kingdoms in case they were attacked. The suzerain was known as the king of kings – the king of all the other kings.

Here are the steps involved in making this covenant at Sinai, as outlined in Exodus 19-24:

1. Israel arrives at Sinai and encamps (19:1-2)
2. God announces his intention to covenant with Israel and the people agree (19:3-9)
3. Preparations prior to the third day, washing clothes, consecration (19:10-15)
4. Assembly before Mt. Sinai on the third day (19:16-25)
5. Proclamation of the Ten Commandments (20:1-17)
6. Further laws and stipulations of the covenant (20:18-23:19)
7. Promise of the Land (23:20-33)
8. Reading the Book of the Covenant and sprinkling with blood (24:1-11)

God's Treasured Possession, Personal Property, Chosen People (Exodus 19:5)

"Treasured possession" (NIV, NRSV), "peculiar treasure" (KJV), "personal possession" (New Jerusalem Bible) is a single word: *segullâ*. The basic meaning of this noun is "personal property."

Deuteronomy 14:2; 26:18; Psalm 135:4; Malachi 3:16b-17, KJV "when I make up his jewels"; Titus 2:13b-14; 1 Peter 2:9.

Q1. (Exodus 19:5; 1 Peter 2:9) From an emotional standpoint, what does it feel like to take out and look over one of your treasured possessions? How was the idea of "treasured possession" fulfilled in Israel? What does it feel like to be God's treasured possession – as we Christians clearly are according to 1 Peter 2:9?

A Kingdom of Priests (Exodus 19:6a)

Israel, then, is either a kingdom *consisting of* priests – people, set apart to God (that is "holy"), who relate to God directly and serve him. Or "royal priests," a cadre of priests *belonging* to Yahweh the King. Either way, it is a position of great privilege and access. 1 Peter 2:9.

Q2. (Exodus 19:6; 1 Peter 2:9) What did priests do in the Old Testament? In what sense are you a priest? How do you function as a priest? In what sense are you a "royal" priest? In what areas can your personal priestly function improve?

A Holy Nation (Exodus 19:6b)

"The adjective *qādôsh* denominates that which is intrinsically sacred or which has been admitted to the sphere of the sacred by divine rite or cultic act. It connotes that which is distinct from the common or profane."

Q3. (Exodus 19:6; 1 Peter 2:9) In what sense is Israel a "holy" nation? What does it mean to be holy? Why do you think that personal holiness is de-emphasized in our time?

Consecrate the People (Exodus 19:10-11)

The word "consecrate" (NIV, NRSV), "sanctify" (KJV) is *qādash*, "to be holy." In the Piel stem, it has the causative sense, "to make holy, to sanctify, to consecrate."

The idea of holiness is prominent in Exodus, Leviticus, Numbers, and Deuteronomy especially. God is pure, holy, full of glory. To approach God, man must prepare himself.

- Take off one's shoes (Exodus 3:5; Joshua 5:15)
- Wash one's clothes and sometimes one's body (Exodus 19:10, 14; Leviticus 16:26, 28; Numbers 8:21; 19:7)
- Abstain from food, fast (Leviticus 16:29; 23:27)
- Abstain from sexual relations (Exodus 19:15)
- Offer sacrifices for atonement for sin (Exodus 12:7; Leviticus 1; etc.)
- Confess one's sins (Leviticus 16:21; 26:40)
- Act justly and keep the moral laws (Exodus 20; Micah 6:8)
- Keep the Sabbath
- Keep other rules of ritual purity

We hold two truths side by side:

1. **The Lord sanctifies us**: "You shall be for me … a holy nation."(Exodus 19:6)
2. **We sanctify ourselves**: "Prepare yourselves…." (Exodus 19:15)

The Ten Commandments and Book of the Covenant (Exodus 20-23)

Exodus 34:28; Deuteronomy 4:13; 10:4-5. They are placed in the ark (Deuteronomy 10:5), which is subsequently known as "the ark of the covenant" (Numbers 10:33; 14:44; Deuteronomy 10:8; 31:9, 25-26).

The Blood of the Covenant (Exodus 24:8)

"Moses then took the blood, sprinkled it on the people and said, 'This is **the blood of the covenant** that the LORD has made with you in accordance with all these words.'" (Exodus 24:8)

Hebrews 9:18-22; Matthew 26:27b-28; Jeremiah 31:31-34; Hebrews 10:4; 1 Peter 1:19

Q4. (Exodus 24:8; Matthew 26:27-28) What is the function of the "blood of the covenant" in Exodus? What is the "blood of the covenant" in the New Testament? How is the Old Covenant similar to the New Covenant? How are they different?

6. The Golden Calf and Moses' Intercession (Exodus 32-34)

The Israelites Worship the Golden Calf (Exodus 32:1-6)

- This practice of combining elements of various religions is called syncretism
- The Apis Bull and the bull-headed Khnum were comparable objects of worship in Egypt.

Q1. (Exodus 32:1-6) Why do you think the people of Israel were so quick to make idols, even after hearing the monotheism of the Ten Commandments that forbade graven images? Why do you think Aaron facilitated their sin? How do you think the golden calf made God feel? What idols do Christian churches allow that lead them away from pure worship of God in our day?

A Stiff-Necked People (Exodus 32:7, 9)

Stiff-necked" is a reference to a mule or ox which would resist the lead rope and refuse to let its master lead it. Instead it would stiffen its neck against the reins.

God's Righteous Anger (Exodus 32:10)

God's anger at sin can't be understood apart from his own holiness, his separateness from sin, his nature utterly opposed to injustice, sin, and human degradation. Our sins offend God's very character. If you can't accept an angry God, then you won't be able to understand him.

Moses Intercedes for the People (Exodus 32:11-13)

The basis of Moses' appeals:

1. Because the Israelites are God's own people
2. Because of God's reputation among the heathen
3. Because of God's promises

The leader stands between God and the people in intercessory prayer.

Moses Reprimands Aaron (Exodus 32:21-24)

Aaron's sin.

1. **Bringing idolatry and syncretism** (32:21), in the sense that he not only passively allowed it to occur, but actually led by supervising the fashioning of the golden calf.
2. **Letting people get out of order and control** (32:25) uses a single Hebrew word twice: *pāraʿ*, "let go, let loose, ignore." Here it has the sense of "to let go, let loose people, that is, remove restraint from them."

Q2. (Exodus 32:21-24) What was the nature of Aaron's sin with the golden calf? Why do you think he won't take responsibility for his actions? Why do you think he gets off so easily? Why must leaders be accountable for their actions? What is necessary for leaders to be able to learn from their mistakes?

Moses Intercedes for the People – Again (Exodus 32:30-35)

On what bases does Moses appeal to God?

1. God's promise to be with Moses personally (Exodus 3:12), not through an intermediary.
2. God's statement that he has found favor with God.
3. Moses' continued to desire to learn from God and please Him – "teach me your ways."
4. God's declaration that the Israelites are "my treasured possession" (Exodus 19:5). Moses reminds God, "Remember that this nation is your people."

Lessons for Leader-Intercessors

1. Leaders are to intercede for their people, even when their people have not acted in a worthy manner.
2. We intercede on the basis of God's promises.
3. We intercede on the basis of our personal relationship with God, forged in prayer. John 16:23-27

Q3. (Exodus 32:11-13, 30-35; 33:12-17) Why is interceding for the people so important in Moses' ministry? Why is this such an important role for pastors and lay leaders today? To intercede effectively before God, why must we know both his character and his promises?

Teach Me Your Ways (Exodus 33:13)

Psalm 103:7; 25:4; 27:11; 86:11

Moses' "Tent of Meeting" Outside the Camp (Exodus 33:7-11)

	Moses' "tent of meeting" (Exodus 33:7-11)	The Tabernacle
Location	Outside the camp	Center of camp (Num 2:2)
Purpose	Inquiring of the Lord and speaking with the Lord face-to-face	Formal worship and sacrifice, and location of the ark of the covenant
Attendants	Joshua	Priests and Levites

Q4. (Exodus 33:7-11) Why is Moses' pre-tabernacle "tent of meeting" so important in Moses' ministry? Why is it called the "tent of meeting"? What would it take for you to spend longer periods of intimate time seeking God? How do you think this would affect your ministry?

Show Me Your Glory (Exodus 33:18-23)

Philippians 3:8a, 12b, 13b-14

Proclamation of the Name of Yahweh (Exodus 34:5-7)

"⁵ Then the LORD came down in the cloud and stood there with him and proclaimed his name, the LORD. ⁶ And he passed in front of Moses, proclaiming, 'The LORD, the LORD, the compassionate and gracious God, slow to anger, abounding in love and faithfulness, ⁷ maintaining love to thousands, and forgiving wickedness, rebellion and sin. Yet he does not leave the guilty unpunished....'" (Exodus 34:5-7a)

Notice that when God revealed his glory, he declared his goodness and graciousness. So here on the mountain God reveals his character. This quintessential statement of God's gracious character is reiterated at least twelve times in Scripture. (Numbers 14:17-19; Deuteronomy 5:10; Joel 2:13; Jonah 4:2; Nahum 1:7; 2 Chronicles 30:9; and Psalms 86:15; 103:8-13; 111:4; 112:4; 116:5; and 145:8)

7. The Tabernacle, Priesthood, and Sacrifices (Exodus 20-31, 35-40; Leviticus 1-17; Numbers 6-10)

A. The Kingdom of God

The key unifying concept to grasp is that Yahweh is Israel's King. Exodus 15:18, Numbers 23:21; Deuteronomy 33:5

The Suzerain or Great King or King of kings makes treaties with kingdoms under him, and in return for obedience and subservience, offers protection and aid. Exodus 19:5-6

Yahweh's Presence in the Midst of His People (Numbers 2:1-3:39)

The very organization of Israel's camp reflected this truth according to Numbers 2:1-3:39. God's presence dwelt in the tabernacle.

Q1. (Numbers 2:1-3:39) Why was the camp of the Israelites laid out as it was? What did this layout teach the Israelites? Why were the Levites and priests camped closer than the other tribes?

B. The Laws of the Covenant

1. The *civil law* that governed the nation Israel. Only binding on the theocracy of Israel. Hebrews 8:13; 9:10; Matthew 21:43

2. The *religious law* that detailed the sacrifices and temple ceremonies required for the forgiveness of sin. Fulfilled by Jesus. Hebrews 9:22b; John 1:29; Matthew 26:28; Hebrews 10:10

3. The *moral law,* underlying principles such as those found in the Ten Commandments. Now fulfilled by the Spirit working in us. Deuteronomy 6:4-5; Leviticus 19:18; Matthew 22:40; Romans 7:6; Galatians 5:18.

CAMP OF DAN (157,600)

Dan (62,700) | Asher (41,500) | Naphtali (53,400)

CAMP OF EPHRAIM (180,100)
Benjamin (35,400)
Manasseh (32,200)
Ephraim (40,500)

Merari (6,200)
Gershon (7,500)
Tabernacle
Kohath (8,600)
Moses & Priests

Judah (74,600)
Issachar (54,400)
Zebulun (57,400)
CAMP OF JUDAH (186,400)

Gad (45,650) | Simeon (59,300) | Reuben (46,500)

CAMP OF REUBEN (151,450)

Arrangement of the Camp of Israel
Numbers 2:1-3:39

C. The Tabernacle

The keys to understanding the tabernacle:

1. It is the throne-room and precincts of the King's dwelling.
2. Moses received the exact pattern on Mount Sinai to be reproduced by skilled craftsmen detail by detail. Exodus 25:9, 40; Hebrews 8:5

Three Names for the Tabernacle

1. **Sanctuary** emphasizes the sacredness or holiness of the place.
2. **Tabernacle**, literally, "tent, dwelling," emphasizes the nearness and closeness of God's presence dwelling with the Israelites in the midst of their camp.
3. **Tent of Meeting**, emphasizing that function of being a place of "meeting" between God and his people.

The Tabernacle Covering (Exodus 26-27)

1. **Tapestry**, beautiful tapestry that decorated the inside of the tabernacle, visible on the ceiling and walls from within.
2. **Goat's Hair**, spun and woven goat's hair, the material commonly used for making tents.
3. **Ram Skins Dyed Red**
4. **Hides**, on the outside of the tabernacle, were apparently from sea cows, dugongs, or dolphins

Cherubim are probably similar to the sphinx or winged bulls or lions found in the Ancient Near East. Striding sphinx. Phoenician, 899–700 B.C. From Nimrud, ivory, 6.9 cm x 7.75 cm. The Trustees of the British Museum.

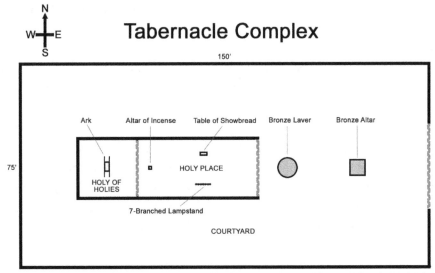

Tabernacle Furniture (Exodus 25, 27, 30)

1. **Altar of Burnt Offering**. The altar was a acacia wood box covered with bronze sheets, about 7½ feet square and 4½ feet high, topped by a grate, filled with earth, with horns at each corner. Here offerings were made to the Lord, both animals and grain.

2. **Bronze Laver or Basin**. This was a basin made of solid bronze set on a bronze stand. It was filled with water for the priests to wash their hands and feet before making an offering or entering the tabernacle.

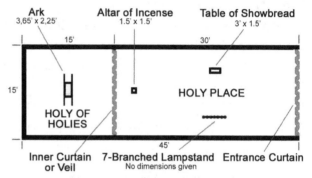

Tabernacle in the Wilderness

Copyright 2011, Ralph F. Wilson (pastor@joyfulheart.com)
Reprint rights granted if copyright information is included

3. **Table of Showbread**. "The bread of the Presence" (NIV, NRSV), "shewbread" (KJV) is literally "bread before the face." The table made of acacia-wood, plated in gold, and measured 3 feet by 1½ feet and 2¼ feet high. It bore 12 flat loaves of bread, one for each of the tribes, which were refreshed weekly. It symbolized providing food for the King in their midst.

4. **7-Branched Lampstand**. The lampstand elevated seven oil lamps high enough to illuminate the entire Holy Place. The lamps were probably open saucers with a wick draped over a lip formed in one end of the vessel burning olive oil. The lamps were to remain lit always.

5. **Altar of Incense**. This altar is 1½ feet square and about 3 feet high, with horns on each corner, and made of acacia-wood plated with gold. It was used to burn sweet-smelling incense in the presence of the Lord.

6. **Ark of the Covenant** (Exodus 25:10-22). The ark in the Holy of Holies was the most holy object of all, a gold-covered acacia-wood chest (dimensions 3¾ by 2¼ feet and 2¼ feet high) that served as the portable throne of Yahweh. The top lid made of pure gold and called the "atonement cover" (NIV), "mercy seat" (NRSV, KJV), *kappōret*, literally, "performance of reconciliation or atonement"[1] or "place of atonement," from *kāpar*, "make an atonement, make reconciliation."[2] At each end of the cover was

[1] *Kappōret*, Holladay, p. 163.
[2] R. Laird Harris, *kappōret*, TWOT #1023c.

a solid gold cherub. These cherubim faced each other with their "wings spread upward, overshadowing the cover" (Exodus 25:20). Portable throne of Yahweh: Exodus 25:22, cf. Numbers 7:89); 1 Samuel 4:4.

Q2. (Exodus 25:10-22) What is the significance of the Ark in the Holy of Holies? What did it represent? Why was it considered so holy? If no one really sat upon it, why was it so important?

Flow of Worship

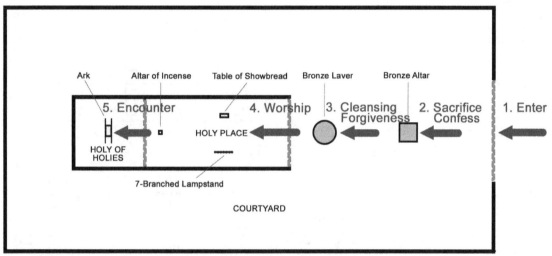

Copyright 2011, Ralph F. Wilson (pastor@joyfulheart.com). Permission to reprint is granted if copyright information is included

1. **Entering**. We enter into prayer to begin to seek God and draw near to him.
2. **Sacrifice and confession of sin** are represented by the bronze altar where sacrifices for sin were made. Christ is our sacrifice and our sin causes estrangement from him. As we confess our sins in humility and look with faith to his sacrifice for us on the cross, we connect with his grace and atonement.
3. **Cleansing and forgiveness** are represented by the bronze laver or basin. We receive his forgiveness and cleansing by faith with thankfulness.
4. **Worship** is the next step. As the priests tended the lamps, the table, and the altar of incense, we offer regular thanksgiving and praise to God in the Holy Place, as a sweet fragrance before him.
5. **Encounter with God** in the Holy of Holies is the ultimate goal. We hear this in Moses' plea, "Show me your glory" (Exodus 33:18) and in Paul's cry, "that I may know him" (Philippians 3:10).

Q3. What does the arrangement of the furniture, the tabernacle, and the courtyard teach us about worship? Why do you come to the bronze altar and the laver or basin before you reach the tent itself?

D. Priests, Levites, and Sacrifices

Priests

Priest in Hebrew is *kōhen*, from which we get the common Jewish surname "Cohen." The etymology of the word is obscure.

1. Ministering to the Lord, worship.
2. Ministering to the people of Israel, atonement

Levites

The present-day Jewish surnames "Levi" and "Levine" come from this tribal name.

Tithing

Supported by the tithes of the people. Numbers 18:8-21, 26; 2 Chronicles 2:2-10; Malachi 3:10; Luke 11:42; 1 Corinthians 9:13-14.

Genealogy of the Priesthood

Copyright 2011. Ralph F. Wilson (pastor@joyfulheart.com)
Permission to reprint is granted if copyright information is included.

Priestly Garments (Ex 28, 39, Lev 8:7-9)

"To give them dignity and honor" (Exodus 28:40). The garments – and differences between the high priest and regular priests is shown below:

	High Priest	**Regular Priests**
Sacred crown of gold, engraved with the words: "Holy to the Lord."	High priest only	None
Turban of linen, different types	*Miṣnepet*	*Migbāʿâ*

	High Priest	Regular Priests
Breastpiece, colorful, like the ephod, with 12 stones representing each tribe, plus a pocket in which to put the Urim and Thummim, which seem to be lots used to seek God's will.	High priest only	None
Ephod, "a sleeveless linen waistcoat" worn over the robe.	Ephod made with gold; blue, purple and scarlet yarn; and finely-twisted linen.	Plain linen ephod, at least in David's time.
Robe of the ephod, made of blue cloth, the hem with alternating embroidered pomegranates and gold bells.	High priest only	None
Sash	Embroidered sash	Regular sash
Tunic, linen, ankle-length	Perhaps checkered.	Plain white linen
Breeches, underwear, linen	Fine-twisted linen	Regular linen
Footwear	None	None

The Sacrifices

1. **Burnt Offering** (Leviticus 1; 6:8-13) the entire sacrifice is consumed on the altar, not just a part. This offering is designed to make atonement for the offerer's sin.
2. **Grain Offering** (Leviticus 2; 6:14-23). It is an offering or gift to God from one's crops. A portion is kept by the priests for their share.
3. **Peace or Fellowship Offering** (Leviticus 3; 7:11-34). This offering was accompanied by the communal celebration of the worshippers who shared in the meat of the offering. There are three sub-types: thank offering, votive offering, freewill sacrifice.
4. **Sin (Purification) Offering** (Leviticus 4:1-5:1; 6:24-30), to purify people from an unwitting sin.
5. **Guilt (Reparation) Offering** (Leviticus 5:14-6:7), that a restitution is required, to make atonement for desecration or mishandling of sacred things.

Special Sacrifices
1. **Morning and Evening Sacrifices** (Exodus 28:38-39; Numbers 28:1-8)
2. **Passover** offerings (Exodus 12; Numbers 9; Deuteronomy 16)
3. **Day of Atonement** (Yom Kippur, Leviticus 16) is the day each year when the high priest seeks atonement for the sins of the whole nation.

Steps in a Burnt Offering (Leviticus 1:3-9)
1. **Sacrifice is without defect** (verse 3; 1 Peter 1:19).
2. **Offer lays his hand on head of animal** (verse 4). Laying on of hands is accompanied by confession (Leviticus 16:21).
3. **Offerer slaughters the animal** (verse 5a).
4. **Priest collects the blood and sprinkles it against the altar** (verse 5b; Leviticus 17:11)
5. **Offerer skins and cuts the sacrifice in pieces** (verse 6).
6. **Priest puts the pieces of the sacrifice on the altar** (verses 7-8)
7. **Sacrifice is completely consumed on the altar** (verse 9).

Q4. (Leviticus 1:3-9) In the burnt offering for an individual's sin: What is the significance of the offerer laying his hand on the animal's head? Why do you think the offerer is to slay the sacrifice rather than having the priest do it? How is the animal's blood significant in sacrifice? In what ways does Jesus' sacrifice on the cross fulfill all of this?

Priests Participate in the Sacrifice (Leviticus 10)

Aaron's older sons, Nadab and Abihu, died before the Lord for "offered unauthorized fire before the LORD, contrary to his command" (Leviticus 10:1)

1. God demands holiness and obedience from his servants. Leviticus 11:44-45
2. God demands a pure heart from those who make offerings to him. Matthew 5:23-24; cf. Mark 11:25
3. God shows mercy when he sees in us a desire to please him, even if we haven't kept all the rules.

The priests are partakers of the altar – as part of the atonement. 1 Corinthians 10:16, 18

8. Rebellion against Moses' Leadership (Numbers 11-17)

Moses' Complaint to the Lord (Numbers 11:11-15)

1. The burden of leadership is too heavy for him.
2. He knows he is inadequate to supply the people's desires.

God answers:

1. God puts some of his Spirit on 70 of Israel's elders (Numbers 11:24-30)
2. God promises abundant meat (Numbers 11:31-34)

Q1. (Numbers 11:11-15) Why do you think Moses is so frustrated in his prayer? What do you think is going on in him emotionally and physically at this point? Does he have any grounds for his complaints, do you think? Do you think this is designed to be a model prayer? Why are we shown this prayer? How did God answer him?

Miriam's and Aaron's Criticism and Punishment (Numbers 12:1-15)

Moses' Cushite wife is only a smokescreen. Cush (*kûsh*) can refer to (1) Nubia, the area along the Nile south of Egypt, (2) a people in Mesopotamia, or (3) just possibly, Midian.

Real issue: a challenge by Miriam and Aaron to Moses' role as God's authoritative spokesman (Numbers 12:2), a power struggle.

Moses, the Humble (Numbers 12:3; 11:11-15; Matthew 5:5; 11:29; Mark 10:42-45)

Aaron and Miriam Rebuked for Speaking Against Moses (Numbers 12:4-9)

"Faithful" is *'āman*. The root idea is firmness or certainty, as we might describe a person as a "solid" leader. The Niphal participle here means "to be faithful, sure, dependable." (Psalm 105:15; 2 Chronicles 16:22)

Q2. (Numbers 12) What was Miriam's and Aaron's motivation for speaking against Moses? Why do people seeking power feel a need to discredit the existing leader? How did Moses handle this provocation? How might he have handled it if he were a proud man? How did the Lord handle it?

Spying Out the Land (Numbers 13:1-25)

Their instructions are to conduct surveillance to determine:

1. Character of the land and its fruitfulness
2. Strength and numbers of the populations
3. Fortification of towns and cities
4. Forestation

They travelled the land from south to north, a distance of about 250 miles each way and were gone 40 days. Report: Numbers 13:27-29. They all agreed on the *facts* of the report. It was at the point of *interpretation* that they differed.

1. Caleb (with Joshua) looked with eyes of faith: "We should go up and take possession of the land, for **we can certainly do it.**" (Numbers 13:31)

2. Ten other spies looked with eyes of unbelief and "spread among the Israelites a bad report about the land they had explored." "We can't attack those people; **they are stronger** than we are (Numbers 13:31-33)

Fear and Unbelief Spread (Numbers 14:1-9)

Bad report fed fears:
- Men would "fall by the sword"
- Women and children would be "taken as plunder"

Met by positive statements of faith:
1. **The Lord will lead us into the land.**
2. **We will consume the people.**
3. **Their protection has been removed.**
4. **The Lord is with us.** Genesis 39:2, 21; Exodus 3:12; 33:14; Joshua 1:5; Deuteronomy 31:23; Psalms 46:7, 11; Matthew 1:23; 18:20; 28:20; 2 Timothy 4:17; Hebrews 13:5b.

Warnings:
1. Do not **rebel**.
2. Do not **be afraid** of the people of the land.

Moses Intercedes Again (Numbers 14:13-20)

1. **God's glory.** The Egyptians and Canaanites will hear about it, and God's previous reputation will be hurt. It would be claimed that since he couldn't bring the people into the land, he killed them (14:13-16).

2. **God's character.** God's character had been spoken to Moses when the glory of God came before him in the cleft of the rock: He both loves and forgives of sin and rebellion (Exodus 34:5-7). Moses recites God's words back to him.

God answered Moses according to the statement of character Moses had claimed before him.

1. **Forgiveness.** God forgives the people, that is, he will allow the people of Israel, not just the descendants of Moses, to be the heirs of the promise.

2. **Punishment.** The 10 leaders who brought the bad report that precipitated the general unbelief were punished with sudden death.

3. **Visiting the sins of fathers on the children**. "Your children will be shepherds here for forty years, suffering for your unfaithfulness, until the last of your bodies lies in the desert." (Numbers 14:33-34)

Israel's sins keep them from entering the Promised Land (14:22-23):

1. Disobedience
2. Testing God
3. Treating God with contempt

Caleb's Faith (Numbers 14:24)

"Wholeheartedly" (NIV, NRSV) is the Piel stem of *mālē'*, "be full, to fill, literally "to be after fully" (KJV). Numbers 26:65; 32:12; Deuteronomy 1:36; Joshua 14:6-15.

Discipleship and Leadership Lessons

1. Godly leaders must possess faith, not just influence. Acts 6:3; 11:24.
2. The majority doesn't necessarily discern God's will.
3. Leaders have a strong influence on the people who respect them.
4. Fear opposes faith and vice versa.
5. Leaders calm fearful people with faith statements.
6. Rebellion against authority can be spawned by fear.
7. Leaders must intercede on behalf of their people's sins.
8. God can forgive the congregation while punishing the offenders. 1 Cor. 3:12-15.
9. The sins of the congregation's fathers are visited upon future generations.
10. Some decisions cannot be undone. Hebrews 12:16-17
11. We must follow Lord wholeheartedly. Joshua 14:6-15.

Q3. (Numbers 14) Why is this failure to enter the Promised Land so serious? What did it represent on the people's part? What did it represent on the Lord's part? In your opinion, was the punishment too severe? Why or why not? If the people had moved in faith, how long would their trip from Egypt to Canaan have taken?

Korah's Rebellion (Numbers 16)

The Levites, whom Korah represented, wanted to have the status of priests.. Numbers 16:8b-10. Moses and Aaron are accused of pride, of setting themselves above the people.

Q4. (Numbers 17) What was the root cause of Korah's rebellion? Which of their accusations were true or partially true? Why is challenging the authority of a spiritual leader so dangerous to the challengers? How is intercession for a sinful people such an important part of a leader's job?

9. Conquering the Transjordan and Moses' Death (Numbers 20-27; Deuteronomy 32, 34)

Moses Strikes the Rock at Kadesh and Is Disciplined (Numbers 20:1-13)

The nature of Moses' and Aaron's sin is two-fold:

1. **Disobedience**. They disobeyed God's instructions to *speak to the rock*. Instead they *struck* the rock and *spoke to the people*, as though they possessed the power to produce water from the rock.

2. **Not sanctifying God**. When Moses and Aaron used the word "we" (Numbers 20:10), rather than giving God glory by declaring God's act of power, it had the effect of compromising divine holiness, which was an unpardonable act of insubordination.

Q1. (Numbers 20:1-13) What did God tell Moses to do to bring water out of the rock? What did Moses actually do? In what way did he sin? What emotions and attitudes were behind his sin, do you think? What must leaders do when they sin in these ways?

Vipers Attack the Israelites (Numbers 21:4-9)

The Israelites begin to complain: lack of water and manna, which they've grown to hate.

Jesus compared the snake lifted up in the wilderness to himself being lifted up on the cross – that those who look on him with faith live. (John 3:14-15)

Q2. (Numbers 21:4-9; John 3:14-15) What precipitated the plague of snakes? Is being impatient with God's provision a sin? Why or why not? What are the points of comparison

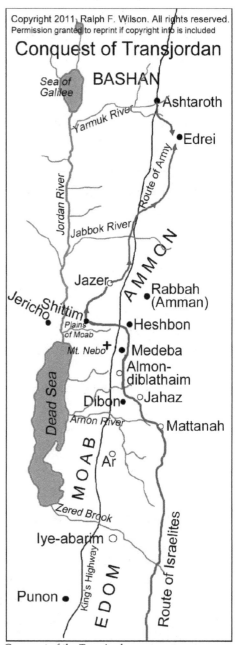

Conquest of Transjordan

Conquest of the Transjordan

between the bronze snake in the desert and Christ on the cross?

Israelite Men Sin with Moabite Women (Numbers 25)

Q3. (Numbers 25; Revelation 2:14) Though Balaam wouldn't prophesy evil against Israel, he was willing to counsel the Moabites how to hurt Israel. How did Balaam's counsel lead Israel into sin? Why was Aaron's grandson Phinehas so honored for his action? What was his reward? Why are we so often zealous to defend the rights of God's enemies and so slow to defend God's honor?

The Death of Moses

When Moses' speech and song before the people were completed – on the same day – God tells him how he will die on Mount Nebo, within sight of Canaan, but never to enter it, Deuteronomy 32:51-52; 35:4

Q4. What about Moses' strengths have inspired you? What about his weaknesses have been a warning to you? If there is one primary thing God has taught you from Moses' life that you seek to apply to yours, what is it?

Appendix 2. The Route of the Exodus

The route of the Exodus has been hotly debated. Since there are no archaeological artifacts from the Exodus itself and place names seldom match places identifiable today, we are left to sort out the probable route based on clues from the biblical accounts and the land itself. Three main routes of the Exodus to Mt. Sinai have been proposed.

1. Northern Sinai Route

The Northern Route sees the "Reed Sea" as Lake Serbonis, then along the Mediterranean coast of Sinai. It finds Mount Sinai in the northern part of the Sinai Peninsula. However, this route was heavily fortified by the Egyptians, since it constituted the route enemies would take to attack Egypt. This route is explicitly excluded by the text:

> "When Pharaoh let the people go, **God did not lead them on the road through the Philistine country, though that was shorter**. For God said, 'If they face war, they might change their minds and return to Egypt.' So God led the people around by the desert road toward the Red Sea." (Exodus 13:17-18)

Moreover, the present Lake Serbonis probably didn't yet exist at the time of Moses.

2. Central Sinai Route

A route directly east of the end of Wadi Tumilat across the center of the Sinai Peninsula doesn't have enough wells to support this body of people and animals.

I've recently seen a variation on this – not held by any reputable scholar – that claims the "real" Red Sea ("Reed Sea") is the Gulf of Aqaba, the "real" Mt. Sinai is Jebel el Lawz in Arabia. The theory holds that Pharaoh's chariots chased the Israelites across the center of the Sinai Peninsula, then down the steep canyon of Wadi Watir, across Nuweiba beach, and a slightly submerged land bridge into Arabia.[1] The problem with this view is that the Scripture shows the confrontation between Pharaoh and Moses at the Red Sea before the trek across the Sinai Peninsula, not after it. It just doesn't fit the facts of Scripture.

---

[1] This view is "explained" in a series of slides on the Grace upon Grace Ministries website. http://graceupongraceministries.org/video-feed It is explained by Russell and Colin Standish, *Holy Relics or Revelation* (Rapidan, VA: Hartland Publications).

3. Southern Sinai Route (Traditional)

Below is a map that shows the traditional route that makes the most sense to me.

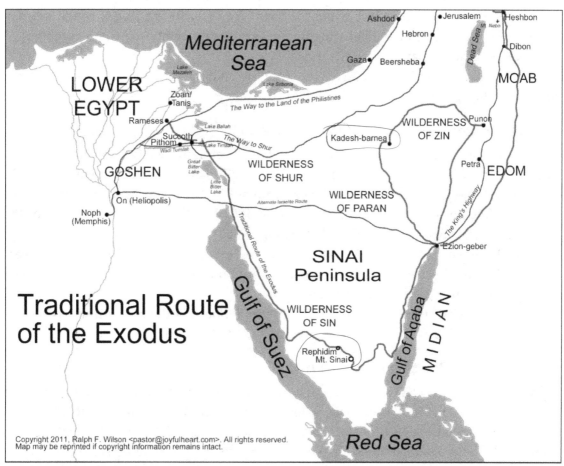

The traditional route crosses the "Reed Sea" at perhaps Lake Timsah or the Bitter Lakes, then down Sinai's west coastlands, then east through the mountains and wadis to a southern Mount Sinai, perhaps Jebel Musa, then back up northeastward by Sinai's east coast and desert to Kadesh-barnea. This route has the advantage that it:

1. Steers clear of nearly all Egyptian presence.
2. The Shur desert was also called the desert of Etham (Numbers 33:8), in the latitude of the east end of Wadi Tumilat. So, moving through that desert for three

days (if the middle way of Seir is excluded) has to be southward along the west coast of Sinai.[2]

3. The west coast of Sinai has a number of known watering places.

Of course, no one knows the route for sure. Very few of the stages of the journey outlined in Numbers 33 have been identified with any certainty, with the exception of Ezion Geber, Kadesh Barnea, and the plains of Moab.

Nevertheless, let's discuss some of the locations that we're more sure about – plus a couple of others.

Ramses, Pithom, and Succoth (Exodus 12:37)

The locations of both Ramses and Succoth have been fairly well established. Scholars identify Rameses ("house of Rameses") as Qantir or Tell el-Dab`a, the ancient Avaris/Pi-Ramesse.[3] It was originally built on the eastern bank of the Pelusiac, the easternmost of the Nile's five ancient branches. Later, prior to 1069 BC, the course this branch of the Nile migrated away from the city, and the site was abandoned.

Succoth[4] (the modern Tell el-Maskhuta) is found in the Wadi Tumilat of the southeast delta.[5] The name Succoth in Hebrew means "temporary shelters, tents, booths," which corresponds to the Egyptian name Tjeku.

Kitchen makes a strong case to identify Pithom ("house of the god Atum") as Tell er-Retabe along the Wadi Tumilat, a few miles due west of Succoth.[6]

Location of the Red Sea or *yām sûp*

We just don't know the exact location of the body of water identified in the text as the "Red Sea." The Hebrew is *yām sûp*, a term used in the Old Testament to identify a number of different bodies of water. *Yām* is used in the Old Testament over 300 times to refer to "sea" and about 70 times for "west" or "westward."[7] The word *sûp* means "reed, waterplant," a general term for marsh plants.[8] What we know as the Red Sea today lies to the south, with two northern branches, the Gulf of Aqabah to the east of the Sinai Peninsula and the Gulf of Suez to the west of the Sinai Peninsula.

---

[2] This analysis draws heavily on K.A. Kitchen, On the Reliability of the New Testament (Eerdmans, 2003), pp. 265-274. See also Peter Enns, "Exodus Route and Wilderness Itinerary," DOTP, pp. 272-280.

[3] P. Enns, "Exodus Route and Wilderness Itinerary," DOTP pp. 272-280, especially p. 273.

[4] Exodus 12:37; 13:20; Numbers 33:5-6

[5] W.L. Thompson, Jr., "Succoth," ISBE 4:648); Kitchen, *Reliability*, pp. 256-259.

[6] Kitchen, *Reliability*, pp. 256-259. J.H. Walton, "Exodus, Date of," DOTP, p. 262.

[7] Paul R. Gilchrist, *yām*, TWOT #871a.

[8] R.D. Patterson, *sûp*, TWOT #1479. Exodus 2:3, 5; Isaiah 19:6; Jonah 2:5.

According to 1 Kings 9:26 and other passages,[9] the term *yām sûp* is used to describe Gulf of Aqabah (Elat), the body of water east of the Sinai Peninsula. Of course, in many many passages, *yām sûp* is the sea of the Exodus.[10]

We conclude, then, that the "Red Sea" (*yām sûp*) refers to some body of water east of the Nile delta. Scholars have found evidence of ancient canals in this area. Here are the primary possibilities of bodies of water we see today along the line of the present-day 101-mile Suez Canal, which opened in 1869. North to south, these are:

Location of Red Sea Crossing

1. Lake Ballah
2. Lake Timsah
3. Great Bitter Lake
4. Little Bitter Lake

Water tables, no doubt, are different now than they were 3,000 years ago, so we can't judge just by what we see today. Some believe that the Gulf of Suez gradually receded over the centuries, its coastline slowly moving farther and farther southward away from Lake Timsah and the Greater Bitter Lake to its present coastline today.[11] "It is plausible, even if they were marshy areas, that the Israelites crossed while the area was flooded, which occurred periodically."[12] The exact spot of the crossing is impossible to determine with certainty, but it probably occurred either at Lake Timsah or at the Great Bitter Lake.

The Sinai Coast

If, indeed, the Israelites took the traditional southern route, it would have been a difficult trip. Beno Rothenberg notes:

> "Sinai's broad southern littoral [area near the shoreline] is for the most part a sandy waste. In the wadi-estuaries and in a few depressions between the sea and the moun-

---

[9] Also Exodus 23:31; Numbers 14:25; 21:4; Deuteronomy 1:40; 2:1; Judges 11:16; Jeremiah 49:21.

[10] Exodus 15:4, 22; Joshua 2:10; 4:23; Psalm 106:7, 9, 22.

[11] "Suez Canal," Wikipedia, 12 Dec 2010, citing Édouard Naville, "Map of the Wadi Tumilat" (plate image), in *The Store-City of Pithom and the Route of the Exodus* (London: Trubner and Company, 1885); S Rappoport, *History of Egypt* (London, Grolier Society, undated, early 20th century), Volume 12, Part B, Chapter V: "The Waterways of Egypt," pages 248-257.

[12] P. Enns, "Exodus Route and Wilderness Journey," DOTP, p. 276.

tains of Sinai the yellow sand is relieved by white patches of chalk and limestone, some-times mingled with loess. In such parts there is water and vegetation: tamarisks, date-palms, and acacias. But the parched soil shrivels and crumples up in the fierce desert heat."[13]

Marah (Exodus 15:23)

Marah has been traditionally identified with Ain Hawara, but there can be no certain-ty. Beno Rothenberg observed in 1957 that Ain Hawara is "a spring now completely buried in sand. Only a cluster of date-palms and a damp spot nearby are there to tell of its existence."[14]

Elim (Exodus 15:27)

It has always been tempting for scholars to try to locate the oasis of Elim.

"Then they came to Elim, where there were twelve springs and seventy palm trees, and they camped there near the water." (Exodus 15:27)

Elim ('êlim) is the plural of 'ayil, "terebinth, great tree," so Elim means "(place of) great trees."[15] Some scholars identify Elim with the modern day Wadi Gharandel, located on the west coast of the Sinai Peninsula and the site of numerous palm trees,[16] but it is by no means proven.

Mount Sinai

The exact location of Mount Sinai (sometimes referred to as Mount Horeb) is un-known. There are three theories as to its general location:

1. **Northern Sinai.** Candidates suggested are Jebel Helal, Jebel Kharif, Jebel Sin Bisher, Jebel Yeleq, Jebel Magharah, Jebel Karkom, or Kadesh-barnea itself.
2. **Arabia.** Mountains suggested are present-day Petra, el-Khrob, or Hala el-Bedr. This has a long tradition, but is unlikely.[17]

[13] Ben Rothenberg, *God's Wilderness*, p. 93, plate 30.
[14] Ben Rothenberg, *God's Wilderness*, p. 94, plate 33.
[15] 'Ayil, BDB 18.
[16] Kitchen, *Reliability*, p. 269, who sees it "possible, but not proven."
[17] Arguments pro and con are presented in Beitzel, *Atlas*, pp. 90-91.

3. **Southern Sinai.** The traditional southern route of the Exodus suggests four possible
peaks, which I think are most
likely, all clustered together:
Jebel Musa ("Mountain of
Moses") is 7,498 feet in eleva-
tion, Jebel Katarina is 8,551
feet, and Ras Safsafa is 7,113
feet. Jebel Serbal (6,739 feet) is
west a few miles, near the
Monastery of St. Catherine.
Which of these peaks is the
real Mount Sinai, God only
knows, but each has its pro-
ponents.[19]

Possible locations of Mount Sinai in the southern Sinai
Peninsula[18]

The location of Rephidim is
unknown. However, many have placed it near the Oasis of Feiran. Yohanan Aharoni
comments:

> "Wadi Feiran is one of the largest and most famous wadis in Sinai. It is 81 miles long
> and begins in the region of Jebel Musa, where it is called Wadi el Sheikh. Feiran boasts
> the chief oasis in Sinai, one of the wonders of the Peninsula. In the heart of the bleak and
> forbidding granite mountains a green parkland suddenly comes into view: over 6 miles
> of date-palm groves, tamarisks, reeds, rushes, and other vegetation, with a small spar-
> kling stream to delight the eye, artesian wells, and even a petrol engine to draw up the
> water. The inhabitants are Bedouin."[20]

Kadesh-Barnea

Kadesh is almost certainly to be identified with Ain el-Qudeirat in the Wadi el-Ain of
the northern Sinai. "The vegetation near Ain el-Qudeirat and its ample supply of water
suit very well the topographical requirements of the wilderness narratives."[21] Ain el-

---

[18] Map relies on Beitzel, *Atlas*, pp. 86-87, map 25.

[19] Kitchen (*Reliability*, p. 270) says, "In practical terms, the immediate conjunction of clear space plus
impressive mountain at Gebel Musa suits the biblical narrative much better than does Gebel Serbal....
Certainty is not attainable, but Gebel Musa may lead Gebel Serbal by a short head."

[20] Yohanan Aharoni in *God's Wilderness*, pp. 135-136.

[21] R.K. Harrison, "Kadesh," ISBE 3:1-2

Qudeirat is the richest spring in the Sinai, having a flow of about 40 cubic meters per hour.[22]

Mount Hor

The actual location of Mount Hor is unknown, but was considered in Edomite territory. Josephus identified Mount Edom as Jebel Nebi Harim near Petra. But a more likely location might be Jebel Madura, about 15 miles northeast of Kadesh at the edge of Edom's territory.[23]

Ezion-geber (Numbers 33:35; Deuteronomy 2:8)

Ezion-geber is almost surely located at Tell el-Kheleifeh at the north end of the Gulf of Aqaba.

Dizahab (Deuteronomy 1:1)

Dizahab must surely be related to the present town of Dahab, as both names are phonetic equivalents and both have to do with places of gold.[24]

Jotbathah (Numbers 33:33)

Jotbathah is quite likely to be the oasis of Taba, located about seven miles south of Ezion-geber on the eastern side of the Sinai Peninsula.[25]

Of course there are many speculations as to other identifications, but these are the most likely.

---

[22] Moshe Dothan, "The Fortress at Kadesh-Barnea," *Israel Exploration Journal*, 1965, pp. 134-51. A number of photos of Kadesh-barnea can be found in *God's Wilderness*, plates 10-17.

[23] Harrison, *Numbers*, p. 272.

[24] Beitzel, *Atlas*, p. 92 and Map 25.

[25] Beitzel, *Atlas*, p. 92 and Map 25.

Appendix 3. References to Moses in the New Testament

Moses is mentioned many times in the New Testament, always positively, though occasionally with reference to the Old Covenant which is contrasted with the New. At no place is he criticized or denigrated, but rather honored.

Moses as Lawgiver

- Purification, Law of Moses (Luke 2:22)
- Cleansing of lepers (Matthew 8:4 ; Mark 1:44; Luke 5:14)
- Divorce (Matthew 19:7-8; Mark 10:3-5; Luke 20:28)
- To Pharisees who cheated widows: Mark 7:10)
- Sadducees on Levirate marriage (Matthew 22:24; Mark 12:19)
- Parable of Lazarus and the Rich Man (Luke 16:29, 31)
- Moses is accuser of Pharisees (John 5:45-46)
- Law of Moses to be observed (John 7:23)
- Moses commanded adulteress be stoned (John 8:5)
- Disciples of Moses (John 9:28-29)
- Stephen accused of blasphemy against Moses (Acts 6:11, 14)
- Stephen relates history of Moses (Acts 7:20-44)
- Circumcision taught by Moses (Acts 15:1, 5)
- Paul accused of turning people from Moses (Acts 21:21)

James J. Tissot, "Moses and the Ten Commandments" (1896-1900), watercolor, Jewish Museum, New York.

- Quotes Moses positively (Romans 9:15; 10:5, 19; 1 Corinthians 9:9)
- Baptized into Moses in the cloud (1 Corinthians 10:2)
- Veil over Moses' face (2 Corinthians 3:7, 13, 15)
- Jannes and Jambres (Egyptian magicians) opposed Moses (2 Timothy 3:8)

Contrast between Old and New Covenants

- Contrast of Moses' law vs. grace and truth (John 1:17)
- Justification from sin by law of Moses limited (Acts 13:39)
- Moses preached in every city (Acts 15:21)
- Death reigned from Adam to Moses (Romans 5:14)
- Moses was faithful, Jesus has greater honor (Hebrews 3:2-5)
- Tabernacle is copy of what is in heaven (Hebrews 8:5)
- Moses confirmed covenant with people (Hebrews 9:19)
- Those who reject Law of Moses die (Hebrews 10:28)

Miscellaneous References

- With Elijah and Jesus at Transfiguration (Matthew 17:3-4; Mark 9:4-5; Luke 9:30, 33.)
- Moses at bush heard from the living God (Mark 12:26; Luke 20:37)
- Moses lifted up snake (John 3:14)
- Moses gives bread from heaven (John 6:32)
- Moses led rebels out of Egypt (Hebrews 3:16)
- Moses didn't mention priests from tribe of Judah (Hebrews 7:14)
- By faith, Moses (Hebrews 11:24-29)
- Moses terrified at Mt. Sinai (Hebrews 12:21)
- Dispute about body of Moses (Jude 1:9)
- The song of Moses the servant of God and of the Lamb (Revelation 15:3)

Moses as the Prophet Prototype of Jesus Christ

- Jesus gives an exposition of references to himself in Law of Moses (Luke 24:44)
- Philip's testimony: Moses wrote about Jesus (John 1:45; 5:46)
- Quotes: God will raise up another prophet (Acts 3:22)
- Moses predicted Jesus (Acts 26:22)
- In Rome, Paul taught Jesus from Law of Moses (Acts 28:23)

CPSIA information can be obtained
at www.ICGtesting.com
Printed in the USA
BVHW010739120821
613993BV00002B/17